Transforming Ireland

MANCHESTER
1824
Manchester University Press

Transforming Ireland

Challenges, critiques, resources

edited by
Debbie Ging, Michael Cronin and Peadar Kirby

Manchester University Press

Manchester and New York

distributed in the United States exclusively by Palgrave Macmillan

Copyright © Manchester University Press 2009

While copyright in the volume as a whole is vested in Manchester University Press, copyright in individual chapters belongs to their respective authors, and no chapter may be reproduced wholly or in part without the express permission in writing of both author and publisher.

Published by Manchester University Press
Oxford Road, Manchester M13 9NR, UK
and Room 400, 175 Fifth Avenue, New York, NY 10010, USA
www.manchesteruniversitypress.co.uk

Distributed in the United States exclusively by
Palgrave Macmillan, 175 Fifth Avenue, New York,
NY 10010, USA

Distributed in Canada exclusively by
UBC Press, University of British Columbia, 2029 West Mall,
Vancouver, BC, Canada V6T 1Z2

British Library Cataloguing-in-Publication Data
A catalogue record for this book is available from the British Library

Library of Congress Cataloging-in-Publication Data applied for

ISBN 978 0 7190 7892 7   *hardback*

ISBN 978 0 7190 7893 4   *paperback*

First published 2009

18 17 16 15 14 13 12 11 10 09   10 9 8 7 6 5 4 3 2 1

Typeset by R. J. Footring Ltd, Derby
Printed in Great Britain by MPG Books Group

Contents

Part III: Social control

Part IV: Power and politics

Tables

Contributors

Michael Cronin holds a Personal Chair and is Director of the Centre for Translation and Textual Studies at Dublin City University. He is the author and co-editor of numerous publications. He is co-editor of the *Irish Review* and a Member of the Royal Irish Academy.

Roddy Flynn is a lecturer at the School of Communications, Dublin City University, where he chairs the MA in Film and Television Studies. He has written extensively on Irish cinema and broadcasting policy and is the author (with Pat Brereton) of the *Historical Dictionary of Irish Cinema* (Scarecrow Press, 2007) and of the forthcoming *Cinema and State: Irish Film Policy Since 1922*.

Debbie Ging lectures and researches on gender, ethnicity and inter-culturalism in the media and is Chair of the BA in Communications Studies at Dublin City University. She is currently writing a book on men and masculinity in Irish cinema.

Peadar Kirby is Professor of International Politics and Public Policy at the University of Limerick. His latest publications are *Explaining Ireland's Development: Economic Growth with Weakening Welfare*, Social Policy and Development Paper No. 37, United Nations Research Institute for Social Development (UNRISD, 2008) and, co-edited with Deiric Ó Broin, *Power, Dissent and Democracy: Civil Society and the State in Ireland* (A&A Farmar, 2009).

Piaras MacÉinrí is a lecturer in the Department of Geography at University College Cork and is Director of the Irish Centre for Migration

Studies (ICMS). He has written extensively about immigration and cultural integration in Ireland and co-authored (with J. King) *Where Is Home? An Educational Resource on Refugees in International and Irish Perspective* (Calypso Productions, 2005).

Mary Murphy is a lecturer in the Department of Sociology, National University of Ireland, Maynooth. She primarily works in the field of political sociology; her research interests include globalisation and welfare states, the political mediation of social policy reform, local governance, gender, social security and welfare to work.

Orla O'Donovan is a lecturer in the Department of Applied Social Studies at University College Cork. Much of her current research focuses on the contributions of patients' organisations and health activists to the production of knowledge, norms and hope about health and healthcare. She recently published *Power, Politics and Pharmaceuticals* (co-edited with Kathy Glavanis-Grantham, Cork University Press, 2008).

Denis O'Sullivan is Associate Professor of Education in the Department of Education at University College Cork. Having taught at all levels of the Irish education system, his research focuses on the sociology of education, adult and community education and educational policy studies. He has recently published a major study entitled *Cultural Politics and Irish Education Since the 1950s: Policy Paradigms and Power* (Institute of Public Administration, 2005).

Sean Phelan is a lecturer at the Department of Communication, Journalism and Marketing, Massey University, Wellington. His work explores the relationship between discourse, ideology and media power, and he has published articles on neoliberalism, the 11 September attacks, the 2003 Iraq war and Aotearoa New Zealand race relations.

Gavan Titley is Subject Leader for Media Studies in the Centre for Media Studies, National University of Ireland Maynooth. His most recent publication is *The Politics of Diversity in Europe* (co-edited with Alana Lentin, Council of Europe, 2008).

John Walsh works as a lecturer in the Department of Irish at the National University of Ireland, Galway, where he teaches sociolinguistics (language planning and policy). He is currently working on a book on the tensions between language promotion and socio-economic development in Ireland.

Acknowledgements

With thanks to the Office of the Vice President for Research, Dublin City University, for publication assistance funding.

1

Transforming Ireland: challenges

MICHAEL CRONIN, PEADAR KIRBY
and DEBBIE GING

In January 2007, the Irish government unveiled its fourth National Development Plan (NDP) to cover the seven-year period from 2007 to 2013. Entitled *Transforming Ireland: A Better Quality of Life for All*, the Plan proposed to spend €180 billion in five priority areas – economic infrastructure; enterprise, science and innovation; human capital; social infrastructure; and social inclusion. Though widely welcomed by commentators as addressing Ireland's many serious economic and social deficits, serious questions were also raised about its viability. It was pointed out that many of the projects promised in its predecessor had yet to be completed and had incurred major cost overruns. For example, only 38 per cent of the inter-urban highways that had been due for completion by 2006 were open by that date and cost overruns had included 92.4 per cent on the Cavan bypass, 98.6 per cent on the Nenagh bypass, 117 per cent on the Drogheda bypass and 306 per cent on the Youghal bypass (McDonald, 2007). Concern was expressed at the lack of adequate oversight mechanisms to ensure value for public monies, particularly as this is the first NDP not to be monitored by the European Commission (the previous ones all having been basically mechanisms to secure large contributions of funding from the European Union). Even before the Plan was launched, the Economic and Social Research Council (ESRI) expressed its fears that it was over-ambitious and would fuel inflation (Morgenroth and Fitz Gerald, 2006). Finally, seasoned observers immediately claimed that it 'has "general election" written all over it', as an *Irish Times* editorial put it (24 January 2007). The newspaper's economics editor, Marc Coleman, concluded: 'That it has snowballed into a catch-all wish list for national happiness will blunt its purpose and impair its implementation' (Coleman, 2007).

The contributors to this book are also concerned about transforming Ireland but believe that the challenges this presents require far more than throwing vast sums of money at poorly analysed, and even more poorly costed, lists of projects. Instead, the challenge of social transformation requires a sustained and thorough critique of the malaise that lies at the heart of today's Ireland, and a mobilising of the resources of Ireland's civil society to address it. For this reason, the book carries the same title as the NDP but a very different subtitle, and it is offered as an alternative approach to the dominant, mainstream view that finds expression in the other text. As such, it offers a real choice – not in the reductionist sense offered us all the time by neoliberal marketeers but in the sense that neoliberal economists and politicians constantly choose to deny.

This is the choice of a society based on different values, on different ways of relating public and private power (or state to market, to use the common shorthand), on different solidarities, and on different geographies of power, both locally and globally. Real choices do exist and if we are serious about transforming Ireland into a sustainable, humane and decent society which can offer a fulfilling quality of life, particularly to its most deprived and vulnerable citizens, then it is imperative that such choices be outlined more robustly and convincingly than is often done. Convinced that the 2007–13 NDP will simply deepen many of the crises and contradictions of contemporary Irish society, since it avoids any critical analysis of their sources in the structures and power hierarchies of that society, the contributors to this book offer a more critical reading of what transforming Ireland entails. This they see as a badly needed contribution to a society caught in the stultifying embrace of a carefully constructed and assiduously policed 'consensus' politics that effectively acts to marginalise and disempower critiques and alternatives. Breaking this embrace requires identifying the ways in which Ireland has changed over recent decades.

A transformed Ireland

Curiosity thrives on enigmas and good political questions are ones we are generally at a loss to answer. If there were easy answers, little time and energy would be needed to find them. For this reason, Ireland in the last three decades of the twentieth century was deeply attractive as a site of scholarly enquiry. The country, in the context of the developed world, was an anomaly. Firstly, there was the economic anomaly of a country which, despite proximity to large British markets and membership of the European Economic Community (EEC), consistently failed to achieve satisfactory levels of economic growth, had the highest net out-ward migration rate of EEC member states in the 1980s and experienced record levels of public debt and youth unemployment. Joe Lee's *Ireland, 1912–1985: Politics and Society* was a forceful indictment of the scale of independent Ireland's economic failure (Lee, 1989) and the title of a collection of essays edited by Therese Caherty and published in 1992 was eloquent, *Is Ireland a Third World Country?* (Caherty, 1992). Secondly, there was the social anomaly of a state in western Europe which banned all forms of artificial contraception, prohibited civil divorce, treated sexual activity between consenting adult homosexuals as a criminal offence and tolerated high levels of clerical interventionism in the educational and health services. The signal failure to separate church and state and the aggressive policing of private morality made Ireland conspicuously dif-ferent from the more general drift towards liberal legislation in post-war Europe. Thirdly, there was the seeming political anomaly of a country mired in ethnic conflict, linked to questions of religion and territory. Thousands of people lost their lives or were seriously injured in decades of strife, and militarisation was an inescapable fact of everyday life in Northern Ireland. The presence of these 'wars of religion' in the pre-Bosnia, pre-9/11 secular vision of an Enlightenment world appeared both scandalous and perplexing. Therefore, as an economic, social and political anomaly, Ireland was attractively puzzling to anyone who cared about the present or future state of the island.

At the beginning of the twenty-first century, what is different is that Ireland, in conventional economic and social terms, is no longer so dif-ferent. In a widely reported survey, *The Economist* declared in 2005 that Ireland was the best place in the world to live,[1] while spectacular economic growth had made Ireland by the dawn of the new century one of the wealthiest countries on the planet:

> Between 1991 and 2003 the Irish economy grew by an average of 6.8 per cent per annum, peaking at 11.1 per cent in 1999. Unemployment fell from 18 per cent in the late 1980s to 4.2 per cent in 2005, and the Irish Debt/GDP ratio fell from 92 per cent in 1993 to 38 per cent in 1999. Throughout the 1990s Irish living standards rose dramatically to the point where the country is now, at least by some measures, one of the richest in the world, and has the fourth highest GDP per capita in the world. (Keohane and Kuhling, 2007: 1)

Ireland in the last decade of the twentieth century shifted rapidly towards the standard neoliberal model of an increasingly deregulated trade in goods, services and labour and the relentless promotion of the market as an arbiter of efficiency, distribution and appropriate response to needs, both private and collective (Allen, 2007). If Ireland was no longer so anomalous in economic terms, changes to social legislation in the 1990s permitting, for example, the sale of contraceptives, removing the prohibition on divorce and decriminalising homosexuality meant that Irish legislation in areas of private morality was closer to the European norm. The IRA ceasefires of 1994 and 1997, the Good Friday Agreement (and more recently the St Andrews Agreement), the decommissioning of weapons and the establishment of a power-sharing assembly in Northern Ireland meant that military conflict was no longer a salient feature of political life on the island.

Therefore, the dominant story repeatedly told by the Irish president on tour, or by political parties making a pitch for the retention of power, or by the Economic and Social Research Institute providing comforting alibis for the status quo, is 'We've never had it so good'. When Tony Fahey, Helen Russell and Christopher Whelan wrote an article in the *Irish Times* on the occasion of the publication of their co-edited volume *Best of Times? The Social Impact of the Celtic Tiger*, they unsurprisingly concluded their paean to the New Ireland by claiming: 'It is therefore easy to agree with President Mary McAleese. In a speech in the United States in November 2003, she said: "If the men and women of Ireland's past could choose a time to live, there would be a long queue for this one"' (Fahey *et al.*, 2007a). The choice is ironically appropriate, as in two key areas of society, health and education, waiting for treatment or to get a school place is the recurrent nightmare of citizens trying to access a public good in a political system that is completely beholden to the logic of the market and the primacy of private gain. While they were waiting to be treated as public patients or trying to find a school that did not have a waiting list of hundreds, the 'men and women of Ireland's past' would have time to reflect on a striking feature of the Irish present, namely, the seizure of language itself by neo-corporate platitudes.

No area of Irish life is immune from the managerial Newspeak of 'stakeholders', 'world-class', 'total quality management', 'excellence', 'best practice', 'strategic plan', 'mission statement', 'key performance indicators', 'customer care' and other corporate shibboleths. In George Orwell's *Nineteen Eighty-Four*, Newspeak is described by the narrator as being 'the only language in the world whose vocabulary gets smaller every year' (Orwell, 1949). The impression of thought control and limited expressiveness is similar for any observer of Irish life as the restricted vocabulary of the business studies vulgate is applied indiscriminately to health, education, the arts, policing, indeed any sector in receipt of public funding. If consultants are the clergy of this new religion of the Word made Pound of Flesh, what explains its all pervasiveness and why does transforming Ireland also involve transforming the way we speak about Ireland? In 2000, the

British sociologist Anthony Giddens opened the century with a solemn pronouncement on the new universal faith:

> Capitalism has become the universal social and economic order of our time. Throughout the twentieth century it has been challenged from right and left, but with the fall of the Communist Soviet Union, it has emerged triumphant and stronger than ever before.
>
> This new capitalism differs from that of previous eras … it is truly global, aided by extraordinary advances in technology and communication, and by unfettered global financial markets. Capitalism has a speed, inevitability and force it has not had before. (Cited in Graham and Luke, 2005: 14)

A key word in Giddens' evangel is 'inevitability'. Resistance is pointless, as fate and destiny are one. There is one 'universal social and economic order' and all must succumb to the overwhelming evidence of its presence and influence. Language, then, merely reflects a ubiquitous reality. There is no other way of 'going forward', no other way of 'thinking outside the box' but to speak the lingua franca of market instrumentalism. To use the language, to speak of students or asylum seekers as 'customers', for example, is already to accept a value system whereby all relationships are defined on the basis of commodified, financial transactions (Holborow, 2007). A further characteristic of the language is the soft fog of euphemism: 'downsizing' is losing your job, 'consultation process' means being told you are going to lose your job; mercenaries become 'private security operatives' and extra-judicial torture mutates into the gentle, Latinate abstraction of 'extraordinary rendition'. The fact that much of the corporate Newspeak originates in the English-speaking world makes Ireland even more vulnerable to wholesale incorporation into the looking-glass world of managerial rhetoric.

However, from the point of view of transformative practices, it is important that we bear in mind that languages have a past and future as well as a present. In other words, the present infestation of public language with the default rhetoric of the market is, in historical terms, relatively recent. When Milton Friedman published his key work, *Capitalism and Freedom*, in 1962, he claimed that he felt he was part of a 'small, beleaguered minority regarded as eccentrics by the great majority of our fellow intellectuals' (Friedman, 1962: vi). Advocacy of an unfettered free market, wholesale privatisation, the commodification of free public services and ruthless tax cuts were ideas considered to be the idiosyncratic beliefs of a chosen few but, through their adoption by key political actors and vested interests, over the decades the dissident credo of the neoliberal sect became the universal gospel of large parts of the developed and developing world (see Allen, 2007: 25–37). Now it is those writers and thinkers in Ireland

and elsewhere who challenge the 'inevitability' of the new 'social and economic order of our time' who are part of a 'small beleaguered minority regarded as eccentrics by the great majority of our fellow intellectuals'. But, ironically, it is the signal success of the neoliberal intelligentsia which points to the potential for their undoing. What they showed with startling clarity was that new ideas and perspectives, no matter how modest their beginnings, have a remarkable ability to shape economic and social realities. The language neoliberal thinkers and their state, corporate and academic cheerleaders have bequeathed us may be universal in its spread, but there is no reason to suppose that it is eternal in its duration. This is not only because of the inevitable contradictions of a system which benefits the few rather than the many but also because beleaguered minorities, articulating the distress of the economic and social majority on the planet, have the potential to destabilise the placid certainties of corporate Newspeak.

A good example of the dominance of a narrow, neoliberal agenda over our way of thinking (and, indeed, the lack of debate about that agenda) was the campaigning for the 2007 Irish general election. What the electorate was offered was repeated (and successful) pandering to a deliberately restricted version of economic self-interest. The only form of forward thinking on offer was fear. Failure to vote for the government parties was portrayed as tantamount to throwing everything away. Paradoxically, for many people, onerous mortgages, high levels of personal debt, crippling price rises and the significant burden of indirect taxation meant that voting for an alternative looked unacceptably risky. In other words, the kind of politics which had backed people into a corner of indebtedness and social anomie was presented as the only way out. Part of the difficulty for the electorate was that there did indeed appear to be no other way out, as the much-touted alternative of Fine Gael and Labour was not an 'alternative' in any meaningful or credible sense of the word. In everything from the lamentable fudge on state complicity in US torture flights through Shannon to the cynical opportunism of belated tax cuts, Fine Gael and Labour played a game whose neoliberal ground rules had been clearly laid down by Fianna Fáil and the Progressive Democrats. No party can ever hope to defeat Fianna Fáil by pretending to be Fianna Fáil. Nobody does Fianna Fáil better than Fianna Fáil. The philosophy of unprincipled populism which has served the dominant government partner so well does not provide a sustainable basis for real opposition.

Ironically, what the 2007 election demonstrated was the perverse triumph of a form of thinking associated in earlier decades with the doctrinaire left, namely, economic determinism. If the economy was held to explain everything and only one form of economic thought was held to be legitimate, then opportunities for debate or contestation were scuppered in advance. The question then became one of choosing between rival sets of consultants to run the business and the incumbents, not surprisingly, got the contract. Thus, a noticeable feature of the election and its aftermath in Ireland has been the unholy alliance of threat and triumphalism. Vote for the neoliberal status quo or face financial ruin and are we not surely living in the Best of Times? If instrumentalist economism is a means of stifling debate, equally effective is a home-grown boosterism, with its coercive rhetoric of self-congratulation. A telling example was provided by Maureen Gaffney in an *Irish Times* magazine supplement on happiness. She informed her readers that:

> We seemed to have used our prosperity as an opportunity to enjoy stable family relationships, to develop our personal expressiveness and to show the world what we're good at. Given Ireland's economic, cultural and religious history – still in living memory – we have embraced prosperity, the good life and personal freedoms with unabashed relish, and we won't lightly let them go. (Gaffney, 2007b: 68)

Who is the 'we' being referred to here? Who apart from self-regarding national elites, who are now richer than ever before, are included in the charmed circle of the chummy pronoun? Self-interest, however, in the context of global meltdown, is self-delusion. The only sustainable form of self-interest is one which looks beyond the picket fences of dynastic self-preservation and moves to broader, collective well-being as a way of ensuring a better life for all. No amount of triumphalist hype – always in Ireland the flipside of an inferiority complex in its over-eagerness to convince – can conceal the real and urgent need for change. The chapters in our *Transforming Ireland* illustrate this.

As the different chapters demonstrate, current Irish society displays many of the worst features of a system dedicated to the ruthless expansion of the self-interest of the powerful. Part I, 'Culture and society', contains three chapters. In chapter 2, John Walsh, examining the case of the Irish language, shows how market-led values do irreparable damage to fragile cultures. Piaras Mac Éinrí in chapter 3 interrogates the nature of racism and a multiculturalism dominated by the perceived needs of the economy, and he re-imagines what a truly multi-ethnic Ireland might involve. The following chapter, by Debbie Ging, looks at the deeply damaging consequences of unrestrained consumerism for the formation of gender identities and relationships. Part II, 'Media and social change', contains two chapters. Chapter 5, by Sean Phelan, illustrates how the Irish media have internalised a neoliberal view of the world and consistently place their coverage of Irish society within the framework of this paradigm. In the following chapter, Roddy Flynn shows, in examining the Football Association of Ireland's attempts to sell the rights to broadcast Republic of Ireland soccer matches to BSkyB, the possibility for public reaction to force governments to stand up to the power of market actors. Part III, 'Social control', contains three chapters. In chapter 7, Michael Cronin highlights the contradiction between the dominant discourse of freedom and choice, and the growth of an ever-more coercive state. Denis O'Sullivan in chapter 8 charts the changing meaning of education in state discourse, from one based on citizenship to one based on the logic of the market. In chapter 9, Orla O'Donovan explores how the pharmaceutical industry has gained increasing power over health information and the treatment of illness, with questionable consequences for our health and general well-being. Part IV, 'Power and politics', contains three chapters. Gavan Titley in chapter 10 examines the politics of Irish mobility and argues that a dominant discourse on cosmopolitanism disguises deep divisions and inequalities in Irish society. In chapter 11, Mary Murphy analyses the changing nature of Irish social policy and current recommendations for its reform, and argues for the importance of greater public debate and activism to ensure a more robust and equitable social policy. Chapter 12, by Peadar Kirby, contests the dominant politics of inequality and maps out what it would take to promote a genuine politics of equality. The contents of this book stand in stark contrast to the constrained nature of public debate in today's Ireland.

Framing public debate

When Pat Kenny interviewed two of the Glen of the Downs eco-warriors on the *Late Late Show* in 2000, many of his questions focused on issues of personal hygiene and on the perceived 'wackiness' of a group of hippies living in trees. Although the interview gave their cause prime-time publicity, the way in which the discussion was framed arguably succeeded in denying them a political voice, thus making it easy for the already sceptical viewer to dismiss them as loony tree-huggers. Such an incident might appear unworthy of much comment. In the greater scheme of things, however, it represents a broader trend of anti-intellectualism in Irish public life that has taken root since the Celtic Tiger years, and is significantly affecting the way in which far-reaching decisions are now being made in Ireland. This book raises a number of pertinent questions about how the cultural, the political and the economic articulate in the new postmodern Ireland. A recurrent trope is how various aspects of Irish cultural life have been hijacked, not only in the sense that culture is becoming increasingly commercialised but also in the way that the mass cultural arena is being used as a kind of ersatz political forum or public sphere. In the explicit rhetoric of neoliberalism, the significance of culture as an aesthetic or political endeavour is almost wholly subsumed by the discourse of corporate profit. Paradoxically, however, it is increasingly at the level of the cultural – through the reiteration of powerful images, words and sound-bites – that common-sense ideas about what constitutes progress, civilisation or the greater good have taken hold. Most Irish citizens are now information rich – however trivial much of the information consumed may be – but are impoverished in terms of time, and this sets the ideal scene for processes of consensus building that are characterised both by amnesia and by a lack of joined up thinking.

Thus, we readily accept not only that 'anti-social' behaviour is on the increase but also the glib, common-sense explanations for this phenomenon that are offered by radio talk-show hosts and pop psychologists. As Steven Poole (2006) has so cogently demonstrated, the persistent reiteration of particular words, phrases and ideas across a broad cultural spectrum effectively sets the terms of the 'debate' by shutting down arguments before they happen and making opposing viewpoints unspeakable. For a common-sense idea such as 'increasing anti-social behaviour' (and the measures necessary to tackle it) to gain credibility, there is apparently little need to interrogate the term itself, to present convincing statistical evidence or to consider a range of alternative perspectives. When it comes to convincing the public that ASBOs (anti-social behaviour orders) or tougher jail sentences are the solution to this problem, the mass media have already done most of the work for the politicians and legislators. In a similar fashion, phrases that signal sea changes in gender relations, such as 'new man', are as much (if not more) the result of media images originating from the advertising of cosmetics to men in the 1990s as they are reflections of material evidence of increased equality between men and women. As our cultural practices as well as our general lifestyles become fuller and faster, contemporary Ireland's more troubling complexities and paradoxes are too frequently drowned out by this culture of images and of noise.

Central to the success of the Fianna Fáil/Progressive Democrat neoliberal project in the period from 2002 to 2007 was a twofold strategy, for which mass culture provided a crucial ideological arena. On the one hand, it was essential to convince the electorate that Ireland is an open, tolerant and, above all, progressive place, one which accommodates difference, dissent and freedom of expression. To a large extent, this discourse has gained a secure foothold through exaggerated accounts of social progress, evidenced not by sociological statistics but by a proliferation of images of 'empowered' women in the entertainment media, the mainstreaming of gay culture and the celebration of cosmopolitanism masquerading as multiculturalism, and in overt manifestations of our sexual liberation from an oppressive, censorious past. Not only has modern Ireland thrown off the shackles of religious oppression but we are now also freed from political correctness, feminism and other forms of identity politics, all strongly associated with the 'nanny state'. Far from posing a threat to the status quo, however, the new bloated counter-cultural images and discourses are inextricably bound up with consumerism. The fair-trade coffee shops, organic foodstuffs, anti-globalisation trainers, sex shops and lap-dancing clubs, gay sitcoms and ethnic restaurants that have become part of daily life are merely new forms of conspicuous consumption posing as dissent: they are both politically unthreatening and good, indeed essential, for post-industrial capitalism.

On the other hand, it is beneath this veil of the liberal, progressive and permissive Ireland that the most insidious forms of intervention become possible. As Michael Cronin demonstrates in chapter 7, there is a vested interest in neoliberal societies in presenting trivial disturbances, such as those caused by bored teenagers or anti-globalisation demonstrators, as major threats to security, in order to justify more coercive forms of surveillance and punishment. Thus, while the radio airwaves in 2006 were frequently dominated by liberals battling it out with Catholic conservatives about the introduction of lap-dancing clubs, a raft of legislation was being rushed in that infringed on citizens' personal privacy and allowed teenagers to be arrested for standing on street corners. Similarly, while in 2002 a high-profile government-sponsored 'Know Racism' campaign focused on the theme of multi-ethnic citizenship, the same government called a referendum in 2004 which led to legislation that denies children of non-Irish parents the right to stay in Ireland if they are born here, thus radically precluding the potential for multi-ethnic Irishness. Quick-fix, short-term solutions to complex problems are acceptable, it seems, once people are convinced that we are moving forward: politically, economically and culturally. What the constant rhetoric of change, development and progress manages to conceal so well, however, is that contemporary Ireland is really caught in a series of holding patterns, all guided by the self-perpetuating logic of the 'free' market.

The decision by the government to build private hospitals on the land of public ones shows that the most flagrant injustices are most successfully performed in clear view. Not only does this move constitute the first step towards a two-tier health system but it also signals the government's intention to continue selling off public assets for private gain, a phenomenon that appears to have bothered significantly fewer Irish people than, for example, whether or not Jade Goody's comments to Shilpa Shetty on the UK's *Celebrity Big Brother* in January 2007 were racist. Crude polls and vox pop interviews still convince the public that Ireland is the best place to live, in spite of the fact that it is among the most expensive in Europe, has high levels of poverty and exhibits the second highest class sizes in Europe (twenty-eight pupils per teacher, whereas best practice indicates that this figure should be below twenty). Exorbitantly priced childcare has forced many women back into the home, while post-feminism's rhetoric of free choice and revival of traditional values frame this economically motivated development as an empowered decision: the fact that it is now a compliment to be termed a desperate housewife, a yummy mummy or a domestic goddess is yet again testament to the power of cultural rhetoric in influencing and legitimating significant socio-economic trends.

Meanwhile, alcoholism, drug abuse and childhood obesity continue apace. However, rather than implementing any sort of effective ban on advertising unhealthy foodstuffs to children (it is merely prohibited on Irish television to use celebrities to promote these foods), Ireland continues to follow the American model – of unregulated advertising – rather than the Scandinavian model. The proliferation of organic and free-range foods on our supermarket shelves gives the impression that food quality has improved, although these foods are no different from those produced in the days before genetic modification and chemical farming. However, they now have more packaging and are flown from different parts of the world at enormous expense to the environment but, most importantly, they are available only to those with high incomes. Cheaper and convenience foods, on the other hand, are of increasingly low quality: packed with sugar, salt, preservatives and additives, they ensure that the health of those on lower incomes will suffer in the long term.

Although there is hard evidence to support the link between nutrition and childhood conditions such as attention deficit hyperactivity disorder (ADHD) (Bateman *et al.*, 2004; McCann *et al.*, 2007), these conditions are often presented in pop scientific discourse as biochemical 'syndromes', thus evading more complex social causes such as poor nutrition and parenting. Indeed, a number of outspoken American scientists and social commentators such as Conrad (2007), Baughman (2006) and Breggin and Scruggs (2001) have questioned the state-sanctioned medicalisation and 'drugging' of children, claiming that most of these conditions are not diseases at all but rather 'common symptoms of emotional discomfiture'. According to neurologist Fred A. Baughman (2006), telling people they have a disease abrogates their right to informed consent and is thus a significant threat to democracy, and he claims that ADHD is 'the greatest health care fraud in modern medical history'. The trends presented by Orla O'Donovan in chapter 9 suggest that unless there is a radical rethinking about the treatment of illness in Ireland, it will not be long before we, too, start administering drugs such as Ritalin to our children, just as we have accepted antidepressant and anti-cholesterol drugs to treat a range of problems that could better be tackled by identifying the causes, rather than the symptoms, of contemporary Ireland's malaise.

Contrary to the official line that Ireland is a progressive nation of free-thinking individuals, a number of key public debates have, in recent years, been driven by astonishingly regressive ideologies. As Debbie Ging points out in chapter 4, bio-essentialism has become hugely popular in the Irish mainstream media. Bio-essentialism posits the notion that a range of 'personality' traits – from gender behaviour and sexuality to criminal tendencies – are genetically encoded rather than socially learned. Supported by pseudo-scientific and pop psychological evidence, this 'common-sense' take on important social developments tends to present them as unavoidable fact, while its true economic motives remain concealed. The discourse of 'brain science' has vast media entertainment value, since battle-of-the-sexes narratives provide advertisers, sitcom producers and radio talk-show hosts with a seemingly endless source of comic material. It also underpins almost all of the self-help literature available on our bookshelves, from sex manuals to relationship guides. Finally, and perhaps more ominously, it has been used to frame a plethora of serious public debates about youth and crime, boys' academic underachievement, male suicide, boy racers, substance abuse and relationship breakdown, all issues that look very different when viewed through lenses of class, urban/rural location or upbringing.

This rise in pop genetic determinism is not coincidental: not only is it used to polarise and control people through their bodies and sexual behaviours, but it also serves to free the state of responsibility for the ill-effects of social marginalisation, by suggesting that certain behaviours are hardwired from birth rather than socially constructed. Such individualistic accounts of criminal behaviour, depression, sexual orientation and relationship failure in turn legitimate highly individualistic solutions. If there is any truth in the claim that the demise of Catholicism has left a philosophical and spiritual void at the heart of Irish life, this has been well and truly filled by the new culture of self-help. The success of the booming self-help market lies in its ability to convince consumers that they are taking affirmative action and control, while in reality they are sustaining both a slavish dependence on commercial solutions to social problems and the continued atomisation of individuals. Self-help teaches us to fudge over and live with the symptoms of a dysfunctional social order rather than illuminating the real causes of the problem or indicating how it might be tackled. Since the causes are deemed to be predetermined (men are from Mars, women are from Venus – fact), the logic goes that there is nothing we can do about them and thus the market perpetuates itself in ever-increasing circles.

To advance any sort of criticism of the new, prosperous Ireland in the media, however, is to lay oneself open to ridicule. Callers to Joe Duffy's show on RTÉ Radio 1 attempting to air alternative viewpoints have simply been rounded on, accused of wanting to return to the days of unemployment, mass emigration and clerical child abuse. Their criticisms appear unreasonable precisely because the rhetoric of freedom of choice is so convincingly perpetuated by a mass media hell bent on giving us the *appearance* of participation, interactivity and democracy: audiences determine the ending of reality shows by text vote, banners run under the screen during the *Late Late Show* letting us know what (an edited version of) the general public thinks of the topic under discussion, leading questions are put to people in the street to determine how the nation feels about everything from immigration to gay marriage. Joe Public has never had so loud a voice in this discursive space, provided his views fit within the already rigged parameters of the debate. Increasingly, complexity and curiosity are perceived as getting in the way of 'what the punters want', which is in turn conflated with 'the public good'. And yet, when public service broadcasting is allowed to do its job, as in the case of the *Prime Time* special on Leas Cross nursing home or Mary Raftery's documentaries on child abuse, governments are forced to take action.

Too often, however, superficial cultural imagery and mass mediated discourses have been used as a convenient foil for the less pleasant material realities of post-Celtic Tiger Ireland. In the realm of multiculturalism, for example, a focus on colourful food, clothing, music and art has served to evade questions of racialisation and inequality, as well as many of the more troubling paradoxes that characterise Ireland's position in the new 'first world' order, for example that we adopt planning laws to prevent non-locals from building in rural areas here but give little if any consideration to the social impact of our own property investments overseas. The highly seductive discourse of progress has effectively distracted Irish people from the fact that processes of consumerism and privatisation have begun to reconfigure core aspects of their lives such as gender, sexuality, health and ethnicity, as well as their understanding of self-governance and community.

How, then, does a transformative politics take told in a country obsessed by wealth accumulation and widely convinced that radical politics has either failed, as in the case of socialism, or completely succeeded, as in the case of feminism? A first step must surely be to cut through the linguistic and visual illusions of progress with which we are surrounded, by understanding and educating about how the media and public relations industries work. Certainly, the current postmodern 'culture of noise' can be regarded as a potentially diverse public sphere in which a multiplicity of viewpoints is heard, but it is essential not to evade questions of power by continuing to ask: who speaks, who listens and whose voices have any impact? Drawing public attention to social injustice, whether through the media, research or activism, is a key step towards influencing government policy on criminal reform, health, education, homophobic bullying or advertising to children. The involvement of young people in politics is also key, a goal that can be achieved only if education is spent not in the sole pursuit of achieving 'leaving cert' points but in instilling in students a sense of civic-mindedness and communal ownership of and responsibility for public space and public assets. In Ireland, the growth of the 'Educate Together' schools is testament to the enduring commitment to the principles of genuine secularism and civil society as well as to democracy, self-government and intercultural exchange.

The contributions gathered here are intended to pose a direct and serious challenge to the defeatist consensus that there is no alternative for Irish society, by proposing workable solutions to the tide of social Darwinism in which the country is becoming swept up. The various contributors argue that the instigation of serious public debate, in which oppositional viewpoints are not dismissed as idealist or 'off beam', as well as community-level organisation around environmental, educational and multicultural issues, could lead to well-thought-out and long-term policies on education, the media, advertising, immigration, crime and security. Crucial to this endeavour is a rejection of a superficial 'public sphere' of sound-bites and images in favour of one based on the material realities of everyday life. Tree-hugger, lipstick lesbian, boy racer, yummy mummy, domestic goddess, decklander, new lad, menaissance man, metrosexual: wherever an ostensibly new, complex or contested phenomenon appears, the knee-jerk reaction has been to stereotype, to simplify and to trivialise, a process which goes hand in hand with that of the widespread commodification of virtually all aspects of our lives. These examples should make us wary of the power of cultural rhetoric. While transformative politics can certainly operate at the level of cultural expression, it is crucial that we do not lose sight of politics as a site of struggle over material, as well as symbolic, power. Social justice is not an obligation we must fulfil by staging feel-good celebrity media events such as Live 8 but a fundamental cornerstone upon which society and our concept of citizenship are built.

A transformative politics

Developing a transformative politics thus requires a theory of social change, in other words, a consideration of how fundamental change happens in society. It is remarkable that this dimension is largely overlooked in discussions of politics – whether among activists, policy makers, the media or even academics. Change is, by and large, envisaged as taking place either through changes to policies and programmes (a technical view of change) or through pressuring or changing power holders, usually political ones but sometimes economic ones (a managerialist view of change). However, a fundamentally conservative bias informs such a view, an assumption that, as Robert W. Cox puts it, 'with respect to essentials, the future will always be like the past' (Cox, 1996: 92). This is the view of change that informs the 2007–13 NDP, a view that sees change essentially as more of the same, just bigger and better. For example, the NDP assumes that the market will continue to provide the dynamic for Ireland's development, that its impact on the environment is sustainable and that Ireland will remain a deeply divided society, since the state has no policy to redistribute wealth and income from the rich to the poor. It is a pretty bleak view of the future for anyone who has a concern for the total good of society, as distinct from a concern for their own self-interest within it.

Of course, even a cursory consideration of broader processes of change over recent centuries reminds us that technical or managerialist approaches to social change have had relatively modest impacts compared with broader and more revolutionary processes, whether of left or right. Even over the course of the twentieth century, the world has been transformed by fascism and communism, by colonialism and then decolonisation, by war and the many attempts to ensure it does not happen again, especially the United Nations, and by the impact of such hugely influential social, political and cultural movements as social democracy, the women's movement and the human rights movement. Recognising this fundamentally shifts the focus of attention to social forces and struggles for power and influence. As Cox has put it: 'Really existing social power relations is the fundamental object of enquiry' (Cox, 2002: 79). Only when these social forces have converged into a particular configuration (such as social democracy or, as at present, neoliberalism) do technical and managerialist approaches become operative. So how do social forces converge into a particular configuration and, more importantly, how might such a configuration be changed? Getting an accurate answer to this question is vital for any hope of transforming Ireland.

Cox's theory of historical structures is a valuable guide here. For Cox sees any particular epoch as being dominated by a particular 'historical structure', namely the 'fit' between three categories of social forces – the material capabilities (how a society produces the goods and services that provision it), the ideas (the intersubjective meanings that constitute the 'common sense' of a particular era) and the institutions (the means through which a particular historical structure is stabilised, institutionalised and

perpetuated) (see Cox, 1996). This account therefore draws our attention
to the interrelationship between the different forms of power that provide
the basis for a stable society, namely, how the economic, cultural/social
and political powers mutually reinforce one another. What is perhaps
most appealing about Cox's theory is that it offers a means of identifying
how any particular historical structure may be changing. Two dimensions are crucial. The first is through the tensions that emerge between
the three forms of social forces that provide the basis for a stable social
structure. In other words, are the economic, cultural/social and political
forces supporting one another or beginning to pull against one another?
Here the role of ideas can provide an early-warning signal, for, as Stephen
Gill has put it, 'knowledge is also a process of social struggle ... between
hegemonic and counter-hegemonic perspectives and principles' (Gill,
2003: 38). Where ideas critical of the dominant social structure come
to the fore, then they undermine the legitimacy of that social structure.
Arguably, the greatest sign that this process is underway today is the
misnamed 'anti-globalisation' movement (misnamed because in truth it is
not against globalisation but is in fact a product of it and by and large is
espousing a different form of globalisation), not primarily because of the
practical impact of its ideas but much more because of its mobilisational
capacity. In other words, its critical message about neoliberalism and the
role of the market is clearly articulating the views of large numbers of
people around the world. The emergence of such a tension within the
dominant historical structure then reveals the second dimension of how
a historical structure changes – namely the emergence of an alternative
historical structure within the bowels of the present, as it were. For, if we
can identify alternative forms of material capabilities, alternative ideas
and alternative ways of organising society, then we are identifying an
alternative historical structure emerging. It may be fragmentary and weak
but so were the democratic and anti-monarchical forces that challenged
societies of privilege in the eighteenth century and the women's movement
that challenged patriarchal societies in the twentieth century. But in these
forces lay the seeds of the future.

There is nothing deterministic about Cox's theory of social change. The
identification of new social forces and the social struggles they give rise to
by no means makes their emergence and strengthening inevitable. They
can be defeated and even driven underground or co-opted into a marginal
but non-threatening position within the institutions of the dominant
historical structure. Arguably, this is the role that social partnership has
played in allowing a neoliberal historical structure to become dominant
in contemporary Ireland (what we know as the 'Celtic Tiger'). But the
contradictions do not go away and the call for social forces to promote

and struggle for alternatives remains. This is the seed of a transformative politics and, for this reason, the editors have asked each of the contributors to this book to identify such potentials within the areas of Irish life they write about. This shows clearly the potential for an alternative historical structure that exists in today's Ireland and, in some cases, the emergence of social forces to promote it. While these can sometimes be dismissed as being of relatively little importance (and such a view is actively endorsed by media and much academic discourse), such a dismissal is based on a very narrow and inadequate view of how social change happens. Putting them in the context of Cox's historical structures invests them with a significance that may more correctly identify their potential. Yet, this potential will be realised only through the activity, creativity, conviction and ingenuity of these social forces.

Note

1 'The world in 2005', *The Economist*, at www.economist.com/media/pdf/QUALITY_OF_LIFE.pdf (accessed April 2009).

Part I
Culture and society

2

The Irish language and Ireland's socio-economic development

JOHN WALSH

This chapter examines the influence of the promotion of the Irish language on Ireland's socio-economic development in both a theoretical and an empirical sense. Drawing on the long-standing tradition that sees Irish as a key resource for national socio-economic development, it rejects the suggestion that the language is irrelevant to the development of modern Ireland and argues that the integration of language planning and socio-economic planning is both necessary and beneficial. It goes on to sketch a theoretical framework, based on disciplines as diverse as development theory and sociolinguistics, in order better to guide understanding of the link between language and development, and to provide a robust defence for the relevance of Irish today. The influence of the promotion of Irish on socio-economic development is then examined in a range of contexts, in the Gaeltacht and elsewhere.

The demographic state of Irish today

Irish, although an official language of the Republic of Ireland and, since 2007, an official working language of the European Union, is also a minoritised language. Due to centuries of language shift to English, Irish persists as a language of spatially defined geographical communities – the Gaeltacht – located mostly along the western seaboard. According to the most recent census (2006), 89,260 people aged three years and over live in the Gaeltacht, 62,959 (70.5 per cent) of whom report that they are Irish speakers. However, only 36,498 (40.9 per cent) claim to speak Irish every day, 13,718 (15.4 per cent) of these within the education system only

(Central Statistics Office, 2007: 82–4). The fact that Irish is a core subject at all levels of obligatory education throughout the Republic of Ireland has been a major factor in creating a situation whereby 1.67 million people, or 41.9 per cent of the population, claimed competence in Irish in the 2006 census. Most of those returned as Irish speakers are of school-going age, rising to 72.5 per cent of eleven- to fourteen-year-olds; percentages for age cohorts over twenty fall dramatically (Central Statistics Office, 2007: 79).

For the first time in 2006, a question was asked in the census about daily use of Irish within and outside the education system. It was reported by 484,812 people (12 per cent of the total population or 29.2 per cent of Irish speakers) that they spoke Irish daily either within the education system only or both within and outside the education system. Only 53,471 people (1.3 per cent of the total population) spoke Irish daily outside the education system. Taken together with the 31,605 people who spoke Irish daily both within and outside the education system, the number speaking Irish daily outside the education system amounts to 85,076 (2.1 per cent of the total population). In Northern Ireland, the 2001 census recorded that 167,458 people or 10.4 per cent of the population had 'some knowledge of Irish', while 4.6 per cent said they could 'speak, read, write and understand Irish'. Knowledge of Irish is much higher among Catholics than Protestants and is strongest in Newry, Derry and West Belfast (Dunn *et al.*, 2001: 10; Northern Ireland Statistics and Research Agency, 2002: 72–3).

Irish is recognised in the constitution as the 'national' and 'first official language' and, since 2003, state bodies have been obliged by the Official Languages Act to enhance their provision of services in Irish. Irish in Northern Ireland is recognised by the Belfast Agreement of 1998. Despite the legal protection, however, Irish remains marginal to the workings of the state in both parts of Ireland.

Language and development: contributions from history

For at least 150 years, writers, commentators and political leaders from a variety of backgrounds have maintained that Irish plays a role in society beyond its obvious communicative function and provides a resource for national development. They have argued that Irish effects social and economic change through its influence on factors such as identity, self-confidence, self-sufficiency, character, cohesion and innovation. In some of the most important historical contributions on the wider role of Irish in society, particularly during the period of the cultural and linguistic revival of the late nineteenth century, and since the 1960s, three themes may be identified in the language–development link. These are:

- Irish as a basis for cultural development (Hyde, 1894; Ó Doibhlin, c. 1973, 2004a, 2004b; Lee, 1989);
- Irish as a basis for social development (Davis, 1843a, 1843b; Hyde, 1894; Blythe, 1958; de Fréine, 1960, 1965; Brennan, 1969; Ó Cadhain, c. 1970; Ó Doibhlin, c. 1973, 2004a, 2004b; Tovey *et al.*, 1989; Ó Murchú, 2003; Kirby, 2004);
- Irish as a basis for economic development (Gaelic League, 1903–10, c. 1936; Moran, 1905; Plunkett, 1905; Lee, 1989).

Some of these contributions were written by academics, but most are the work of journalists, polemicists and political leaders. Most lack an explicitly theoretical basis, which leaves them vulnerable to criticisms that they do not explain the relationships which they posit between language and development. Therefore, they require further investigation in the light of relevant bodies of theory.

A typology of language, culture and development

This chapter outlines three overarching approaches to the language–development relationship: the minority language promotion approach; the socio-cultural development approach; and the economic growth and modernisation approach. It then suggests a new theoretical framework which guides the remainder of the study.

The minority language promotion approach

The minority language promotion approach is the name given to a cluster of perspectives which theorise the position of a given minority language in relation to a majority language, and which prioritise the promotion of the weaker language. It is based on a number of theoretical foundations, most of which can be said to fall under the banner of 'macro-sociolinguistics', the branch of sociolinguistics which deals with 'macro' issues such as language policy and planning (LPP) (Coulmas, 1998: 1).

One body of theory posits that language influences cognition and is linked intimately to culture. It is based largely on the 'linguistic relativity principle', known widely as the 'Sapir–Whorf hypothesis', which holds that each language influences differently the ways in which its speakers conceptualise the world (Lee, 1996: 30, 84–7). While some scholars have rejected the hypothesis out of hand, Fishman has modified and refined it (1989, 1991, 1996, 2000). He has argued that language and cultural identity are linked in three ways: indexically, symbolically and in a part–whole fashion (1991: 20–4). These theories go some way towards substantiating the essentially psychological arguments advanced by many of the historical authors: that Irish is an integral part of national cultural identity and that promoting it has a positive influence on society.

Fishman's theory of reversing language shift (RLS) considers the condition of endangered languages in relation to their marginalisation by the dominant global socio-economic model (1991: 6). RLS is a process which reduces 'anomie and alienation' and is 'a potential contribution to overcoming some of the endemic sociocultural dislocation of society' (Fishman, 1991: 6–7). RLS considers more explicitly the links between promoting a traditional language and overcoming the underdevelopment of that language's speakers and, in this sense, it contributes to understandings of the language–development link.

A rights-based approach to language promotion situates it in the growing corpus of international language law. In a trenchant defence of 'linguistic human rights', it is argued that the failure to grant such rights leads to the denial of other social, cultural and economic rights and the danger of inter-ethnic conflict (Phillipson *et al.*, 1995: 2, 7). Therefore, this approach posits a connection between a failure to respect linguistic rights and a range of social, economic and political problems.

Finally, theories of LPP deal with direct interventions in favour of a specific language. There are many models (Ricento, 2006) but it will suffice to mention just two here. Mac Donnacha's 'integrated language planning model' stresses the importance of 'nurturing and strengthening the language community'. This raises the possibility of closer integration of language and development through the hypothesis that supporting the development of the community of speakers consolidates their language (Mac Donnacha, 2000: 19–20). Secondly, Fishman's 'graded intergenerational disruption scale' – which contains eight stages to be undertaken in order to stem the decline of a given language – gives his RLS theory further transformative powers as a general theory of social change, rooted in language (Fishman, 2000: 458).

Although sociolinguistics offers some rich insights into aspects of the language–development link, its main weakness is that it does not intersect adequately with theories of development. Therefore, the next two approaches turn to theories of development itself, firstly socio-cultural development and then economic growth and modernisation.

The socio-cultural development approach

Recent innovations in development theory contribute to an analysis of the language–development link. Many of these come from the field of human development, but insights are also provided by cultural political economy and the economics of language.

'Human development' as a concept emerged only in 1990, in the form of the first *Human Development Report*, published annually by the United Nations Development Programme. The Programme's concept of development is fundamentally different to the dominant paradigm (see below): growth is a means by which human development is to be achieved, not an end in itself. Growth in itself is not sufficient, but must be translated into improvements in people's lives (United Nations Development Programme, 1992: 12). The origins of human development are diffuse, but it has its roots in the social well-being approach pioneered by development economists such as Sen (1999: 3). While the original concept of human development was measured by adult literacy and education, life expectancy at birth and per capita income, more recently the role of culture in development has been considered (United Nations Development Programme, 1996: 55). The *Human Development Report* of 2004 was dedicated entirely to culture and included some brief references to language (2004: 60–4). The strength of the human development approach is that it takes a broad view of development, which includes economic growth but which prioritises other social and cultural factors, many of which were posited by the historical authors as outcomes of the promotion of Irish: social cohesion, self-confidence, initiative, participation and empowerment. Culture is seen as giving meaning to the process of development, by embedding it in people's everyday experiences and shared identity. This approach contains few references to language, however.

The cultural political economy of development provides another source of guidance on the language–development link. Taking Kirby's definition of the 'political economy of development' as the ways in which market, state and society interact to achieve socio-economic development (2002a: 96, 129), the cultural political economy of development may be understood as the influence of *culture* on these interactions between market, society and state. Tucker posits a connection between the denial or suppression of a specific cultural identity and the exclusion of such a group from development (1997: 6–7), while Stavenhagen (1990) and Hettne (1995) pay attention to culture and social movements. Therefore, the tripartite division of market, state and society may be further refined to consider the role of *civil* society in the development process – dynamic collective action in the public sphere – rather than society in general (Marshall, 1998: 74; Giddens, 2002: 439–41, 684). Although the tripartite division is a useful tool of analysis, the weakness of cultural political economy is the marginal role which it accords to language.

Finally, the 'economics of language' approach is also relevant to the language–development link. Criticising the failure of mainstream economics to consider language as a factor worthy of sustained attention, Grin has argued that economics and linguistic variables influence each other (1996: 30–5). While much work remains to be done on the causal links between language processes and economic processes, Grin (2003) concludes that there is far more circumstantial evidence today than before that linguistic diversity is worth cultivating from an economic viewpoint. This approach is useful because it deals predominantly with the relationship between language and economic variables, but its weakness for the present study is that it does not consider the link with *socio*-economic development in general.

In general, therefore, while the socio-cultural development approach is appropriate to analyse the influence of *culture* on development, it is not sufficient to analyse the influence of *language* on development, because discussion of language remains marginal. The minority language and socio-cultural development approaches exist in opposition to the third category, the economic growth and modernisation approach.

The economic growth and modernisation approach

Development studies as a distinct academic discipline did not emerge until after the Second World War, in response to the destruction of some western countries and the political decolonisation of parts of Asia, the Middle East and Africa. It was during the same period that the terms 'developed' and 'undeveloped' entered common usage, as did 'First World' and 'Third World'. Development has deep roots in historical theories of economics and sociology, and it has been profoundly influenced by the economic growth and modernisation paradigm (Remenyi, 2004: 25). During the early period, development was associated almost exclusively with major institutions such as the World Bank and the International Monetary Fund, which between them divided the world into 'developed' and 'developing' states (Martinussen, 1997: 5; McKay, 2004: 45).

The modernisation thesis has been employed widely throughout the period since development emerged as a distinct discipline. It emphasises the importance of industrialisation and growth and underlines the inevitability of a linear, evolutionary transition to the modern. Frequently, proponents of this approach have criticised 'traditional cultures'. For instance, Ayres (1944) argued that the development of a society was inhibited by traditional culture and that science, not sensibility, drove development. Modernisation was 'irresistible' and acceptance of 'the industrial way of life and all the values that go with it' was the only 'alternative' (cited in Barry,

1987: 9). Lewis (1955: 433) wrote that 'illiterate' societies whose cultures are not based on modern science would find it very difficult to modernise, but that change was inevitable. Rostow (1968: 4) argued that every poor society could take solace from the hope of 'take-off' to 'the age of high mass-consumption'. Later, he hinted that cultural factors, such as 'tribal attachment', may have slowed down the transition to mass consumption (Rostow, 1990: 501). Other theorists of modernisation have spoken of 'advanced' and 'backward' countries or peoples (Baran, 1958: 91; Myint, 1958: 93), underlining the ethnocentrism of this approach. In the field of sociology, Talcott Parsons, 'theorist of modernity', also favoured a scientific evolutionary approach to social change and represented a strongly American cultural outlook (see Hamilton, 1985; Robertson, 1991).

Although there are few direct references to language in these works, because the minority cultures disparaged by many of the theorists were intimately associated with ancestral languages it can be argued that such languages would similarly be viewed as impediments to progress. The Sapir–Whorf hypothesis, which emerged before the heyday of modernisation theory in the 1950s and 1960s, posited that language and culture were intimately linked (see above). Therefore, the view that language and culture were two sides of the one coin ensured that the dismissal by modernisationists of minority *culture* was equally a rejection of minority *language* (May, 2001: 159).

Conclusion

The dominant economic growth and modernisation approach is not an appropriate lens through which to view the influence of the Irish language on Ireland's socio-economic development. It is too narrowly focused on economic growth to analyse the broader and more holistic concept of development, and its opposition to 'pre-scientific', 'illiterate' or 'tribal' cultures rules out any constructive engagement with the view that a minoritised language such as Irish benefits a country's development. Both the minority language promotion and the socio-cultural development approaches have more to contribute to understandings of the influence of Irish on Ireland's development. These contributions can be drawn together in a new framework, a *linguistic political economy of development*. This framework facilitates an analysis of the ways in which a minority language in particular, as opposed to a minority culture in general, influences the interrelationships between market, state and civil society and their achievement of developmental outcomes. Applied to Ireland, the linguistic political economy of development guides an investigation of how the Irish language influences the market–state–civil society nexus and the developmental outcomes which emerge from it. This is the map which guides the remainder of this chapter.

Case studies

Using the theoretical framework, the language–development link is now examined in an empirical way through a series of case studies, two in the traditional Gaeltacht, one in the institutional setting of the Gaeltacht development agency, Údarás na Gaeltachta, and two in urban areas. The case studies are based on document analysis and semi-structured interviews with a variety of stakeholders representing the three approaches to language and development outlined above.

The Gaeltacht

Two Gaeltacht areas were chosen: South Conamara in County Galway, which exhibits high levels of both language vitality and socio-economic development (although there are pockets of deprivation) and Na Déise in County Waterford, which exhibits relatively high socio-economic development and low to moderate language vitality.

In the strongly Irish-speaking Gaeltacht of South Conamara (Central Statistics Office, 2004b), development was found to emerge from a dynamic interaction between civil society, state and market. Irish appears to exert a strong influence on this interaction, particularly on certain state actors and civil society. The private sector, whose business is not generally directly related to Irish, is less amenable to this influence, but the growing number of language-based industries is slowly changing this. Irish has been given an additional boost in the area by the presence of several key institutions (state, voluntary and private) charged with language promotion, which are located along the coastal strip west of Galway City. These institutions include the national television and radio stations TG4 and RTÉ Raidió na Gaeltachta, the headquarters of the Gaeltacht development agency, Údarás na Gaeltachta, and the Department of Community, Rural and Gaeltacht Affairs, as well as the office of the language commissioner and several independent television production companies, language schools and language-based industries. This has guaranteed a local presence for Irish and a steady supply of well paid and prestigious employment for local people competent in Irish. Were it not for the relatively strong position of Irish as the community language, the cluster of language-based institutions and industries would not be possible. Such employment, in turn, improves public perceptions of Irish, due to its additional functionality in the area.

The resilience of Irish in Conamara may also have been supported by the strong tradition of activism, perhaps best illustrated by the Gaeltacht civil rights movement of the 1960s and 1970s. This movement played a key role in the campaign which led to the establishment of several Gaeltacht Irish-language institutions such as Raidió na Gaeltachta and, in later years, Údarás na Gaeltachta and TG4. However, the linguistic political economy of development in South Conamara is a very delicate equilibrium, vulnerable to external shocks. The combination of high development and relative normalisation of Irish is threatened by a set of factors that include the nature of industrialisation itself, the mobility of the workforce, the planning system (which has facilitated urban sprawl well into the Gaeltacht), the dominance of the growth-led and modernisationist approach to development and the anglicising influence of central and local government, despite official policy in favour of Irish (Walsh, 2005).

The case study of Gaeltacht na nDéise in County Waterford reveals that the relative resilience of Irish there has had a positive impact on socio-economic development (Central Statistics Office, 2004b). Were most people in the community to cease regularly using Irish, and were key local institutions to switch to English, there would not be enough fluent and habitual speakers of Irish to ensure the continued presence of large language-based industries such as the independent television production company or local Irish language college. The area has benefited considerably economically from inward investment due to its Gaeltacht status. Local civil society has also harnessed the language for social ends, by drawing on this resource to guide community development and to engage with the state over the issue of housing sprawl extending into the Gaeltacht. The question of insensitive planning is the most pressing local question at present and threatens to dilute significantly the local Irish-speaking population. Na Déise, like many other Gaeltacht communities, finds itself at the centre of a struggle between opposing approaches to language and socio-economic development. The anglicising influence of local government, combined with its growth-led and modernisationist approach to development, exists in tension with generally under-resourced and under-staffed community and voluntary groups, representing the socio-cultural or minority language promotion approaches, or a combination of both. The vulnerability of this Gaeltacht community underlines the need for more local expertise in language planning, in order to strengthen the influence of Irish on the political economy of development (Walsh, 2005).

It is concluded from these traditional Gaeltacht case studies that Irish positively influences the political economy of development in the Gaeltacht, but that this influence varies from place to place. For instance, the influence of Irish tends to be stronger in areas where the market contains firms whose operations are directly related to Irish itself, or which implement strong internal policies in favour of Irish. This is clearly the case in South Conamara. However, the influence of Irish is felt even when the number of habitual speakers is relatively low, such as in Na Déise, when local civil society explicitly draws upon it as a resource for development by raising awareness of it and integrating it into daily activities. The presence of strongly Irish institutions in an area is also likely to strengthen the role of Irish in the state–civil society–market interplay, and is a necessary part of future micro language planning initiatives (Walsh, 2005). In general, however, the Gaeltacht case studies underline the challenge of consolidating an Irish-speaking geographical community in the context of a neoliberal and strongly monolingual state.

Údarás na Gaeltachta

Another case study investigates the ways in which the influence of Irish on development is understood by Údarás na Gaeltachta, the state development agency for the Gaeltacht. Údarás was established in 1979 following a campaign, led mainly by Gaeltacht civil society, for a more democratic and language-focused agency than its predecessor, Gaeltarra Éireann. However, although the legislation (the Údarás na Gaeltachta Act, 1979) under which Údarás was established gave the impression that the promotion of Irish would be to the fore, it remained, like Gaeltarra, firmly focused on industrialisation and rooted in a growth-led and modernisationist approach. In terms of the theoretical framework, therefore, both Gaeltarra and Údarás achieved development primarily through a state–market interplay (grant aid to industries) but the influence of Irish on this interplay was largely incidental. However, a series of reports representing both the socio-cultural and minority language promotion approaches raised concerns that industrialisation had hastened anglicisation and that a more holistic developmental approach was required (Comhairle na Gaeilge, 1971; Gaeltarra Éireann/ SFADCO, 1971; Anson, 1982; Ó Cinnéide *et al.*, 1985). Such criticism culminated in the report of the Gaeltacht Commission of 2002, which revealed a linguistic crisis in the Gaeltacht and a rapidly changing economic structure. The Commission called for the radical restructuring of Údarás na Gaeltachta in order to reflect the new sociolinguistic and socio-economic situation (2002: 17; Ó Cinnéide *et al.*, 2001).

Údarás na Gaeltachta responded to the criticism and in 2005 announced a review of its roles and responsibilities. The origins of the review can be dated to the mid-1990s, when the sheer success of the industrialisation strategy led to full employment in much of the Gaeltacht, but also prompted concerns about negative linguistic consequences as workers from outside filled local job vacancies. Údarás attempted to diversify its operations into other sectors thought to be more culturally appropriate, such as the social economy, cultural tourism, the traditional arts and industries based directly on Irish.[1] In terms of the theoretical framework, this represents a re-orientation away from a primary state–market nexus to a more holistic engagement with both civil society and market. However, the organisation has said it is restrained by the legislation from expanding its areas of responsibility beyond a narrow industrial development role.[2] As of March 2009, the Údarás Act was still being redrafted to facilitate this change.[3]

Shortly after the review was announced, Údarás published a new development policy for the years 2005–10. The strategy document paints a picture of an organisation broadening its focus from that of a narrow industrial development agency to an unprecedented type of institution with a wide range of developmental and linguistic functions. The Irish language is given a higher profile in the document than any other area of policy:

> As far as Irish is concerned, language protection and development initiatives will be given a language planning basis, the approach to language consolidation among client companies will be reviewed … alliances to consolidate and reclaim Irish will be created with local communities, more effective use will be made of local organisations funded by Údarás in order to develop a comprehensive campaign of language planning, consolidation and development throughout the Gaeltacht, attempts will be made to increase substantially the number of language-based projects, and robust lobbying will be carried out on behalf of Irish speakers with other sections of the public service. (Údarás na Gaeltachta, 2005: 3–4, translation)

In what amounts to a reversal of the emphasis of twenty-five years, employment creation is placed close to the *end* of the list of policy priorities for the years ahead. Even this aspect of policy is linked to Irish: employment opportunities related to the Official Languages Act, public service training, translation and the arts, cultural and educational sectors are emphasised (Údarás na Gaeltachta, 2005: 9). There are also references to strengthening links with the community and voluntary sector, and to broader development, comprising social as well as economic aspects (Údarás na Gaeltachta, 2005: 3).

The document represents a significant modification of Údarás na Gaeltachta's traditional industrialisation strategy, and a shift from achieving development through a state–market interaction largely separate from language to a more holistic state–market–civil-society interaction *based* on the consolidation of Irish. Although it does not state explicitly that promoting Irish influences Gaeltacht development, it is reasonable to infer from the strong emphasis on Irish that development *without* it would be deemed incomplete or flawed. There is also considerable emphasis on community development and underdeveloped areas. Therefore, both the minority language promotion and the socio-cultural development approaches are stronger than was previously the case. However, given the fact that the success of Údarás was always measured in terms of employment creation, and that it has deep roots in the modernisationist approach, it may be too early to reclassify it. Furthermore, the strategy is very recent (May 2005) and cannot be implemented in full without legislative change (see above).

It is concluded that, through the work of Gaeltarra and Údarás, Irish has positively influenced the *economic* development of the Gaeltacht in the past, but that the ways in which that link are understood are changing fundamentally. The state would have invested in these areas anyway, but without separate institutions it is reasonable to infer that investment would not have been as sustained or systematic. However, in the past the influence of Irish was *indirect*, rather than direct, as it simply provided the mechanism required by the state to intervene economically. The *direct* influence of Irish on Gaeltacht *economic* development through, for instance, language-based industries has been relatively weak to date, but will be strengthened if the new Údarás policy is successful. The attention to the social aspects of development also illustrates the extent to which the organisation is shifting its priorities.

Urban areas

The urban areas of Galway City and West Belfast were also chosen in order to investigate empirically the influence of Irish on socio-economic development *outside* the traditional Gaeltacht. Cities have long been centres of anglicisation in Ireland and, therefore, the revitalisation of Irish in them amounts to a counter-cultural struggle, an attempt to reverse a potent symbol of cultural dislocation stretching back to the Norman invasion (Maguire, 1991: 13). Although it contained large numbers of Irish speakers when the state was established (Government of Ireland, 1926), Galway City is now heavily anglicised and there is virtually no difference between the percentage of its residents who speak Irish daily (9.4 per cent) compared with the rest of the country (9.3 per cent) (Central Statistics Office, 2004a: 14, 17, 59). However, there is strong interaction between Galway and the strongly Irish-speaking Gaeltacht area to the west. A report published in 1988 on the socio-economic impacts associated with the Galway Gaeltacht found that the total gain to Galway City businesses from the state intervention in the Gaeltacht and associated economic activities in

1987 was £13.1 million, €28.4 million in today's values (Ó Cinnéide and Keane, 1988: 30).[4] The authors concluded that state Gaeltacht investment contributed handsomely to the prosperity of Galway City, and recommended that city businesses show 'language courtesy' to their Gaeltacht customers by increasing the amount of Irish used (pp. 36–8).

The report coincided with the establishment of Gaillimh le Gaeilge (literally 'Galway with Irish'), a non-governmental organisation with state backing designed to promote Irish among Galway businesses. Gaillimh le Gaeilge has coordinated the introduction of bilingual menus, bilingual signage, refresher courses for Irish-speaking staff and an annual award for the business deemed to have done the most to promote Irish. An originally sceptical business community has supported the project and the city centre in particular has a strong bilingual appearance. However, with the exception of a study on the cost-effectiveness of Gaillimh le Gaeilge (Grin and Vaillancourt, 1999), no detailed research has been carried out on the effects of the project on levels of language use.

All three approaches to language and development are to be found in Galway City. Many city businesses, while willing to give limited support to Irish through, for instance, the erection of bilingual signage, are hostile to more robust language planning and tend to promote instead the modernisationist approach. The minority language promotion approach is spearheaded by voluntary language bodies, while the City Council and City Development Board represent the socio-cultural approach. In terms of the theoretical framework, Gaillimh le Gaeilge links state, civil society and market on the basis of Irish, with the aim of consolidating it. It contains the potential to strengthen considerably the influence of Irish on development, through, for instance, the establishment of closer alliances with the tourism industry and other elements of civil society which promote Irish. Although Galway is influenced linguistically by the Gaeltacht, the city is another example of how even a weak Irish language community can be harnessed, using targeted initiatives, for developmental ends (Walsh, 2005).

West Belfast contains the highest proportion (11 per cent) in Northern Ireland of people who claim to be able to speak, read, write and understand Irish (Northern Ireland Statistics and Research Agency, 2002: 73). The area also contains some of the highest levels of disadvantage in Northern Ireland, a legacy of the devastation of the Troubles (Northern Ireland Statistics and Research Agency, 2003). However, the changing political climate has led to an ambitious project of linguistic and socio-economic regeneration in West Belfast, an embryonic linguistic political economy of development in action. The 'Gaeltacht Quarter' project, centred on the Falls Road, envisages the Irish language influencing the combined efforts of social groups, government agencies and private business to create development. There are plans for a board of twelve organisations involved in socio-economic development, community development, the Irish language, urban regeneration, education and health, and state funding is currently being sought (Dutton, 2004; Walsh, 2005).

It may be concluded from these urban case studies that Irish influences the socio-economic development of both West Belfast and Galway City, but that the link is understood in different ways. In West Belfast, Irish is commonly viewed as a cohesive force which contributes to the *social* and *psychological* well-being of the community, reflecting strongly elements of the socio-cultural approach. The unique political context of West Belfast has also been a contributing factor (Maguire, 1991: 99). This does not rule out the possibility of *economic* benefits, as language-based employment is envisaged by the Gaeltacht Quarter project. However, despite the announcement of ambitious plans in 2004, at the time of writing, the Gaeltacht Quarter project had yet to be established formally. In Galway City, there is more emphasis on the direct *economic* benefit of Irish, due to the work of Gaillimh le Gaeilge, but social and cultural benefits are also emphasised. However, the lack of coordination of Irish-language activities in Galway, and the lack of research on the effects of Gaillimh le Gaeilge, are restraining factors.

Language policy and planning (LPP)

The case studies above draw attention to the need for greater coordination of LPP efforts, at both micro and macro level. Despite over eighty years of language policy under independent government, there is no comprehensive national LPP framework in existence and Irish remains a marginal policy issue. Such a gap has been identified by many commentators as a key weakness in Irish language planning (Gaeltacht Commission, 2002: 17; Ó Flatharta, 2004; Walsh, 2006, forthcoming). Although many worthwhile projects exist,[5] these tend to operate in isolation from each other and there is no overarching strategy to unite them. The aims of the language policy are unclear. In 1965, the Irish government retreated from the original policy of re-gaelicisation in favour of bilingualisation, a vague concept (Government of Ireland, 1965: 10). Similarly, LPP and socio-economic development policy tend to operate in isolation from each other, as illustrated by the paucity of references to Irish in key national documents on development (Government of Ireland, 1999, 2002; Department of Enterprise, Trade and Employment, 2006). Although an all-Ireland body for language promotion, Foras na Gaeilge, has been in existence since late 1998, it has yet to publish its detailed intentions in relation to LPP, based on international best practice in these fields. At the end of 2006, the government issued a statement on the Irish language and promised to develop a twenty-year strategy within two years (Government of Ireland, 2006). Work on the strategy began in 2008 and was expected to be completed by mid-2009. Such a long-term approach should lead to greater coordination of LPP efforts (Walsh, forthcoming).

Conclusion

This study indicates that the promotion of Irish positively influences Ireland's socio-economic development. The Gaeltacht case studies revealed that the state's intervention in these areas, on the basis of their linguistic distinctiveness, has brought considerable *economic* benefits. Historically, the influence of Irish on such economic development was indirect, but due to the comprehensive new Údarás na Gaeltachta strategy, Irish can be expected to exert a more direct influence on Gaeltacht economic development in the future. An indirect and largely *social* influence apparent in the Gaeltacht case studies was the perception that Irish was a resource which contributed to well-being and self-confidence and which could be harnessed for community development. The strongest evidence was apparent in South Conamara, where Irish remains dominant. Such a finding prompts the question: what benefits accrue to the vast majority of communities elsewhere where Irish is *not* dominant? Census returns reveal that much of the official Gaeltacht is now indistinct linguistically from the rest of Ireland, so separating Gaeltacht from non-Gaeltacht is a false dichotomy. To use the terminology of the first Gaeltacht Commission, of the 1920s, the entire state is in essence a 'Breac-Ghaeltacht',[6] where Irish is used frequently by a minority through social networks and is supported passively by a majority, most of whom have some knowledge of it.

It follows from this that the findings of the weaker Gaeltacht and Galway City studies are relevant for the Republic of Ireland as a whole, because there is very little difference between levels of Irish in these two areas. The applicability of the West Belfast study to other situations in Ireland is limited by the unique political circumstances and the strong association of Irish with nationalist cultural identity. Such conditions do not apply in the Republic, but it is reasonable to conclude that the example of West Belfast could be applied to other nationalist areas of Northern Ireland. The main difference between the influence of Irish on development in the largely English-speaking areas and the small number of strongly Irish-speaking Gaeltacht areas is that there are fewer employment opportunities based on Irish (direct economic influences) in the former due to the smaller number of habitual speakers. Therefore, the influence of Irish on the strongly Irish-speaking Gaeltacht appears to be both *economic* and *social*, whereas it is largely only *social* in the rest of the country. This does not rule out the possibility of creating more language-based employment outside the Gaeltacht (see below). Overall, the empirical research underlines the tension in Irish-speaking communities between, on the one hand, the predominantly monolingual, modernisationist and anglicising ideology of the state and market and, on the other, the efforts – mostly by civil society – to consolidate Irish and link it with socio-economic development at local level. This is the most serious obstacle to proponents of the minority language promotion approach.

Recommendations for policy

Because the chapter has established a link between the promotion of Irish and Ireland's socio-economic development, it is appropriate to recommend granting the language a more central role in development policy. At a conceptual level, this means broadening the concept of development itself, a stark challenge given the dominance of the growth-led and monolingual approach in Ireland at present. The academic community, both sociolinguists and other social scientists, has a central role to play in presenting new frameworks for interpreting development, and in providing appropriate training in LPP. There is also a need for greater cooperation between language and development agencies. A starting point would be the identification of key stakeholders in both fields and the creation of a national coordinating structure, perhaps under a future National Development Plan (Walsh, 2004). Employment creation based on Irish has been limited to date, but coordinated efforts could create significant job opportunities through, for instance, a formalised national structure of adult education, including the provision of teaching resources, the training of teachers and the establishment of language learning centres. The Irish-language media, which has grown considerably in recent years, could be further consolidated, although in privately owned media Irish is either marginal or absent entirely (Watson, 2003; see also Roddy Flynn, chapter 6 in this volume).

Further economic and social opportunities could emerge from a coordinated national structure of micro-level Irish-language initiatives, based in physical centres. There is no structure similar to the Welsh *Mentrau Iaith* ('language ventures'), local Welsh-language 'one-stop shops' providing various services (Campbell, 2000; Williams, 2000; Mac Giolla Chríost, 2006). Such physical spaces are urgently needed in every Irish community as points of reference and to ensure the delivery of services through Irish. The Official Languages Act, which is bringing about a gradual improvement in public services in Irish, needs robust political support, and should be strengthened to cover the private sector, as is the case in Catalonia (Hall, 2001). Some of the above elements are already in place, but their impact is lessened by the absence of a national planning framework for Irish, setting out clear targets and ensuring that various language planning initiatives are coordinated and their effectiveness monitored. The absence of such a framework is a serious weakness in national LPP and means that the full contribution of the Irish language to Ireland's development is not being exploited. It is to be hoped that the twenty-year government strategy for Irish will begin to address that weakness.

Notes

The author wishes to thank those people who made themselves available for interview while this study was conducted between 2001 and 2005, many of whom have wished to remain anonymous.

1 Interview with G. Ó Tuathaigh, Professor of History, National University of Ireland, Galway, 19 April 2004.
2 Interview with P. Ó hAoláin, Deputy Chief Executive, Údarás na Gaeltachta, Na Forbacha, 10 December 2004.
3 Interview with P. Ó hAoláin, Chief Executive, Údarás na Gaeltachta, 26 May 2006.
4 Conversion information provided by Barry Condron, Central Bank Economic Analysis Unit, 21 July 2006.
5 For instance, the Department of Community, Rural and Gaeltacht Affairs provides limited funding for a small number of micro-level language planning initiatives in selected Gaeltacht areas (Department of Community, Rural and Gaeltacht Affairs, 2004).
6 'Breac-Ghaeltacht', literally 'speckled Gaeltacht', was defined by the Commission as an area where between 25 and 79 per cent of the population could speak Irish. By contrast, 'Fíor-Ghaeltacht' ('true Gaeltacht') referred to areas containing at least 80 per cent Irish speakers (see Walsh *et al.*, 2005).

3

If I wanted to go there I wouldn't start from here: re-imagining a multi-ethnic nation

PIARAS MAC ÉINRÍ

The well known BBC late-night news programme *Newsnight* reviewed the hit Irish movie *Once*, a kind of love story between two musicians, one Irish and one Czech, on 12 October 2007. Presenter Kirsty Wark observed that immigration in Ireland seems to have 'largely been a happy experience'. Populist Irish economist and pundit David McWilliams published a book on Ireland's economy and society (McWilliams, 2007a) in which he addresses the issue of immigration by suggesting that Ireland can avoid the difficulties experienced by other countries by importing the right sort of immigrants, that is to say, highly skilled people and, notably, members of the global Irish diaspora. All will be well, it seems, if Ireland uses the 'soft power' of the diaspora and if one can imagine 'a greater Ireland that transcends geography, where the country is the mother ship and the tribe is the nation' (McWillliams, 2007b). He also says:

> The Israelis have followed an ethnic immigration policy, where every Jewish person in the world is given 'the right to return'. This has been at the expense of the Palestinians, but as we have no 'Palestinians', an Irish right to return would threaten no one. If managed properly, the more people we have in the country, the more dynamic it will be, with a greater sense of a national project. (McWilliams, 2007b)

I consider Wark's comment to be too insouciant, although unsurprising because it forms part of a current received myth of how well – indeed, by inference, how much better than anyone else – Ireland is thought to be handling immigration. McWilliams' idea, by contrast, is pernicious and dangerous but also goes to the heart of how Irish people tend imagine themselves as a nation. I wish to explore the implications of this thinking

and to suggest that unless it is challenged and changed, it will not be possible to lay the basis for a successful multi-ethnic society.

Mainstream Ireland has imagined itself in mono-ethnic, mono-cultural
tribal terms since the foundation of the state, even if this never corre-
sponded to the realities. Moreover, the decoupling in the 1998 Belfast
Agreement of the territorial claim to a thirty-two-county Ireland from a
state of 'Irishness', while undoubtedly helpful in laying the groundwork
for the peace process, may also have had the unfortunate side-effect of
reinforcing an emphasis on virtual Irishness, an 'Ireland of the mind'.
Indeed, the effect of this move has arguably been to re-inscribe and re-
encode Irishness in terms of bodies, not territories, as was all too clearly
evident in the 2004 referendum in the Republic on citizenship rights,
which removed the hitherto automatic right to citizenship conferred on
any child born in Ireland.

In considering the situation of foreigners and ethnic minorities in
Ireland before the 1990s, the condition of indigenous religious minorities
probably offers the most instructive paradigm. De Valera's 1937 constitution did not recognise Roman Catholicism specifically as the religion of
the state, despite the wishes of some that it should, and did recognise the
place of a number of other confessions. Nevertheless, the public culture of
the country was and remained overwhelmingly Catholic. Insofar as there
were migrants and minorities in Ireland, they were expected, in a conservative and consensus-based culture, to know their place – a silent and
subordinate one. I recall a local Italian family, part of the community of
post-war Italian migrants, mainly from Casalattico (Reynolds, 1993), who
ran the local fish-and-chip shop in Kilmacud, Dublin, as such families did
in many of the new and growing Dublin suburbs in the 1950s and 1960s.
It was thought odd that they spoke a foreign language at home but at least,
people said, they were Catholics.

We have now entered a new era in Irish history. It would be disingenuous
to argue, on the grounds that Ireland has always had immigration and
diversity, that the acceptance of the current substantial scale of immigration should automatically be seen as unproblematic. It is certainly true
that the presence of the 'other' in the form of immigrants of various
ethnic backgrounds was not unknown in Ireland before the Celtic Tiger
generation (Rolston and Shannon, 2002; Garner, 2004). But I can also
say, as a matter of simple fact and as someone who subsequently lived
for several years in various ethnically mixed cities in other countries, that
I had never, in the period before I left Ireland for the first time in 1971,
met or spoken with a black or Asian person, although I was familiar with
the local Italian family already mentioned and grew up with (Irish) Jewish
next-door neighbours. Until the late 1990s, this – never meeting ethnic

others – would have been a not untypical experience of most Irish people who had not themselves become migrants.

How, in light of this history, should one characterise the discourses of 'race', immigration and integration in Ireland today? I draw on a number of key articles which have already sought to address some of these issues (McVeigh, 1992; Mac An Ghaill, 2002; Fanning, 2002, 2007; Rolston and Shannon, 2002; Garner, 2004; Gray, 2006; Lentin and McVeigh, 2006). The new reality is one of dynamic, contradictory and rapidly evolving discourses; more research and analysis are needed. In the meantime, however, I would argue that, with the exception of a very generalised and deep-rooted phenomenon of anti-traveller racism, more widespread and virulent than any other comparable sentiment in Ireland, in the present state of our knowledge we do not know enough about the persistence, level and extent of *overt* racism in Ireland today. What is more useful at this juncture is to explore the negative factors *already latent* in Irish attitudes, and which began to come actively into play once Ireland became an immigrant society. Few thinking people would now assert that the mass of the population is free of any prejudice. Nor could it be reliably argued that there is no institutional racism, or that the state should be absolved of its responsibilities in respect of addressing this. The evidence for widespread anti-traveller discrimination is overwhelming. But it is necessary to consider, in McVeigh's (1992) phrase, the *specificity* of Irish racism and to examine how it may become activated in a more dangerous and virulent form.

Political discourses and public opinion concerning migrants

Irish politicians do not usually openly express racist views, though there have been exceptions. Cork TD Noel O'Flynn attacked asylum seekers in 2001, saying the country was being 'held hostage by spongers, wasters and con-men' (Riegel and Niland, 2002), something which did him little subsequent harm with the electorate. Taoiseach Bertie Ahern was critical, describing the remarks as neither 'educated' nor 'tolerant', although characteristically he took no punitive action. O'Flynn later used Dáil privilege to accuse 'illegal immigrants' in general of 'misbehaviour on the streets', of having chosen a life of crime and, most seriously, of 'causing hostile public reaction because of their anti-social behaviour and abuse of Irish hospitality'.

> Mr. O'Flynn: Am I to tell the citizens of Cork that they have no right to express views on events such as occurred at the North Quay Centre a few days ago? Must I tell them not to complain about being pushed off the

pavement by illegal immigrants because that would be racist? Will I tell shopkeepers in Cork that they are to close their eyes to the intimidation they are suffering when some groups of illegal immigrants enter their shops and steal from them? Some, as Deputies know, have chosen a life of crime, including credit card scams and drug dealing. Is this the behaviour of people who entered this country looking for asylum? Surely they should be behaving themselves and conforming with the laws of this country. (*Dáil Debates*, vol. 547, 31 January 2002)

Few Irish parliamentarians have, however, used such offensively crude language as Deputy O'Flynn. One should also bear in mind that no less a person than Jacques Chirac, subsequently President of the French Republic, expressed the following view about immigrants in 1991:

Comment voulez-vous que le travailleur français qui travaille avec sa femme, et qui, ensemble, gagnent environ 15,000 francs, et qui voit sur le palier à côté de son HLM, entassée, une famille avec un père de famille, trois ou quatre épouses, et une vingtaine de gosses, et qui gagne 50,000 francs de prestations sociales, sans naturellement travailler … si vous ajoutez le bruit et l'odeur, hé bien le travailleur français sur le palier devient fou…. Et ce n'est pas être raciste que de dire cela. (Chirac, 1991)

How do you expect the Frenchman who works, together with his wife, for about €2,500 per month, and who sees on the landing beside his own in the public housing scheme, a family, with a father, three or four wives, and twenty or so children, who get €8,300 in social payouts, without of course working … if you add the noise and the smell, well then the French worker on the landing gets mad…. And it's not racist to say that. (Author's translation)

It is also noteworthy that in Ireland there is no substantial, explicitly anti-immigrant party similar to the Belgian Vlaams Belang, the British National Front or the French Front National. The sole political anti-immigrant movement which exists in Ireland, the Immigration Control Platform, appears to be little more than an occasionally updated website.[1] Its leader, Áine Ní Chonaill, has stood for election on a few occasions, as has another party member. The votes obtained were negligible. In 2007 Ted Neville obtained 804 votes for the party in Cork South Central, while Ní Chonaill got 926 votes in Dublin South Central on her last outing in 2002, in spite, or perhaps because, of a high media profile.[2] One other individual, Justin Barrett, came to national prominence in 2004 when he ran for the European elections on an independent, anti-Nice, anti-abortion, anti-immigrant platform. He obtained 10,997 votes in an electorate of 806,598, a derisory figure of 1.4 per cent of votes cast,[3] but even this almost certainly had more to do with his extreme anti-abortion and anti-EU views rather than his stance on race and immigration.

For the sake of completeness, it should also be mentioned that more exotic views on race, immigration and identity in Ireland are expressed from time to time. These are nearly always to be found in the virtual world of the internet, on US-based servers protected by the First Amendment of that country's constitution. The views expressed on these websites, as well as on late-night talk radio and other such outlets, can hardly be described as representative.

The hard evidence about public opinion on these topics is limited and usually based on very broad surveys such as Eurobarometer and the European Values Study (1981–2004).[4] The reliability of such clipboard- and telephone-based polling is questionable, especially when the subject matter is sensitive, and its broad-brush character is frustrating. That said, a few tentative but somewhat contradictory conclusions can be drawn from the available data about Irish attitudes compared with those of other EU states. The data from the 1999 European Values Study showed that the EU average who agreed with the proposition that countries should main- tain their 'own customs and traditions' was 42 per cent; the figure for the UK was 45 per cent, whereas that for Ireland was 57 per cent. Obviously, this suggests a relatively conservative stance on the preservation of the mainstream or traditional culture. On the other hand, the response to the proposition on immigration 'let anyone come if jobs available' was 55 per cent in the case of Ireland compared with just 38 per cent for the UK and an average 49 per cent for the survey as a whole – showing a more liberal attitude in Ireland. The most recently published Eurobarometer (2007) shows that 56 per cent of Irish people agree that 'immigrants contribute a lot to Ireland', while 34 per cent disagree and 9 per cent do not offer an opinion. Rather more Irish people (23 per cent) than the European average (19 per cent) listed 'fight illegal immigration' as a policy area that the EU should prioritise, but when asked to identify the most important policy issues facing the EU, Irish people placed immigration in only ninth position. Asked whether 'people from different ethnic backgrounds enrich our culture', the EU average for agreement was 65 per cent; the figure for Ireland was slightly lower, at 62 per cent. A significantly larger proportion of Irish people than others favour targeted measures to assist migrants in the workplace. Yet surveys of migrant and minority groups in Ireland, although few in number, suggest they experience relatively high levels of racism and racist abuse, especially in the case of those of a different colour (e.g. McGinnity *et al.*, 2006). Moreover, attitudes to the traveller community remain stubbornly negative (Hayes, 2006). And we know that unemployment rates among West Africans with refugee status or leave to remain are persistently high: more than 70 per cent in a Cork survey (Coakley and Mac Éinrí, 2007).

A 'raceless' society?

A notable feature of recent debates has been the claim that those who accuse mainstream society and its politicians of 'racism' are the very people who are themselves introducing a 'racialised' discourse into Irish society. By implication, the critics are, perversely, the originators of the very phenomenon which they seek to criticise. In effect, older claims that Ireland was a 'classless' society are replicated by a modern claim that it is a 'raceless' one. An example of this rhetoric may be found in the following passage (on the Constitution Bill 2004) from former junior government minister Tony Killeen:

> Aside from the constitutional amendment, we must look closely at the issue of racism in Ireland. It is frequently argued that the Irish are more prone to racism than other nations. I do not believe this is the case. However, a small number of media outlets deliberately contrive to contribute to racist feelings and perhaps racist actions. There is legislative provision to outlaw this but it never seems to be proceeded with. I wonder if the occasional media story, almost always in one of two publications, does more damage than the woolly thinking and feather-headed, neo-liberal cant *which does much damage by annoying ordinary people.* Until recent years the people of this country have not been exposed to any great extent to people of African or oriental origin. Genuine wonder is sometimes confused with racism.
>
> The Irish people will not make up their minds on the proposed referendum on grounds of racism. Genuine concerns may arise as a consequence of the manner in which provisions are made for non-nationals. The quicker such concerns are dealt with – they are usually dealt with fairly quickly – the better for all concerned. Such speedy action helps *to avoid the kind of problems that feed the latent anti-immigrant feeling that sometimes lies undisturbed.* (*Dáil Debates*, vol. 584, 22 April 2004; emphasis added)

In reality, the myth of a raceless society was challenged a long time ago. From McVeigh's groundbreaking 1992 article 'The specificity of Irish racism' onwards, it became necessary to address the reality of the reception of the 'other' in Ireland (whether indigenous or foreign born). This was accompanied by an interrogation of Irish identity itself: as Alana Lentin, the foremost writer and thinker in Ireland on these matters, has put it, 'who are the "we"?' For McVeigh, Irish racism contains indigenous and imported components. He correctly dismisses the notion that Irish people, as the victims of racism and colonialism, cannot themselves be guilty of racism, before he goes on to consider the extent to which Irish racism has been influenced by ideas imported from elsewhere and how far it shows indigenous features of its own. He argues that the fact that there were, until the recent past, very few black people in Ireland is beside the point, as racism does not require the presence of the racialised 'other'. McVeigh (1992) suggests that Irish racism falls into five categories:

1 the 'diffusion' of racism from Britain;
2 the involvement of Irish people in the process of western imperialism;
3 the Irish diaspora;
4 the 'grafting' of racism on to internal forces, notably sectarianism and nationalism;
5 the existence of an endogenous anti-traveller racism.

I would add a sixth category, which did not yet exist in Ireland in the early 1990s. This is the type of differential racism common in other countries experiencing the complex and interrelated effects of globalisation and the restructuring of the economy. Informal evidence suggests that in Ireland's workforce, where certain sectors reflect increasingly racialised patterns of employment, indigenous workers occupy a dominant position, while somewhat less favourable conditions are offered to other EU migrants, and non-EU migrant workers, whether legal or undocumented, are frequently exploited. This conforms to the pattern of segmentation well described in other countries. Furthermore, if (as for instance in the United States) persons of colour or migrant workers are associated largely or exclusively with certain kinds of poorly paid work, it is a short step to the self-justifying belief that this is the only kind of work they are able or qualified to do. There is anecdotal evidence to suggest that this is already happening in Ireland.

In terms of the general climate of opinion in the EU, it is commonplace to note the resurgence of right-wing nationalism and its associated sentiments of xenophobia and racism in 1990s and 2000s Europe. A number of reasons have been advanced, including the collapse of the European left following the fall of the Berlin Wall and the effects of growing globalisation. Balibar notes that this rise of racism is to be seen in the east as much as the west. A notable example is the case of Russia, across a span from skinhead extreme-right racists to ultranationalist parliamentarians. Balibar connects the 'virtual hegemony of these movements' among a growing 'desocialised' segment of young unemployed people with the advent of neoliberal economics and the failure of representative politics, though he argues that a window still exists for collective democratic action (Balibar, 1996). There must be some concern that this type of racialised indigenous disaffection on the part of 'those left behind', that is, those who have not profited from the Celtic Tiger, may also emerge in Ireland.

Finally, much has been written about the 'cultural turn' (Stolcke, 1995) of contemporary racism – a form of 'racism without race'. As Mac An Ghaill puts it:

> A main element of the 'new racism' is the deracialisation of race, involving the displacement of an older racial vocabulary in public arenas, in which explicit references to race are now coded in the language of culture. (Mac An Ghaill, 2002)

One must keep in mind that whiteness (like masculinity) is not some kind of natural ground but itself a construction, and in practice a defence of privilege. Oliver Cromwell Cox argued over sixty years ago that race/class relations *are* basically labour/capital/profits relations (Cromwell Cox, 1948). The extensive contemporary literature on whiteness (e.g. Allen, 1994; Roediger, 1999) reminds us that 'race' as a social construct serves as a constitutive element in the operation of market capitalism. Even if 'race' is nowadays construed in more complex ways and even if the categories 'black' and 'white' are inadequate reflections of much more varied contemporary realities in multi-ethnic mixed societies such as many contemporary European ones, the analysis of underlying socio-economic structures as rooted in class-based inequality and its clear inflection by ethnicity and gender remains valid. A pertinent illustration of this can be found in the way in which ethnicity, gender and workplace marginalisation intersect in the increasing out-sourcing, in Ireland as elsewhere, of caring, nurturing and personal services – everything from childcare, domestic service and retirement home services to the sex industry – to women from Majority World countries. A dominant feature of all these activities is the location of women as marginal and disempowered subjects and the inscription of the female body as the locus of objectified processes and transactions based on a structured and profoundly gendered inequality.

The role of the state

Turning to the role of the state, it will be evident that it cannot be regarded as a neutral actor, above all in a neoliberal, globalised era. French academic Michel Wieviorka (2002) argues that differentialism – the categorisation of people by their 'communal identity', which lies behind the entire philosophy of multiculturalism – is itself the enemy, whether expressed by racists or by multicultural anti-racists, because it encodes a structural and oppressive inequality which classifies people by ethnicity or some other factor rather than as individual free subjects. But that is to accept an implied premise that its opposite, state-enforced universalism, is itself inclusive and egalitarian, whereas French universalism, for instance, was in practice anything but inclusive. Can the state be inclusive and emancipatory, recognising individual rights and freedoms but also validating our various communal belongings? And will the 'mainstream' accept some dilution of its hitherto hegemonic position? This is the circle to be squared.

If one accepts Goldberg's thesis of the 'racial state' (Goldberg, 2002), a further dilemma arises. How is it possible to engage in good faith with the state if it is also itself responsible for the very exclusion of migrants which any effective integration or inclusion strategy must address? In Ireland until 2007 this dilemma was exacerbated by the arrangement whereby the same government department – Justice, Equality and Law Reform – was responsible both for the *policing* of Irish citizenship and immigration policy, in what can be seen as an expression of Irish modernity and exclusion, and for the *integration* of migrants, supposedly following a logic of inclusion. Happily, this changed with the creation of a new ministerial portfolio for integration, located in a different department, Community, Rural and Gaeltacht Affairs. However, it will be evident that real or effective integration, however defined, cannot take place unless the state has mediators and spokespersons in civil society; yet, equally, it is not clear how such stakeholders can address the power imbalance still encoded in the current system. This does not mean that civil society stakeholders have no agency, but the cards are heavily stacked against them, especially in the case of migrant-led organisations.

Ethno-cultural nation versus hypermodern state: the diaspora as grounds for identity discussions?

A brief reference has already been made to the diaspora, in relation to McWilliams' appropriation of it in his soft-edged future fantasy. By contrast, McVeigh suggests that the diaspora might be seen as a 'source' of racist thinking. I would argue rather that there is a crucial fault-line between discourses of diaspora and nation, on the one hand, and the territorially bounded modern state, on the other, and that this offers a way of reading contemporary Irish attitudes to 'race' and identity.

Those who framed the key legislation on nationality and citizenship, the Irish Nationality and Citizenship Act 1956, already had to deal with the dilemma of reconciling nationhood, citizenship and identity. Who belonged, discursively, to the nation and how would the nature of the relationship between the (only partially realised) territorial entity of the state and the embodied citizens of the nation be defined? How could members of the nation who lived outside the state be spoken of? The Dáil and Seanad debates of the mid-1950s throw interesting and sometimes entertaining light on the matter but also foreshadow issues which are now of direct, everyday relevance and not merely theoretical pertinence. The definition of citizenship was manifestly based on a biologically defined nation:

> Mr. Walsh: In my opinion, the draft legislation contained in this Bill is desirable, as it extends the number of our Irish stock who will be, or who may become, citizens of the country. Ireland is indeed a mother country and her sons and daughters have peopled many lands. They brought the Faith to many races and have assisted in building up and have contributed to the development and administration of many countries throughout the world.
>
> Although a big percentage of our people emigrate or require to emigrate, due to economic reasons, I believe that one day most of them hope to return to end their days in their own country, to be buried beneath the green sod, to be mourned by those near and dear to them in their native land. Sometimes, however, it is their children who come back, and it is right, therefore, that there should be adequate provision to permit our emigrants, or their descendants, to return to Ireland as their country even though they may have become naturalised citizens of another country. (*Seanad Debates*, vol. 46, 16 May 1956)

An opposition TD, Anthony Esmonde, in welcoming the Bill, noted that:

> It is our aim and object to extend as far as possible citizenship to those who certainly have Irish blood in their veins and I welcome particularly the return to Ireland under our own Government of many people who emigrated in bygone days. I am now referring to those whose forefathers perhaps emigrated some generations back. (*Dáil Debates*, vol. 154, 29 February 1956)

While there was clearly a general consensus on biological Irishness, some concerns were expressed about the rather loose additional discretionary category of 'Irish association', through which citizenship might also be granted by the minister. A person might, it was feared, acquire an entitlement to Irishness on dubious or spurious grounds. It is perhaps significant that persons of 'Arab' and 'Asiatic' background illustrate this concern:

> One could even imagine an Asiatic, playing, say, in an Irish band in New York, being regarded as sufficiently qualified under that definition. (*Seanad Debates*, vol. 46, 16 May 1956)

> For instance, it appears to me that under this, if an Arab in Cairo drinks a glass of Irish whiskey it would qualify him for citizenship under this particular provision. (*Dáil Debates*, vol. 155, 22 March 1956)

But it is clear that the overall definition of citizenship is framed in such a way as to include as far as possible people 'of Irish blood', whether living in Ireland or not. This approach was further emphasised in another contribution from Deputy Esmonde, which foreshadowed in a remarkable way the 2003 Supreme Court *Lobe and Osayande* case[5] – which removed the more or less automatic right since the late 1980s for parents of Irish-born children to be given leave to remain in the state – and the 2004 citizenship referendum, by almost fifty years:

> It is undesirable that we should have people in this country with rights of citizenship who might be not exactly satisfactory, from the standpoint of Irish culture and Irish thought, or to the overwhelming majority of the Irish people. It may well be argued that anyone who is born here would, as a baby, inherit the national outlook on culture, and acquire the national outlook from the people in the country itself, but it is reasonable to assume from sub-section (1) of Section 6 that if you are giving nationality to anyone who is born in this country, you are also giving the right to the parents of that person, be it a male or a female child, even though they are not themselves obtaining citizenship, to remain in this country. You cannot very well, if you give citizenship to someone born in Ireland, say to the parents: 'We do not like the look of you; you are unsatisfactory from our point of view; we think you ought to get out.' You cannot very well do that, if you give to the child itself Irish citizenship. (*Dáil Debates*, vol. 154, 29 February 1956)

It is reasonable to ask whether such attitudes still underlie the construction of Irish identity in the current day, at least informally and perhaps passively, in the minds of sections of the general public.

In spite of the above lofty aspiration, the state has done little, in practice, to embrace the diaspora. How can this anxiety to deny any real agency to the diasporic Irish, in spite of their admitted legal and 'ethnic' status, be interpreted? It seems reasonable to explore this question in terms of a developing tension since the 1950s between the 'ethno-nation', which can be constructed (as, for example, in even McWilliams' vague gestures) to embrace a global concept of deterritorialised identity, on the one hand, and, on the other, the emerging modern state, defined by the trappings of European statehood, notably a desire to control, confine and police. While it may have been politically unacceptable in 1956 to deny citizenship to the 'broader Irish nation', any concrete effects of granting it could be largely nullified by denying to such citizens outside the state any meaningful active expression of that citizenship, such as the quintessentially participatory exercise of the franchise. By marked contrast, other traditional high-emigration countries, such as Poland and Italy, sought no such containment.

Social and historical developments in the 1980s and 1990s changed the terms of this debate. Perhaps the main change was the positive shift in Anglo-Irish relations which emerged from the New Ireland Forum of the mid-1980s, the precursor to the eventual 1998 Belfast Agreement.

Insofar as the South in 1998 abandoned its territorial claim on the North, expressed in the words of articles 2 and 3 of the 1937 constitution, it became necessary to replace this aspiration with a definition of national identity which expressed an explicit disjuncture between nation, territory and state. It is interesting that the amendment adopted in that year does specifically address the diaspora, but once again in a way which denies its members any meaningful agency:

> It is the entitlement and birthright of every person born in the island of Ireland, which includes its islands and seas, to be part of the Irish Nation. That is also the entitlement of all persons otherwise qualified in accordance with law to be citizens of Ireland. Furthermore, the Irish nation cherishes its special affinity with people of Irish ancestry living abroad who share its cultural identity and heritage.

From the point of view of politics in Ireland in both jurisdictions, this amendment was a liberating move. However, the deterritorialisation of identity, well foreshadowed as a desirable, even an ideal, development in Richard Kearney's writings of the late 1980s (Kearney, 1988), had other consequences. The notion of a 'virtual identity' of Irishness, floating free of its territorial origins, had a powerful resonance for people of the diaspora, amplified by President Mary Robinson's outreach to them in the period 1990–97 (Robinson, 1995). But it also inevitably reinforced the notion of a community based on blood. Indeed, the language used by President Mary McAleese since 1997, as distinct from that of her predecessor, President Robinson, has if anything served further to emphasise this point, as 'the global Irish family' replaced the somewhat more neutral 'diaspora'. This shift sets up a clear dichotomy in *affective* terms between, on the one hand, notions of 'family' and extended kinship (which readily includes emigrants *outside* Ireland and their descendants) and, on the other, outsiders *within* Ireland, considered strangers and firmly 'othered'. This is well illustrated in the public and political endorsement in Ireland of the current work of the Irish Lobby for Immigration Reform.[6] Many prominent Irish politicians have made speeches supporting this lobby's campaign to regularise the undocumented Irish in the United States (a number often grossly inflated to 50,000, but in reality far smaller). Meanwhile, the often difficult situation of undocumented migrants in Ireland is very rarely voiced.

A Habermasian solution?

Steven May quotes Habermas' view that 'a correctly understood theory of citizenship rights requires a politics of recognition that protects the individual in the life contexts in which his or her identity is formed'

(Goldberg and Solomos, 2002). This formulation seems promising in its attempt to combine civil republicanism with a politics of identity (Taylor, 1994). It may, however, be argued that such a conception of identity is too 'thin' in the anthropological sense. It may not be able to provide the kind of ontological reassurance that differentialists say must accompany the fight against discrimination and the battle for equality if people are to have a sense of loyalty to and identity with the overarching civil entity of the state. There remain the troubling issues of how a differentialist approach is not to lead to the perpetration of ongoing structural inequality (notably in such fields as gender rights) and how the state's own potentially conflicted role as both gatekeeper and facilitator can be appropriately challenged so as to develop a genuinely inclusive state and society.

The difficulty for Irish anti-racists is as much about means as about ends. A process of inclusion and consultation which is based on partnership and consensual approaches, successful as this has been in many respects in Ireland (especially in the economic sphere of controlled pay bargaining), is unlikely to succeed in addressing and redressing problems of exclusion, injustice and ethnic othering. New kinds of participation are needed, yet it is noteworthy that the current notion of 'active citizenship' has largely bypassed any serious consideration of the place of migrants and their voices. The Taskforce on Active Citizenship, appointed in 2005, for instance, has no migrant members.[7]

An analysis based on a literal acceptance of the remorseless logic of the 'racial state' would suggest that it is not possible to engage meaningfully with state actors. Yet the alternative of leaving the field free for a kind of triumphalist postmodern simulacrum of diversity and the appropriation by the state of the *language* of inclusion, equality and diversity, while simultaneously denying an actual voice to all those (including migrants and ethnic 'others' themselves) who wish to promote a radical *politics* bringing these about, could only reinforce both *de facto* assimilationism and a climate of institutional racism. A new, more dialectical politics is needed to get beyond such empty consensus, to an acknowledgement of shifting, multiple, hybrid, sometimes conflicting positions, which can accommodate ongoing and productive change.

To move towards a somewhat more optimistic conclusion, it is worth noting that the notion of 'family' may itself be de-essentialised, and this is happening in contemporary Ireland, as elsewhere. Presidents Robinson and McAleese have both sought to recognise many different kinds of 'family', traditional and non-traditional. Within the diaspora, one may take heart from the position adopted by the Irish Immigrant Center in Boston. Under the motto 'serving all nations', its multi-ethnic and multilingual staff treat all visitors equally.[8] No one is unencumbered by various kinds of collective belongings, but it must still be possible to construct a radical politics which can recognise and live with traditions, while simultaneously challenging and subverting any notion of a fixed, privileged and unchanging inheritance.

Finally, in order to challenge this mythic mono-culturalism, a counter-history is now needed, one which tells the history of the country and its multiple peoples and diasporas, not, as overwhelmingly in the past, in the tribal sense of a 'core nation' beset by successive invasions, but in terms of an accretion of encounters and syntheses over many centuries, making the Irish people the already multi-ethnic, non-tribal nation they are today. The challenge is not so much one of recognising Ireland's 'new' diversity but of validating the diversity which was always there but which has largely gone unrecognised.

Notes

1 See www.immigrationcontrol.org.
2 See www.electionsireland.org.
3 See www.electionsireland.org.
4 The European Values Study is run by the University of Tilburg. See www.europeanvalues. nl. The website gives the 1999 data for Ireland.
5 Judgement title 'Lobe & ors -v- Minister for Justice, Equality & Law Reform, Osayande & anor -v- Minister for Justice, Equality & Law Reform and ors', 28 January 2003. Available from www.courts.ie.
6 See www.irishlobbyusa.org.
7 See www.activecitizen.ie.
8 See www.iicenter.org.

4

All-consuming images: new gender formations in post-Celtic-Tiger Ireland

DEBBIE GING

'We learn to think of our desires in terms of the commodities produced to meet them, we learn to think of our problems in terms of the commodities by which to solve them.' (John Fiske, 1990: 182)

Over the past ten years, conspicuously new images of and discourses on gender have appeared in Irish shopping malls, on Irish billboards, in the Irish news and entertainment media and on the shelves of Irish bookshops. Radio shows, television programmes, online chat-rooms, magazines, daily newspapers and self-help books are all increasingly populated by a range of new male and female typologies: from new men, new lads and metrosexuals to domestic goddesses, desperate housewives and yummy mummies. This chapter looks at how the recent rise in consumerism is affecting the ways in which we mediate and talk about gender behaviours, identities and relationships in contemporary Ireland. It maps out a number of key debates in contemporary gender studies and considers how the changes discussed here are likely to affect Irish society unless proactive measures are taken to ensure a more egalitarian gender order. Many of the developments discussed here, enmeshed as they are in global cultural processes, are not specific to Ireland. However, their reception in and impact on a society which, like all others, has its own history of gender relations, and thus its own unique 'gender-scape', is of obvious concern to anyone with an interest in social and cultural change in Ireland.

The changes addressed here are the result of a number of mutually compatible developments, the most noteworthy of which are: firstly, the decline in western societies of second-wave feminism and its replacement with a broadly post-feminist cultural discourse (Tasker and Negra, 2007);

secondly, the growing popularity of bio-determinist discourses on gender;[1] and thirdly, the move towards an increasingly commercial media-scape. Although recent statistics on gender in Ireland and the rest of Europe point to significant equality deficits,[2] a new (liberal) discourse of progress has emerged in relation to gender in post-Celtic-Tiger Ireland which has little to do with material (in)equality or the representation of citizens in the public sphere. Within this new rhetoric, freedom is understood less as the legacy of second-wave feminism and increasingly as something given to us by an open, liberal market, which celebrates female empowerment in the form of 'girl power', is inclusive of sexual diversity and ironicises the antiquated sexism of a bygone era. Indeed, as this chapter will demonstrate, much recent debate about gender in Ireland is underpinned – both implicitly and explicitly – by the assumption that equality is a *fait accompli* and that feminism's work is done. However, contrary to the justifiable assumption that such a climate of post-feminism might render gender issues less prevalent in popular imagery and discourse, the opposite is in fact the case. In recent years the popular media have displayed a near hysteria with the obsolescence of gender equality on the one hand, while actively reviving a 'war-of-the-sexes' discourse on the other.

In tandem with this development, ironic sexism and stereotypes have made a spectacular comeback in the entertainment media, with large-breasted, pouting babes in hotpants at one end of the spectrum and emotionally challenged hard men hell-bent on the adolescent pleasures of 'Lad-land' (cars, soccer, beer, gangsters and pornography) at the other. This repolarisation of gender identities is particularly evident in the dominance of an aggressive but allegedly ironic 'gender war' rhetoric, which pervades all aspects of media culture, from advertising copy to radio quizzes: women and men are pitted against one another in a bid to see, it would seem, which set of stereotypical traits is 'better'. The irony underpinning this new, brash sexism lies in the claim that the stereotyping of women as obsessive shoppers or shoe fetishists and of men as domestically inept, relationship-averse larger-louts is so blatant and so passé that we can now laugh at its anachronisms. This, however, is where the paradoxes of the irony argument begin: because precisely this type of essentialist thinking about gender is now emerging in more serious fora, which serve not only to challenge social construction theory but also to rationalise and justify the gender stereotypes that contemporary advertising both lampoons and simultaneously reaffirms.

Gender has become an increasingly popular prism through which to view a broad range of contemporary social ills, many of which might be better explained by using other analytical variables, such as class, ethnicity or sexuality. Thus, suicide, anti-social behaviour and academic

underachievement are increasingly discussed in male-versus-female –
rather than in class-based – terms. In addition to this centre-staging of
gender is another striking development, namely the growing prevalence
of essentialist or bio-determinist accounts of gender difference. This is
increasingly evident not only in the ostensibly ironic gender stereotyping
that has become a key feature of popular cultural imagery but also in
serious media debates about male disadvantage, fathers' rights, domestic
violence, childcare and anti-social behaviour. Brain size, serotonin,
testosterone, endorphins, bipolarity and synaptic connections are terms
no longer confined to the specialist lexicons of psychiatry, neuroscience or
biochemistry but have become the staple fodder of discussions about men,
women and the relationships between them on a host of popular daytime
talk shows and phone-in radio programmes. To take just a few examples:

> Biologically, whether feminists like it or not, boys are genetically more
> disposed than girls to achieve academically. On average, men's brains are
> 15 per cent larger than women's, which is roughly twice the difference in
> physical proportions. (John Waters, *Irish Times*, 27 August 2001)

> We have forgotten that social structure is what protects males from
> the volatility of their nature…. The young males of all primate species
> indulge in heart-stopping risk-taking and experimentation…. The peak
> of aggressiveness and antisocial behaviour occurs in the late teens and
> early 20s, corresponding to the peak of testosterone at that age. (Maureen
> Gaffney, *Irish Times*, 28 February 2004)

> It's a woman's primary role to nurture…. Women by temperament are
> more caring, more forgiving, more tolerant and have a greater empathy
> with the children that they have given life to. (Eamon Dunphy, *Ryan
> Tubridy Morning Show*, 7 December 2006)

These commentators are not exceptional voices: their opinions and the
discursive parameters within which they are framed are part of a much
wider shift towards essentialist thinking in science, therapy and popular
culture (Rosalind Gill, 2003: 50–1) that is characteristic of most advanced
capitalist societies today. According to Maija Holmer Nadesan:

> More recently, the public has been bombarded with a 'scientific' discourse
> that implies a bio-genetic essentialism through its explication of phenomena
> such as intelligence, sexuality and aggression as neural-biological outcomes
> of genetic factors affected by natural selection. (Holmer Nadesan 2002: 403)

Why, however, is this prioritisation of the biological over the social so
attractive and conducive to a neoliberal economy? For Holmer Nadesan,
the objectives and outcomes of such a discursive shift are clear: because

'the discourse of "brain science" renders populations visible in new ways', it enables them to be problematised and subsequently dealt with in a manner that legitimises the extension of governmentality over potentially threatening populations. Thus, hyperactive children can be managed with Ritalin rather than through radical changes to diet, parenting or state-supported services. Depression, conceived of as a chemical imbalance, can be addressed through quick-fix medication rather than through costly and time-consuming qualitative research on how the pressures of modern life affect people's sense of self-worth. Similarly, biochemical explanations for criminality, particularly in relation to young men, can be used to justify heightened surveillance and tougher jail sentences, while the social causes of male marginalisation are ignored.

Besides fostering complex and ostensibly non-invasive forms of governmentality, however, it is important to recognise that 'brain science' is inextricably bound up in the logic of everyday consumerism.[3] This is well illustrated by an article written by psychologist Maureen Gaffney in the *Irish Times* magazine, in which she claims that women fall in love with shoes and handbags not because they have been relentlessly objectified by western visual culture for hundreds of years or aggressively targeted by modern advertising since its inception, but because they are 'fulfilling their evolutionary destiny' (Gaffney, 2007a). According to Gaffney, women in early human societies:

> specialised in child rearing, nesting and foraging for food, while males hunted for meat and defended their territory. By necessity women evolved to have better peripheral vision than men, enabling them to see in a wider arc and monitor any danger approaching the nest or any subtle changes in the environment.

She goes on to explain that these sensory skills make women:

> avid and effective foragers of luxury goods…. Women lovingly fondle silk and cashmere, sniff perfume with a look of rapt attention on their faces, and talk about colours such as taupe and eau de nil.

In Ireland, as in Britain and the United States, the shift towards neo-liberal government and its concurrent commercialisation of the media-scape have been key drivers in facilitating the discursive and representational repolarisation of gender. The trajectory from a public-service broadcasting model to one whose core objective is to sell audiences to advertisers sets up an entirely new dynamic between the broadcast media and their audiences. As well as marginalising those demographic groups that are of little interest to advertisers, this model addresses consumers in increasingly gender-reductive ways. This is particularly evident in the growth of gender-specific cultural genres such as chick-lit, chick-flicks and lad mags, as well as in the way television programming is becoming increasingly organised around the marketing not only of gender-specific products but also of new, gender-specific viewing contexts. The launch of Channel 6 (now 3e), Ireland's first dedicated entertainment channel, is a case in point. Aimed at a core audience of fifteen- to thirty-four-year-olds, the station made clear the gendered niche markets it intended to deliver to advertisers. 'Boys Night' on a Tuesday evening was sponsored by Paddy Power bookmakers and featured the usual line-up of job- and relationship-averse, yet sex- and soccer-hungry, 'losers' (Messner and Montez de Oca, 2005) who have come to characterise 'Guyland' (Kimmel, 2008). 'Girls Night', on the other hand, was dominated by programmes such as *Dharma and Greg* and *Sex and The City*, with product-placement inserts showing female friends giggling and enjoying low-calorie sparkling drinks together.[4] As Andrew Wernick (1991) has commented, the market has become the core organising principle of social life, giving rise to increasingly diffuse and convoluted forms of pro-motional communication. Channel 6/3e exemplifies what Wernick refers to as promotional culture: it is not just the ads that are selling lifestyles, brands and identities but rather the entire televisual 'supertext' (Browne, 1987).

The formats supported by commercial media, therefore, are highly conducive to the use of simplified images and sound-bites. Ideas, on the other hand, which challenge common-sense assumptions are generally not media-friendly, since they require complex foregrounding and con-textualisation (Herman and Chomsky, 1994). This partly explains why so much entertainment media space is currently taken up with the vox-pop 'surveys' and diluted snippets of deeply flawed yet highly accessible and apparently objective scientific 'facts' that fuel the jokey, blokey antagonism characteristic of the rapport between male radio jocks and their female side-kicks. However, the complexity and media-unfriendliness of the alternatives are not the only reasons why genetic-determinist ideas have succeeded in assuming such a central, even banal, position in Irish social discourse. Not only does the shift towards a 'liberal' gender-scape justify new forms of governmentality and generate highly lucrative markets in the sex, fashion, cosmetics and children's toy industries, but it also frequently serves to free the state from assuming its responsibilities in promoting gender equality, in tackling the problems associated with social exclusion and in safeguarding children. The remainder of this chapter seeks to demonstrate in detail how free-market economics have conspired with a broadly post-feminist culture to support a distinctly neoliberal political agenda on gender which, beneath its liberal rhetoric, is both deeply regressive and potentially highly coercive.

The post-feminist paradox

Neoliberals, unlike conservatives, understand only too well that reactionary interventions are not required to get reactionary results. Global market forces, when left to their own devices, will ensure that the worldview of a powerful minority becomes normative: in other words, that the most reductive and most lucrative discursive constructions of gender will prevail. While these are generally also the most conservative ones, a number of key social and cultural shifts have occurred which ensure that they come packaged in a discourse of progress, empowerment and free choice. The most significant development of the past twenty years has been the trajectory from a feminist to a post-feminist framing of gender issues. This paradigm shift is colossal, not only because it represents a new set of assumptions about gender but also because it has effectively relocated the discursive arena within which these assumptions are addressed, from the realm of the political to that of the cultural (Tasker and Negra, 2007). According to Tasker and Negra (2007: 1), 'Postfeminism broadly encompasses a set of assumptions, widely disseminated within popular media forms, having to do with the "pastness" of feminism, whether that supposed "pastness" is merely noted, mourned or celebrated'. They go on to explain that 'Postfeminism does not always offer a logically coherent account of gender and power but through structures of forceful articulation and synergistic reiteration across media forms it has emerged as a dominating discursive system' (2007: 2–3). Unlike second-wave feminism, therefore, post-feminism cannot be understood either as a distinct mode of political activism or as a coherently developed ideology, but rather as a set of discursive responses – often serving contradictory agendas – to the perceived successes and failures of feminism.

Post-feminist culture is characterised by number of key developments. The first and most visible of these is its capitulation on feminism's rejection of the sexual objectification of women. This is defended using a number of arguments – men are also objectified, regressive portrayals of women are ironic, feminism robbed women of their 'innate' femininity – some of which suggest a return to essentialist concepts of gender identity and most of which are deeply enmeshed within the logic of consumer capitalism and commodity fetishism (Ging, 2007a). One outcome of this *volte-face* is that women no longer need to be liberated from the cosmetics and fashion industries, since freedom, in the post-feminist scheme of things, is most readily expressed in terms of the ability to consume, as L'Oréal's ubiquitous advertising campaign so frequently reminds us ('because you're worth it'). Perhaps the most important defining feature of post-feminism, however, is the widespread acceptance of the myth that gender equality has been won, in spite of the fact that Irish women continue to be under-represented in politics, industry and the professions, and continue to earn less than men (Central Statistics Office, 2006). Indeed, it is upon this optimistic rhetoric of the 'level playing field' (McMahon, 1999) that many of the more flagrant inequities and contradictions of the contemporary gender-scape are often justified. Now that what is (re)imagined as a harsh, humourless feminism is past, the dual discourses of equality and empowerment facilitate a more flexible and playful discussion of gender: it has thus become acceptable to claim that men are from Mars and women are from Venus, to view lap-dancing as liberating or to assume that women retreat from public life on the basis of empowered choices. At the level of cultural representation, which, as Tasker and Negra (2007) rightly point out, is post-feminism's central discursive arena, this has brought about a proliferation of images of women as variously self-indulgent, narcissistic, irrational, hypersexualised and often violent creatures who conflate pornography with freedom and consumerism with self-worth.

Finally, post-feminist culture tends to be underpinned by a postmodern aesthetics of parody, pastiche and irony (Whelehan, 2000; Tasker and Negra, 2007), which is by no means coincidental. As Whelehan (2000) has so cogently illustrated, using irony to underscore post-feminist culture's many contradictions and 'trouble spots' has served as a useful escape clause against claims of sexism, elitism and gender essentialism. It is against this particular cultural, political and economic backdrop that the mainstreaming of a pornographic aesthetic has been possible in Ireland: the Wonderbra phenomenon, which stirred up a degree of controversy in the early 1990s, has since been widely appropriated by Irish advertising agencies to sell everything from yoghurt to holidays. Scantily clad women drape themselves over cars at the annual 'Toys 4 Big Boys' exhibition at the RDS (Royal Dublin Society Exhibition Centre), in the style of 1970s soft pornography. Posters in third-level institutes of education advertising everything from hiking clubs to debating society events feature wide-eyed, pouting females in bikinis. Post-feminism gives us a fun take on porn, premised upon the notion that a minority of humourless, embittered feminists lost out to a more open-minded and progressive lobby.

It is important to point out, however, that this analysis does not assume a top-down, 'hypodermic needle' model of media influence. We cannot conclude, simply because certain discourses and images have become widespread, popular or accepted, that they are being interpreted or used in uniform ways. As strategies for the advancement of gender equality go, 'girl power' may be a deeply flawed concept, but that is not to say it does not help many pre-pubescent and adolescent females to negotiate some of the limitations imposed on them by traditional, more passive models of femininity. As Flanagan and Booth (2002: 3) have pointed out in relation to the new images of hypersexualised and often violent femininity that prevail in cyberspace, the discursive terrain of popular culture is 'a space in which there is oppression as well as room for tactical and oppositional manoevres'. Similarly, media images that celebrate tough, underclass masculinities, such as those found in gangster films or rap music, may serve to valorise the identities of young, marginalised men (Ging, 2006, 2007b) who more readily find themselves demonised in the news media (Devlin, 2000). Without concrete empirical studies of its reception, however, we know very little about how ironic gender stereotyping is actually being understood. In two substantial studies about men's media consumption and film-viewing practices (Ging, 2005, 2007b), there was very little evidence that contemporary images of male machismo and female submissiveness were understood as tongue-in-cheek references to yesterday's gender norms. On the contrary, the research showed that ironic sexism was poorly understood – at best, irony was used as shorthand for 'don't take things too seriously' – since the back story of lad culture's humorously antagonistic interplay with feminism is clearly something that happened too long ago to have any real meaning for fifteen- to twenty-four-year-old male audiences (Gauntlett, 2002).

In Ireland, the broadly celebratory acceptance of the commercialisation of sex may have been intensified by a collective sense of liberation from a censorious and highly repressive brand of Catholicism. However, that both the political and the visual economies of pornography remain highly male dominated is consistently evaded in the rhetoric of liberalism, as are the everyday realities of the abuse and exploitation of women in the sex industry. Certainly, there is an important distinction to be made between pornography and prostitution, yet, as Kon and Riordan (1996) point out in the context of eastern Europe, pornography's overt commodification of women's bodies has contributed significantly to the reassertion of patriarchy and of a burgeoning sex industry. The Irish studies cited above indicate that most young Irish men mobilise liberal rhetoric when discussing pornography, wherein it is generally agreed that women do this kind of work out of choice – 'They're getting paid', 'They chose their career', 'They're not complaining'. However, a majority of the study participants were also deeply uncomfortable with the idea of their girlfriends, mothers or daughters engaging in such activities. This double-speak is perhaps one of the most confounding paradoxes of the new liberalism. Irish women may be finally freed from Catholicism but they must now negotiate the dual forces of bio-determinism and commodification, which have equally high stakes in the regulation of their bodies.

Hard-wiring masculinity

Nowhere is the language of genetic determinism so prevalent as in contemporary discourses about Irish men and masculinity. In recent years, *Irish Times* journalist John Waters has been to the fore in extolling the virtues of the mythopoetic strand of the men's movement, made famous by Robert Bly's highly influential bestseller *Iron John* (1992). Bly's argument is premised on the notion of innate masculine characteristics: he contends that women have become too involved in the 'civilising' of men and that, if contemporary social ills are to be tackled, men must reclaim their lost power and reject 'feminine' influences such as excessive emotion, sensitivity or indecisiveness. Most of the American men's groups and the literatures they have produced have been founded by and cater to middle-class, and mostly white, American men, whose response to social change has been described by Kimmel and Kaufman (1995: 263) as 'the cry of anguish of privileged American men, men who feel lost in a world in which the ideologies of individualism and manly virtue are out of sync with the realities of urban, industrialized, secular society'. The perception that men are becoming increasingly feminised and disempowered is central to a politics of gender that is underpinned by strict sex-role stereotyping based on biological difference. Men's relationship to the feminine is thus a crucial dividing factor: while most sociologists and psychologists argue that it is men's suppression of the feminine and the imperative to strive towards an illusory masculine ideal that is at the root of male social problems such as juvenile crime, alcohol and drug abuse, suicide and mid-life crisis (Horrocks, 1994, 1995; Clare, 2000), others contend that criminality and social problems arise from modern society's failure to raise young boys according to a strict model of traditional masculinity, which prioritises paternal authority and represses the feminine (Bly, 1992; Farrell, 1993, 1999).

   In Ireland, what Harry Ferguson (2002) has referred to as the 'social problematisation of masculinity' has occurred around a number of 'flashpoint' issues, including male violence and anti-social behaviour, the alleged feminisation of education, fathers' rights and male suicide. What is striking about the framing of these debates is the way in which they have been underpinned by the gender-essentialist rhetoric of the American men's movement[5] and of self-help literature, which has banded with a reactionary Catholic lobby to produce a highly volatile and distorted public discussion on these issues. As Anne Cleary's (2005) work has shown, suicide has been discussed and debated predominantly along the lines of gender, with male suicide being constructed as a response to men's inability to deal with advances in female power. Factors such as social class, sexuality, alcohol and drug use and urban/rural location, which might have carved up the picture in a significantly different way, were largely ignored in this debate, although they are beginning to emerge in more recent public discourse. According to Cleary (2005: 156), 'A binary divide between masculinity and femininity drives much research around emotional and psychological issues despite contrary evidence about the across-gender fluidity of emotional lives' (Connell, 2002; Frosh *et al.*, 2002).

This essentialism is also prevalent in recent debates about male violence and anti-social behaviour in Ireland. As Maurice Devlin (2000) has pointed out, working-class male youths are routinely pathologised in the Irish news media, and the young male is constructed 'as a belligerent, wilful creature, naturally avaricious and aggressive, in need of constant punishment if he is to learn the "avoidance of transgression"' (Mariani, 1996: 136). With increasing evidence of anti-social behaviour among young middle-class men, this rhetoric of gender determinism has become even more commonplace, as it helps to evade more probing questions about social maginalisation and its causes, while at the same time justifying the need for increased levels of parental and state authority. During the Brian Murphy trial,[6] for example, psychologist Maureen Gaffney attributed the upsurge in this type of male violence to 'a collapse of the old authority structures', which, she claimed, has allowed young men's 'natural' testosterone-fuelled aggression to go unchecked and untamed. In line with much bio-determinist thinking on gender, analogies with the animal kingdom were implied, so that her account of homosocial male behaviour read much like the voice-over for a nature documentary. She wrote:

> In the competition for women, testosterone rises, as though to mobilise the male for the rivalry ahead. (Correspondingly, testosterone falls in men who are approaching marriage and withdrawing from the competitive world of seeking a mate.) (*Irish Times*, 28 February 2004)

However, as Mariani points out:

> The fact that antisociality itself is a culturally-constructed concept has been buried under an avalanche of research purporting to locate its cause in 'individual vulnerabilities' that give rise to personality syndromes like attention deficit/hyperactivity disorder (AHDH), conduct disorder (CD), oppositional defiant disorder (ODD), and antisocial personality disorder (APD). (Mariani 1996: 136)

In recent years, a proliferation of television documentaries, such as *Why Men Don't Iron* (Channel 4, 1998) and *Testosterone* (Channel 4, 2003), have used 'brain science' to mobilise biological essentialist theories of gender and to establish links between testosterone and male aggression. According to Mariani, this is a complex way of liberating governments of responsibility for the damage caused by hegemonic masculinity, and of securing the patriarchal status quo. She contends that biological essentialist accounts of criminality ('bio-criminology'), by focusing on congenital dis-orders in the young, downplay the role of environmental and sociological factors: thus, the behaviours of abused children and poor black chil-dren – 'any child ready to point an accusing finger at the system' (Mariani, 1996: 143) – are more readily attributed to congenital neurotransmitter dysfunction or to brain injury incurred in the birth canal (since, it is claimed, *in utero* exposure to testosterone makes the male brain less pliant than the female brain and thus more susceptible to injury in the birth canal) than to abusive or dysfunctional childhoods. While the research acknowledges that socially excluded males are more prone to anti-social behaviour, the prevailing view is that environmental factors are primarily catalysts or triggers that affect only susceptible individuals. Mariani claims that cultural and sociological explanations, which see excessive discipline and the repression of emotion as the problem, have been eclipsed by biological essentialist and individualising frameworks, which function to justify stricter disciplinary measures. Pathologising the problem of white boys out of control, she maintains, is a way of explaining, containing and treating anti-social behaviour, for example by putting them on Ritalin, which has obvious benefits for the pharmaceutical industry, while at the same time maintaining the patriarchal order of things:

> Thus, tramps ride the rails, not because a cataclysmic economic depression has thrown them out of work, but to satisfy a perverse pleasure in vaga-bondage arising from 'defective inhibition'. The 'delinquent' runaway is impelled by a congenital contempt for authority, not the nightmare of savage beatings. (Mariani, 1996: 147)

'Raunch culture' for the under-twelves

The rise of genetic determinism and of 'raunch culture' (Levy, 2005) raises even more important questions about children, who are neither familiar with the ideological back stories of lad culture and post-feminism nor capable of detecting and successfully decoding irony. In Ireland, the chil-dren's media, fashion and toy industries have been hugely influenced by American imports over the past twenty years, which has succeeded in creating highly gender-polarised markets through processes of consump-tion. Gender-neutral clothing and toys have all but disappeared from Irish shops, while the gender coding of advertisements for toys and games has become so extreme that television advertising and product packaging rarely depict male and female children playing together.[7] At the level of media representation, girls are becoming increasingly sexualised and passive, while boys are depicted as rejecting emotion and engaging in exaggerated performances of aggression and bravado. Against the wider backdrop of a dominant discourse of genetic determinism, this state of affairs is often presented as natural, even inevitable.[8]

There is no conclusive evidence, however, to support the hypothesis that girls and boys have natural or genetic predilections for different types of play, while there is a considerable body of research which shows that social conditioning – through parents, carers, teachers, peers and media images – is the primary cause of differentiated gender behaviours (Condry and Condry, 1976; Hyde, 1981, 1984, 1985, 2005; Giddens, 1982, 2001; West and Zimmerman, 1987; Lightdale and Prentice, 1994; Epstein and Johnson, 1994; Hyde and Plant, 1995; Steele, 1997; Epstein, 1998; Frome and Eccles, 1998; Kimmel, 2000; Sandberg and Pramling-Samuelsson, 2005). Those parents who resign themselves to the genetic 'inevitability' of their children's orientation toward sex-specific toys and games might ask themselves why, if boys are hard-wired to play with guns and girls' predilection for Barbies is genetically ordained, so much money needs to be spent on such aggressive marketing and forceful colour coding of these products. Moreover, those who actively discourage their male children from playing with female-coded toys surely need not worry: if masculine traits are encoded into the male genes from conception, superficial acts such as playing with dolls or tea sets should not, according to this logic, upset the child's hard-wired, biologically destined masculinity.

The blatant sexualisation of girlhood in child-directed advertising and marketing imagery raises further questions about consumerism's impact on children's self-identity. High-heeled shoes and boots are available in many Irish shoe shops for children aged five and upwards. T-shirts with 'porn star' written across the chest are widely available for the same age group. Major chain-stores sell g-string and bra sets for girls ranging from five to ten years of age. Bratz dolls, now far exceeding sales of Barbie, combine pre-pubescent, wide-eyed innocence with the clothing and make-up of the prostitute or dominatrix.[9] Increasingly, seven-year-old girls making their Holy Communion use highlights and fake tanning.

There is a confounding double-speak at work here, whereby viewing paedophile images is a serious crime but using a paedophile aesthetic to sell toys and make-up to children is not. For all its rhetoric about a society of free choice that engenders liberal, open debate, post-Celtic-Tiger Ireland has not yet succeeded in having an honest public discussion about this topic. Paedophilia is portrayed by the Irish media as transgressive, abject or 'other', with paedophiles routinely constructed as anti-social 'outsiders', (homo)sexually repressed priests or disturbed celebrities. According to

Harry Ferguson (2002), the revelations of clerical abuse by the media, while they have played a crucial role in giving voice to those who have been silenced by an oppressive, autocratic and deeply patriarchal culture, have also served to skew the realities of child abuse in Ireland:[10]

> The 'paedophile priest' has become a key symbol of danger to children, a social construction which is entirely a media event implying clear links between celibacy and child sexual abuse. Significantly, while there are many more convicted sex offenders who are married heterosexual men, malestream [*sic*] heterosexual masculinity within and without the Irish family has not been problematised. (Ferguson, 2001: 43)

The point here is not to argue for a causal link between the media's sexualisation of children and the incidence of paedophilia. There is no evidence to support such a link, and it is worth noting that children have been sexually abused throughout history, irrespective of how they were dressed. There is also an important distinction to be made between the production of images that involves the physical or emotional harming of children and that which does not. Nonetheless, research conducted in Canada (Steed, 1994: 138) shows that as adult sex offenders 'got older, they found their predilections reinforced by mainstream culture, movies and rock videos that glorify violent males who dominate younger, weaker sex objects'. What is of more concern here, however, is the potential impact of mediated messages that boys do things and girls look pretty on how people think about children and on how children think about themselves. Given the tendency documented in the psychological literature for most victims of abuse to feel varying levels of guilt or responsibility for what has happened, the media's sexualisation of pre-adolescent girls is unlikely to help children in tackling abuse or sexual harassment. Teaching girls to view themselves as passive sexual objects, albeit heavily cloaked in girl power's lippy catch-phrases, is unlikely to equip them with the confidence or sense of self required to deal with the realities of female sexual objectification or to make them feel that society valorises and supports their resistance.

In the absence of concrete ethnographies of reception, however, the impact of such imagery on the attitudes and behaviours of children as they develop remains unclear. Certainly, research shows that children are discerning and media-savvy consumers of popular culture. However, while boys and girls actively use what they consume – clothes, toys, games – to construct their identities, the extreme gender coding of these products arguably limits the repertoires from which they feel they can choose. Peer pressure, combined with the widespread popularity of gender-determinist thinking, would appear to make it difficult, especially for boys, to experiment or cross boundaries. This gender 'straight-jacketing' is arguably at odds with the notion that, as adults, these men and women will have equal status in their jobs or be able to conduct egalitarian relationships. In this micro-universe of Power Rangers and Bratz, it appears that the seeds are being sown for a highly lucrative future market of adult men and women who understand themselves as polarised, incompatible and unable to communicate. Today's children are set to become tomorrow's self-help generation.

When Venus and Mars collide: the self-help solution

The explosion in self-help literature, CDs and DVDs is both a cause and a symptom of the new essentialism, and the impact of bestselling books such as John Gray's *Men Are From Mars, Women Are From Venus* (1993) and Deborah Tannen's *You Just Don't Understand: Men and Women in Conversation* (2001) cannot be underestimated. As Michael Cronin demonstrates in chapter 7 of this volume, the creation of anxieties around modern living makes individuals increasingly dependent on private or corporate solutions. Rather than questioning the structural causes of gender inequality and instigating social change, transformation takes place through the individual consumption of (self-help) therapy. While most self-help therapies that address problems of gender relations give the impression of taking radical individual action to change things, they ultimately serve to preserve the status quo. Instead of tackling the root causes of inequality, they teach individuals how to gloss over and live with the symptoms. Explanations of men and women as coming from different planets fit with common-sense assumptions, and do not challenge the existing economic and social structures into which people have become enmeshed. From the New Age-inflected literature, which draws upon theories of yin and yang, to the Christian end of the self-help market, with its call for a return to wifely subservience, this literature consistently ignores the social in favour of the biological.[11] Most importantly, because the supposed incompatibilities between the sexes are presented as ordained, the demand for dating agencies, self-help books and sex and relationship counselling is potentially infinite. Love, sex and procreation have become highly complex emotional danger zones, which the common human apparently cannot negotiate without the help of 'expertise'.

The new essentialism has taken root in the Irish media to such an extent that reviews of self-help literature have ceased even to acknowledge that the 'nature thesis' might be contentious. In a recent *Irish Times* review of a book entitled *Babyproofing Your Marriage*, co-authored by Irishwoman Cathy O'Neill and two other mothers who found their relationships coming under strain after the birth of their children, Kate Holmquist

(2007) fails to question any of the deeply problematic theories and methodologies upon which the book is based. Like the raft of other self-help books which ostensibly critique yet in reality rehearse and perpetuate myths about motherhood,[12] these approaches ensure that childcare and home-making remain the emotional responsibility of women. Manuals about balancing family life and work aimed at men do not exist, nor does anybody seem to think they should. The eternal post-feminist conundrum – of how to juggle children and career – is thus constructed as a problem exclusively for women. Paradoxically, it is a common feature of much post-feminist discourse to blame feminism for landing women with this 'second shift', while refusing to acknowledge that the real source of the problem lies with both men's and women's unwillingness or inability to divide housework and childcare equally.[13] As Anthony McMahon (1999) has so cogently illustrated, the dominance of a progressive or optimistic rhetoric of gender equality has effectively blocked progress on these issues. Though it is difficult to measure, the influence of self-help therapies has undoubtedly been instrumental in compounding and sustaining the centrality of post-feminist and bio-determinist discourses in Ireland.

Finally, the gender-difference hypothesis provides industry and the professions with a useful strategy for channelling women in and out of the workforce as economic needs arise. Increasingly, it is also used within industry to encourage women into particular types of activity as well to allow companies to score corporate and social responsibility points for their ostensibly pro-female policies. An article on the Microsoft website uses 'brain science' to claim that women make better managers:

> In the past few decades, researchers have discovered physiological variations in the brains of men and women. For example, male brains are about 10% larger than female brains. But women have more nerve cells in certain areas. Women also tend to have a larger corpus collusum [*sic*] – the group of nerve fibers that connects left and right hemispheres. That makes women faster at transferring data between the computational, verbal left half and the intuitive, visual right half. Result: Women are more flexible and find it easier to multitask. Men are usually left-brain oriented. That often makes them better at solving abstract equations and problems.[14]

As Aileen O'Carroll (2006) points out, an almost identical discourse was also used by the president of Harvard in 2005 to explain why women were under-represented in science. Under his presidency, the number of tenured jobs offered to women at Harvard dropped from 36 per cent to 13 per cent. O'Carroll makes a crucial point:

> The idea of gender differences can be used to either exclude women (as in the position of women in Harvard) or to attract more women (as in the call

centre workers). The malleability of the idea of difference, and the different political uses to which it is put, should make us very wary of arguments that take difference as their starting point.

Conclusion

The Celtic Tiger years have led us into new discursive arenas, in which ideological consensus is increasingly achieved at the level of the symbolic, the rhetorical and the discursive. Although it is difficult to determine or measure the extent to which consumerism and its associated imageries are affecting how people actually 'do gender' in their daily lives (West and Zimmerman, 1987), there is widespread evidence to suggest that attitudes to gender are being (re)constructed through subtle processes of consumption and economic rationalisation, which are channelled through an increasingly profit-driven media. As Phelan, drawing on Billig's (1995) work, points out in chapter 5, ideological production is sometimes most usefully conceptualised in terms of 'banal' representational practices, rather than through indices of explicit, or intentional, neoliberal bias. The rising popularity of bio-determinism across a wide range of interconnected industries – from self-help therapy to computer games – means that these ideas infiltrate our lives and relationships in subtle but presumably significant ways.

Rather than adopting a fatalistic liberal response to these developments, however, Irish people have the possibility to intervene or to call for intervention. At the level of education, the Educate Together model is an excellent example of collective self-determination, whereby parents and educators have formed democratically run cooperative schools based on the principles of gender equality and cultural inclusion. At secondary level, there is an ongoing and urgent need for further gender mainstreaming initiatives such as those already implemented by the Gender Equality Unit of the Department of Education. However, if these are to succeed, both parents and teachers must confront their own prejudices in relation to gender and actively tackle the subtle instances of sexism and homophobia which too often go unchecked. As Sadker and Sadker's (1994) three-year study in the United States so aptly demonstrates, teachers who consider themselves to be gender egalitarian are often not conscious of the vastly different ways in which they treat boys and girls. In recent years, the non-secular nature of Irish education has been highlighted by the Congress of Catholic Secondary Schools Parents' rejection of the Exploring Masculinities programme, on the grounds that it encourages positive attitudes to homosexuality and gay marriage (Oliver, 2001). In this context, popular discourses of progress and inclusion are especially paradoxical.

Furthermore, there is a need for increased lobbying on the part of parents to have child-directed advertising on Irish television banned. The Broadcasting Commission of Ireland's children's advertising code prohibits celebrities from advertising food or drink for children and stipulates that advertisements for fast food must carry a health warning (Shaw, 2004). However, this is far a cry from the Swedish model, which has banned all advertising to children under twelve years of age, and from countries such as Norway, Austria, Belgium and Denmark, which impose tight restrictions on advertising around children's programmes. However, given that roughly 50 per cent of Irish children watch non-Irish channels (Shaw, 2004) and the internet presents another vast source of advertising, it is clearly not possible to protect children from what has become a widely promotional culture (Wernick, 1991). Increasingly, efforts and resources need to be devoted to the teaching of critical media literacy in schools. While a media component has been introduced into the primary curriculum and into the English syllabus for the Junior and Leaving Certificates (O'Neill, 2000), this is far from adequate, given the extent to which young people engage with mediated messages and images on a daily basis. To date, a more vocational and market-oriented emphasis on digital literacy has tended to overshadow a more critically oriented model, and there is clearly a growing need to involve students in the broader philosophical, ideological and political debates around modern mass media. As media reception research with male teenagers in Ireland has shown (Ging, 2005), evidence of media literacy is by no means synonymous with an ability to decode media ideologically. Thus, the introduction of media studies curricula which foster a culture of critical reflection and questioning is one very tangible way in which education policy might respond to the growing gender apartheid facing children.

Related to this is the need for an open discussion about the sexualisation of children through consumerism and the way in which the mainstreaming of a pornographic aesthetic is (re)constructing – at least discursively – male and female sexuality and desire. Research (Ging, 2005) indicates that many young men are blind to the gaze economy of popular culture, which dictates that it is still mostly men who look and women who are looked at, and so it is important to render consistently visible the inconsistencies and paradoxes of the post-feminist rhetoric of the level playing field or 'ground zero' (Kimmel, 2008). Finally, it is crucial that men become involved in the debate about childcare, and that male accounts of the pressures of balancing career and childcare are acknowledged and listened to. It is also up to women to facilitate the sharing of this responsibility, by rejecting the unbalanced and limiting parameters within which the debate has been framed by self-help literature, women's magazines and post-feminist discourse generally.

The increasingly commercial media-scape in Ireland has enabled deeply conservative images and ideologies of gender to proliferate. Meanwhile, the increased visibility of homosexuality, the perceived freedoms of 'raunch culture' and the broad acceptance of the myth that equality has been achieved have serviced a convincing rhetoric of progress and, in doing so, have ultimately served to gloss over the persistence of substantial material inequalities between men and women. In addition to this, neoliberalism's mutually beneficial rapport with bio-determinism has arguably diminished the responsibility of the government vis-à-vis a range of social problems, including crime, anti-social behaviour, social exclusion and paedophilia, since it locates these problems in the genes, hormones or brainwaves of individual bodies.

While the successes of feminism have been undoubtedly monumental, they have also been dramatically overplayed by the popular media, with the result that the feminist movement is either held in contempt or is considered to have been so successful as to have rendered itself obsolete, or both. Indeed, the expediency with which a complacent and often regressive discourse on gender has assumed centre stage in the last decade in Ireland is extraordinary. That said, blunt 'hypodermic needle' models, which assume that people passively absorb media messages, do not account for the complexity of our engagements with mass culture. Considerable research remains to be done on how genetic-determinist and post-feminist discourses are influencing the ways in which we think about and 'do gender' in Ireland. Until we begin to explore in detail the actual meanings and uses generated by post-feminist images and discourses, as well as by Mars–Venus accounts of gender relations, it remains unclear whether and to what extent Irish people will accept, resist or negotiate the messages of a highly Americanised consumer culture, in which men and women are being increasingly constructed as polarised rather than united.

Notes

1 It is important to stress from the outset that this chapter is not an attempt to convince the reader that gender is socially and culturally constructed. A vast body of distinguished sociological and psychological researchers (among them John Condry and Sandra Condry, Anthony Giddens, Michael Kimmel, Michael Kaufmann, Harry Brod, Janet Shelby-Hyde, Lynne Segal, Máirtín Mac an Ghaill, Chris Haywood, Raewyn Connell, Margaret Matlin, Deborah Cameron and Judith Butler) have long identified and discredited the flawed premises and methodologies upon which biological essentialist theories of gender difference are founded.

2 In 2006, only 14 per cent of TDs in Dáil Éireann were women, which is well below the average European Union rate of 23 per cent, and in 2004 women's earnings were 65.7 per cent of men's (Central Statistics Office, 2006: 10).

3   The Brantano shoe company ran an advertising campaign in 2007 which featured a fictional institute founded by Professor Anne-Marie Brantano, who first discovered the 'slingback synapse'. This is a prime example of a discourse which straddles both ironic sexism and genetic determinism, thus simultaneously parodying and normalising woman's 'natural' disposition toward shoe shopping.

4   The website of Channel 6 (www.channel6.ie; the channel was rebranded 3e in January 2009, http://3e.tv3.ie) proclaimed that 'Channel 6 will aggressively advertise throughout launch year with a very substantial multi-platformed campaign designed to raise awareness of the station and direct viewers to particular shows and themed nights. This campaign will be advertised at weights previously unheard of in Ireland for a TV station.'

5   The men's movement is by no means a unified political grouping; it also has radically different connotations in different parts of the world. In spite of this, the expression has been used predominantly in the media as an umbrella term to describe those men's groups whose agendas include – at a political level – the recuperation of male power and privilege (usurped by feminism) and/or – at a personal level – the rediscovery of the 'masculine self'.

6   Brian Murphy, aged eighteen, was kicked and beaten to death outside a nightclub in south County Dublin in August 2000. His assailants were young middle-class men and the attack was apparently without motive.

7   Irish advertising to children is virtually unregulated. The Broadcasting Commission of Ireland has succeeded in banning only advertising for junk food products that are endorsed by celebrities or cartoon characters.

8   See, for example, Kate Holmquist's article in the *Irish Times*, 3 November 2007, in which she argues that the sexism in toy advertising is justified because boys and girls are hard-wired to be different. Boys, she argues illogically, should not be encouraged to play with tea sets and ironing boards because they will have to do enough ironing and cooking when, as adults, they discover that women will no longer iron their shirts or serve them dinner. Why, in that case, girls should be given these toys is unclear. Holmquist concludes her article, with a 180-degree turn, by claiming that children have never been more aware of the fluid nature of gender identification, evidenced by the increasingly inventive ways in which they play with flexible notions of gender!

9   Bratz Babies come accessorised with nappies, bottles and rattles as well as earrings, make-up and handbags.

10 Statistics from the Dublin Rape Crisis Centre show that, in 2005, 19.6 per cent of reported child sexual abuse cases were perpetrated by fathers, 16.2 per cent by brothers, 26.8 per cent by another male relative and 30.2 per cent by another known person. Only 3.4 per cent of cases were perpetrated by strangers (Dublin Rape Crisis Centre, 2005).

11 Examples are Laura Doyle, *The Surrendered Wife: A Practical Guide to Finding Intimacy, Passion, and Peace With a Man* (2001), and Leanne Payne, *Crisis in Masculinity* (1995).

12 See also Susan Maushart, *The Mask of Motherhood: How Becoming a Mother Changes Our Lives and Why We Never Talk About It* (1999), and Joan Williams, *Unbending Gender: Why Family and Work Conflict and What To Do About It* (2000).

13 A report launched by the Equality Authority in June 2008 shows that significant inequalities persist in Ireland – to the disadvantage of women – in terms of the amount of paid and unpaid work done by men and women (Equality Authority, 2008).

14 Microsoft Small Business Centre, at www.microsoft.com/smallbusiness/resources/management/leadership_training/do_women_make_better_managers.mspx (accessed 15 February 2007).

Part II
Media and social change

5

Irish neoliberalism, media and the politics of discourse

SEAN PHELAN

The notion that the media have a significant role to play in legitimating the dominant ideology is hardly a revelation. The insight has long formed the kernel of critical assessments of mass media and journalism, though this broad theoretical position has been challenged by those who emphasise the ability of audiences to 'resist' media constructions of the social world. Unsurprisingly, this critical perspective sometimes finds little favour among media workers, who can be instinctively hostile towards an argument that interrogates the professional assumptions of journalistic objectivity and autonomy. This nod to some of the central debates of journalism and media studies is worth foregrounding, as they inform any considered reading of a chapter anchored in the assumption that Irish media practices play a significant role in the constitution of what the present volume calls 'Irish neoliberalism'.

This chapter explores one central question: what is the nature of the relationship between Irish news media and Irish neoliberalism? My analysis gives only a cursory account of how the question might be conceptualised in its broadest sense and focuses more specifically on Irish newspaper texts. However, before addressing the specific media question, my analysis begs an outline consideration of a more fundamental one: what is this 'thing' that we call 'neoliberalism'? One can hardly go about trying to assess its ideological manifestation without formally conceptualising it. The need for definitional self-awareness and caution extends to the category 'media'. I argue that if the question of neoliberal influence in media is to be satisfactorily explored, one needs to avoid a reductive analysis of *the* media, which glosses over the possibility of *some* plurality of perspectives within mainstream media.

My analysis is organised into four distinct parts. First, I theorise neo-liberalism with particular reference to the Irish context, and argue that it is most usefully understood as a malleable ideology that can assume different discursive forms. Second, the relationship between neoliberalism and media production is briefly discussed. Third, I present a general overview of the relationship between neoliberal discourse(s) and journalistic representation, drawing on the evidence gathered in a doctoral study (Phelan, 2003). Fourth, I supplement my general overview with a close reading of a particular *Irish Times* article, which shows how a neoliberalised logic structures putatively 'objective' forms of journalism. The scope of my chapter precludes any satisfactory engagement with the question of how Irish media might be transformed, though I would hope that the analysis is, in itself, suggestive of transformative possibilities.

Theorising neoliberalism as discourse(s)

It is generally recognised that neoliberalism is open to different rhetorical and policy inflections (Kirby, 2002a; Allen, 2003). Yet, as a conceptual shorthand for describing a paradigmatic shift within capitalism, it is fated to be sometimes used in ways that can presume too much doctrinal coherence. This is an important point. Neoliberalism is not a 'thing' or an 'it' (Hay, 2001) but a label that gives conceptual shape to the cumulative effects of various actions and processes that have altered the trajectory of global capitalist accumulation since the 1970s (Harvey, 2005). And, understood in those (over)ambitious terms, its use as a shorthand is a necessary part of critically identifying the ideological pedigree of the changes that have altered profoundly the character of Irish society since the late 1980s.

But this still begs the definitional question: how does one *specify* the contents of the label 'neoliberal'? The use of the term risks two distinct pitfalls. The first is the overly reductive use of a *necessarily* reductive term, where neoliberalism's expanse becomes so broad, its implications so monolithic, that the fact of its different manifestations is effectively unheeded, or belittled as 'merely' a matter of rhetoric. The second pitfall involves a more exacting use of the term, where neoliberalism is more narrowly understood in terms of overtly neoliberal political identities (e.g. Charlie McCreevy, the Progressive Democrats, the *Sunday Independent*, the *Sunday Business Post*). This use of the term is understandable. But the problem here is that it orientates the analyst towards an agent-centric view of neoliberal power and, because they do not self-identify as such, attention is deflected from other, supposedly non-neoliberal political, media and cultural actors.

Mindful of these pitfalls, this analysis offers a theorisation of neo-liberalism that seeks to recognise its ideological malleability and reach. To this end, I introduce a broad analytical distinction between two 'ideal types' of neoliberal discourse: transparent and, following Bourdieu (1998), euphemised neoliberalism (Phelan, 2007a).[1] A transparent neoliberal discourse can be understood with shorthand reference to the ideological identity articulated in the works of theorists like Hayek (1960) and Friedman (1962) and, politically, by the pro 'free market' stance of Irish politicians like Michael McDowell and Charlie McCreevey, and media intellectuals like Moore McDowell and Kevin Myers. A euphemised neo-liberal discourse can, in contrast, be understood with indicative reference to the discourses of the 'third way' and 'social partnership' (Fairclough, 2000) or, indeed, the personal political identity of Bertie Ahern. The latter certainly stretched credibility when he proclaimed himself a 'socialist'. Yet his quite skilful cultivation of a media-savvy identity of 'conciliatory', 'consensual' and 'pragmatic' can be understood as a personalised embodiment of this euphemising form.

The formal understanding of discourse that underpins my analysis follows Laclau and Mouffe (1985), who conceptualise discourses as 'structured totalities' (p. 205) that articulate relatively fixed relations between different signifiers.[2] The definition can be given a straightforward illustration. A transparent neoliberal discourse can be understood as the construction of a structured totality that seeks to articulate a (relatively) fixed relation between key signifiers such as 'market', 'individual' and 'freedom'. In other words, the fixing of meaning becomes a way of describing the emergence of a hegemonic politics where the market is constituted as the *natural* guarantor of individual freedom. Yet, as a description of a discourse's structure, this gives us only half the picture. Laclau and Mouffe also observe how any discourse is constituted through its establishment of a discursive frontier with an antagonistic 'other', which, in the case of transparent neoliberalism, would be 'socialism' or, more specifically, the kind of social democratic 'Keynesian' identities that structured the general character of western political economy up until the 1970s (Beaud and Dostaler, 1997). What gives this basic structuralist insight a post-structuralist inflexion is Laclau and Mouffe's recognition that, although difficult to shift, the location of this hegemonic frontier is open to political movements that are the site and outcome of discursive struggles.

Thus, reformulated in the conceptual vocabulary of Laclau and Mouffe, the two ideal types of neoliberal discourse can be understood as distinct, yet overlapping, 'structured totalities'. The two discourses share a common genealogy that has its (immediate) political origins in the transformation of the global political economy that has taken place since the

1970s and its (immediate) theoretical origins in the influence of seminal neoliberal thinkers like Hayek and Friedman (see Harvey, 2005). Where the two discourses most obviously differ, however, is in their mode of *self-identification* with an overtly neoliberal identity.

A euphemised neoliberal discourse generally avoids either over-identification with the market or excessive dis-identification with the state or the collective, and instead constructs its identity around signifiers such as 'social partnership', 'modern', 'non-ideological' and the 'national good'. It seeks to debunk any doctrinal assumption of a stark antagonism between state and market, and asserts itself as a 'pragmatic' appropriation of the 'common-sense' elements of a more transparent, ideologically moti-vated neoliberalism. In other words, by emphasising how 'our pragmatism' is *relationally* different to 'their ideology', a euphemised neoliberal identity can endeavour to assert itself (irrespective of the implausibility of the gesture!) as 'non-ideological'; or, as I have suggested with respect to Ahern, to construe itself as overtly identifying with other ideologies.

So, how might this distinction, as cursorily reviewed here, help us understand the dynamics of the Irish case and this chapter's particular interest in media? Two points, in particular, should be emphasised. First, the distinction highlights the fact that neoliberalism is not bound to a fixed set of representational practices. Neoliberal discourse is a dynamic and contaminable construction that is capable of being articulated with fragments of other political discourses and identities (Fairclough, 2003). The distinction cautions us, therefore, against accepting simplistic accounts of how neoliberalism is articulated, and emphasises instead the enduring capacity for political differences within a paradigm of broad ideological sameness (Jessop, 2004).

Second, my distinction emphasises the relational nature, both *inter-nationally and intranationally*, of neoliberal identities. The shift towards a more neoliberalised politics in the Ireland of 1987 onwards needs to be situated in a wider international context, where the most obvious referent that Irish political and media elites had for 'neoliberalism' was Thatcherism. The fact that the Irish case was hegemonically understood as avoiding the antagonistic class politics of the latter[3] contributed to the naturalisation of an assumption that, because it was not Thatcherism, the politics of the Celtic Tiger and social partnership can somehow be regarded as non-ideological.[4]

Finally, it should be stressed that discourse analysis transcends a narrow concern with analysing language *only*. Laclau and Mouffe (1985) develop Foucault's account of discourse as that which structures the link between language and social practice; indeed, they radicalise the latter's insights by rejecting any ontological distinction between discursive practice and social practice (Chouliaraki and Fairclough, 1999). A comprehensive discourse analysis of the relationship between neoliberalism and Irish media would, therefore, also need to consider how the production, distribution and consumption of newspaper texts is discursively constituted, though this chapter is centred on a more conventional analysis of newspaper texts.

Neoliberalism and Irish media production

This chapter does not have the space to consider adequately the different dimensions of news media analysis. However, I want to make some observations about the process of media production, as it would be a mistake to disembed my specific concern with the neoliberalisation of media texts from a wider political economy assessment (Herman and McChesney, 1997).

One can identify five general ways in which the Irish 'journalistic field'[5] has been and is being reconstituted according to a neoliberalised logic.[6] First, the neoliberalisation of the Irish media is most obviously manifest in the increased competition within, as well as across, markets. One clear consequence is that Irish media production is now more firmly embedded in globalised networks of media ownership.

Second, a neoliberal logic has structured, through a combined process of top-down corporate mergers and changes in bottom-up consumption practices, a general technological convergence of production processes both within and between so-called 'old' and 'new' media (Quinn, 2005). The *Irish Times'* June 2006 purchase of the 'myhome.ie' property website for €50 million[7] is indicative in this respect, as it was a move that repositioned journalism as only a part, if still the central thrust, of the *Irish Times'* 'brand' identity.

Third, a neoliberal logic has contributed to an increased tabloidisation of news content across the journalistic field. The distinction between 'serious' and more popular 'tabloid' media remains a meaningful professional shorthand. But the distinction is increasingly porous in a context where a market logic – at least when internalised by those with most power within the newsroom hierarchy – determines that even the more 'high brow' *Irish Times* must give front-page attention to the winner of *Big Brother* (see *Irish Times*, 28 July and 22 August 2001).

Fourth, elements of a 'tabloid' sensibility also inform the reconfiguration of the (hardcopy) newspaper as an object. The last two decades have seen the reconstitution of newspapers, especially weekend and Sunday editions, in terms of a formula of supplement packaging, where the paper is now an amalgam of magazine, lifestyle, comment, review, news, property, business and sports sections. This chapter does not have the space to explore this diverse range of genres. But it seems reasonable to surmise that some sections, most obviously the once thriving property supplements, are likely to have played a significant role in the banal legitimisation (Billig, 1995) of Irish neoliberal and consumerist discourses.

Fifth, one can characterise the neoliberal turn as having a simultaneous decentring and recentring effect on the constitution of the Irish journalistic field. Several decentring characteristics are discernible: the emergence of a greater diversity of local radio, which is conceivably decentring the place of RTÉ in the national imaginary; the analogous pressures faced by RTÉ in the television market, which, for cable subscribers at least, now offers direct access to a globalised range of consumer choices; the increasing 'Murdochisation' of the Irish print media sub-field, which hypothetically decentres the relative political importance of more traditional newspaper brands; and the decentring of an 'old media' landscape by technological and cultural developments that are challenging the very notion of what constitutes 'journalism'. Yet it is the central contention of this chapter that these decentring trends have been accompanied by a process of ideological recentring, which has seen the Irish journalistic field become increasingly embedded in assumptions that naturalise and legitimise the 'truth' of neoliberal discourses. I will illustrate this argument through a brief overview of how Irish newspapers represented the privatisation in 1999 of the Eircom telecommunications company and a 2002 EU summit, followed by a closer reading of a more recent *Irish Times* text. My examples are purposefully selected but have an indicative value that transcends their particular contexts.

Neoliberalism discourse(s) and Irish media representation

The media representation of the Eircom stock market flotation in July 1999 offered a chance to assess Irish newspapers' attitudes towards neoliberal policy decisions.[8] I examined all editorial references to Eircom from the start of 1999 until the end of 2000, a post-flotation timeframe when the fate of the company was marked by a progressive share price slump that antagonised many of its shareholders.[9] I evaluated editorial texts in six broadsheet newspapers, the *Irish Times, Irish Independent, Sunday Independent, Irish Examiner,*[10] *Sunday Tribune* and *Sunday Business Post.* I chose to analyse the opinionated genre of editorials, because they enabled me to examine how institutional elites within Irish newspapers explicitly identified with neoliberal assumptions.

The decision to fully privatise Eircom was editorially endorsed by all six newspapers. In addition, all of them affirmed the notion that direct state involvement in a modern telecommunications market is archaic, and all encouraged – some more evangelically than others – the notion of public participation in the stock market. The tone of the editorials was often celebratory. This was especially the case in the weeks immediately before and after the flotation, when the privatisation was sometimes invoked to establish political distance between the country's newfound enthusiasm for the market and the 'bad old days' of a more statist, monopolistic Ireland (*Irish Times*, 22 April 1999). The *Irish Independent* editorial published the day after the flotation was especially heady, situating the privatisation as a gleeful symbol of the country's arrival on an international stage:

> On Wall Street yesterday the Minister for Public Enterprise, Mary O'Rourke, looked like a little girl opening her birthday presents. And no wonder. Wall Street, like the Dublin and London markets, had pronounced the Telecom flotation a big success. (*Irish Independent*, 9 July 1999)

The euphoric nature of the editorial discourse faded in tandem with the decline in the company's stock market fortunes. However, none of the papers renounced their support for the privatisation. Instead, they offered a generally convergent diagnosis of the share price decline that desisted from seriously interrogating, though some vaguely lamented, the logic of the global market or the initial decision to fully privatise the company.

These findings are unsurprising. The privatisation of Eircom had the support of the main political parties and trade unions, and so the high degree of editorial consensus accords with the well documented view that the range of opinion expressed in mainstream media converges with that found in the political field.[11] However, rather than terminating my analysis with the blanket conclusion that the six papers are 'all neoliberal', I want to briefly consider editorial differences, since these help illuminate the different ways that newspapers can articulate neoliberal identities.

Some papers asserted an unproblematic neoliberal stance. The *Sunday Business Post* asserted a triumphant, sometimes ideologically belligerent rhetoric that exalted the virtues of the market. The neoliberal identity of the *Irish Independent* and *Sunday Independent* was similarly transparent. Both editorial stances were given a populist inflection that championed a new, more 'democratic' era of share ownership. The stances of the other three papers were more complex, but shed light on the often euphemised nature of Irish neoliberalism. The *Irish Times'* stance was a hybrid of transparent and euphemised neoliberal discourses. On the one hand, it celebrated the 'historical' policy move yet, on the other, assumed a temperate editorial voice that insisted future privatisations should be decided on a pragmatic, 'case by case' basis.

The editorial voice of the *Sunday Tribune* was marked by similar tensions
and fissures. Literate neoliberal discourses were articulated with the fragments of other political economy discourses, some of which assumed an
interrogative posture towards the ascent of the market. For example, one
editorial distanced itself from a blinkered commitment to privatisation by
reproaching what it categorised as the '"stack 'em up high and sell 'em
approach" that the Government (especially its PD [Progressive Democrat]
members) seems to be adopting at present' (*Sunday Tribune*, 9 May 1999).
Another appropriated an equality discourse to highlight complacent aspects
of the new Ireland and spoke to a less affluent public, for whom the purchase
of telecom shares was a remote prospect: 'Now such is the relative wealth
many – *but most definitely not all*[12] – enjoy in the booming Irish economy
that the 1.2 million registrations for shares in the share offer is met with
almost a casual shrug' (*Sunday Tribune*, 20 June 1999). Similarly, the *Irish
Examiner*'s support for the Eircom privatisation did not preclude it from
drawing on an anti-privatisation discourse to reproach the government for
its 'obsession with selling off state assets' and 'its Thatcherite policies [which
do] not inspire confidence' (*Irish Examiner*, 10 December 1999).

What does this brief overview of Eircom editorials tell us about the
structured relationship between media representation and Irish neoliberalism? On the one hand, it shows how the editorial stance of all
six newspapers was constructed around clear identification with the neoliberalised logic of the privatisation policy. Yet it also shows how different
journalistic field identities persisted within this sphere of 'constrained
heterogeneity' (Jessop, 2004: 162). The differences between the papers
cannot mask a fundamental ideological sameness across the editorials.
However, the differences should not be occluded either, as they offer
insights into how Irish neoliberal hegemony is partly sustained through
discourses that often euphemise – perhaps unconsciously – their ideological identification with the 'truths' of neoliberalism.

The latter point applies with particular respect to news reportage. The
genre can be conceptualised as one where journalists typically adhere to a
set of objectivity codes that seek to avoid biased identification with certain
perspectives. One can surmise, then, that if reportage contributes to the
hegemonic constitution of an Irish neoliberalism, it will do this mainly
through subtly privileging certain neoliberalised understandings of the
social and political world.

Let us consider this argument by examining how both the *Irish Independent* and the *Irish Times* represented the gathering of EU leaders at the
2002 Barcelona summit.[13] The summit was officially convened to advance
the so-called 'Lisbon agenda', the strongly neoliberalised blueprint for EU
economic reform that was formulated at the 2000 Lisbon summit. Media

interest in the Barcelona summit's formal agenda was, however, displaced by a number of other summit-related events, including violent clashes between Spanish police and what both papers called 'anti-globalisation' protesters, and the issue of Irish ratification of the Nice Treaty.

I want to focus here on the depoliticised way the specific reform agenda was represented. The framing in both papers took its basic narrative cue from the 'primary definition' (Hall *et al.*, 1978) of the political situation proffered by elite sources like Tony Blair, who was quoted as saying 'There is no-one really arguing about the direction. There may be some arguing about the pace of the movement' (*Irish Times*, 17 March 2002). The 'some' was code primarily for the French, whose prime minister, Lionel Jospin, was consistently framed as half-hearted about the reform agenda. His ambivalence was markedly at odds with the perspective advanced by other sources. The *Irish Times* referenced four sources who specifically alluded to the reform agenda, each of whom was a prime minister and, with the exception of Jospin, all assumed a favourable disposition towards the fundamental goal of reform. The *Irish Independent* cited twelve sources (mainly national and EU political figures) and Jospin was again the only one represented as hesitant about reform.

The framing of the issue in both papers followed the logic of the sourcing patterns to construct an institutional political world favourably disposed towards what the *Irish Independent* called 'badly needed reforms'. The elite 'reform' agenda was sometimes represented as alienated from the concerns of ordinary people. Intertextually taking his cue from what he described as Blair's 'ironic assessment' of the summit as a 'joy', Denis Staunton's analysis of the summit in the *Irish Times* on 18 March 2002 spoke to a reader bored by a technocratic agenda 'dominated by dull, economic issues, many so complicated that only a handful of officials in Europe's capitals understand them fully'. This assessment could, in some ways, be read as an indictment of an abstruse reform agenda. Yet it also suggests an obvious, unexplored contradiction, since a separate *Irish Times* report by Staunton on the same day noted that 'more than 200,000 people gathered in Barcelona to protest against the EU's economic policies'. Why is a 'dull', 'complicated' agenda the reason for protest by 'more than 200,000 people'? Why were the perspectives of groups involved in the protests not directly sourced by either paper?

In fairness, the papers did give generic voice to protesters' concerns, though the legitimacy of the voice – as if 'it' were a singular one – was diminished by vague, abstract attributions of agency: '*their leaders* have promised'; 'More than *200,000 people gathered … to urge …*' (*Irish Times*); '*they* were protesting [*sic*] the liberalisation agenda' (*Irish Independent*). Both papers also made clear distinctions between the 'violent' protests of 16 March and the peaceful protests organised by trade unions of 15 March. However, with the foregrounding of visual images of violent exchanges between the police and protesters, the most prominent aspects of the coverage reinforced stereotypical associations between the 'anti-globalisation' movement and political violence.

Two inter-related conclusions can be drawn from this brief overview. First, it shows how both papers reproduced a political world where the goals of economic reform met with little legitimate resistance. This TINA-like[14] logic is not spontaneously created by journalists. But it is (re)articulated through banal processes of journalistic representation. Resistance may have been flagged in the form of protester objections and French obstinacy. Yet the reader's knowledge about the former was hampered by a diminishment of agency and hackneyed 'anti-globalisation' stereotypes, while sourced-based and paper-formulated explanations of the latter reinforced, rather than challenged, a neoliberal logic. This neo-liberalised assessment of the French position emerged through a discourse which established parallels between ambivalence towards the market, a controlling state, self-interested political behaviour and the timidity of politicians in the face of trade union power.

Second, it shows how newspapers tacitly and sometimes explicitly identified with a reform agenda, despite much of the coverage exuding a sense of fatigue ('leaders were deadlocked', 'leaders struggled', 'leaders scrambled') with what was represented as the perennial discussion of EU reform. The fundamental rightness of the neoliberalised agenda was basic-ally presupposed – as exemplified by the political consensus emerging from the choice of sources and the failure to explicate satisfactory narrative links between the official summit agenda and the civic protests.

The neoliberalisation of the *Irish Times*

I now want to consider the framing effects of neoliberal discourses in more detail through a close reading of a single *Irish Times* piece. My analysis focuses on a page-length, multi-article examination of the Swedish social and fiscal 'model' in the *Irish Times* of 19 December 2005. Billed under the heading 'Agenda', the feature spread followed normal journalistic con-ventions of balance and impartiality in that, of the three intertextually linked articles, two were positioned as 'for' and 'against' opinion pieces. The 'for' text was authored by Paul Sweeney, economic consultant to the Irish Congress of Trade Unions, and expressed a position that identified strongly with the more egalitarian character of Swedish society (Sweeney, 2005). The 'against' text was written by the neoliberal economist and journalist Constantin Gurdgiev (2005) and assailed the 'Irish left' for its naïve identification with Swedish 'socialism' and failure to recognise how 'the Nordic spirit of egalitarianism is, itself, increasingly turning away from state intervention in the lives of its citizens'. What interests me here, however, is the third article, written by the paper's then economics editor, Marc Coleman (2005), which was implicitly coded as the more neutral complement to the two overt opinion pieces.

Under the headline 'Swedes warm to Ireland's low-tax regime', the article was anchored in the assumption that 'a growing number of people on the left in Ireland' saw the Swedish model as a 'rallying point' for an alternative Irish social model. The implicit irony, intimated in the headline, is how the Irish model seemed to be functioning as a contrary rallying point for some in Sweden. The text was superficially coded as balanced and impartial. Perceived failings and merits of the Swedish model were identified; as Coleman observed, 'with one of the world's highest standards of living, Sweden has as much baby as it has bathwater'. However, when examined more closely, one can discern a text firmly embedded in a neoliberalised logic that worked to delegitimise both the Swedish model and the 'Irish left'.

The article began with an interrogation of what was generically categorised as 'the Irish left' and 'the left'. This left perspective was given no direct voice; the only representative figure cited was Socialist Party TD Joe Higgins, though there were generic references to 'trade unionists', 'public sector union(s)' and the 'big [Irish Ferries] March in Dublin'. While this reductive labelling can, in one sense, be regarded as a mundane journalistic act, it can, in the wider context of the article, be interpreted as an archetypal neoliberal move, as the subject position giving 'voice' to the political identity of 'the left' was also the one interrogating it. This is to say that the text established, in its opening paragraphs, a clear othering relation between a 'left' identity and what, later in the text, was identified as a 'free market' one – a discursive move redolent of the subject position strongly disidentifying with socialism that centred the prototypical neoliberalism of Hayek (1960) and Friedman (1962).[15]

This neoliberalised representation of 'the left' is affirmed in other respects. The coding of a left political stance as naïve and embedded in romantic forms of political identification is intimated by the characterisation of the left as 'celebrating' a Swedish model that 'inspire[s] admiration' and is regarded as a 'noble contrast' to the Irish case. The logic of these rhetorical moves is rendered explicit later in the text, when Coleman observes:

> Many [on 'the left'] hope that Irish Ferries will rekindle a new form of the old Boston versus Berlin debate. Berlin has long since lost its lustre. But in seafaring tradition, trade unionists are looking north to that most constant of stars in the social democratic constellation – Sweden.

There is a lot to unpack in this short extract. It triumphantly presupposes a Boston victory over Berlin and gratuitously deploys a 'seafaring' metaphor to make a sarcastic aside to the Irish Ferries dispute. It also clearly constructs left, trade unionist and social democratic identities in terms of a starry-eyed utopianism that is coded as an ideologically bankrupt search for political alternatives.

This pejorative characterisation of 'the left' is interspersed, in turn, with a representation of the Swedish model as antiquated. This is anchored in the text's choice of Swedish sources, all of which function as argumentative resources undermining the credibility of the Swedish model. The first source is 'Johnny Munkhammer' (*sic*), who is described as a representative of the 'free market Stockholm network'.[16] Munkhammer is referenced twice in the article and, given his 'free market' billing, is unsurprisingly framed as a strong critic of the Swedish welfare system. His stance is given a more generalisable authority by the statement that immediately follows his first comment: that 'such critics are growing in number'. The claim is supported with reference to the 'Swedish Confederation of Business'. The organisation is not sourced. Instead, Coleman reflects on a personal meeting he had with Confederation delegates who visited Ireland in November, who, despite Coleman's flattering observations about 'Sweden's excellent transport system, education system and good record of research and development … were still adamant that they had much to learn from Ireland'. Subsequent e-mail correspondence with Coleman[17] confirmed that there is, in fact, no Swedish Confederation of Business. The article should have indexed the Confederation of Swedish Enterprise, which, it turns out, previously employed Munkhammer as a 'senior policy adviser'.[18] Thus, while the statement that 'such critics are growing in number' can be read as implying an organic popularisation of Munkhammer's stance beyond a specific 'free market' milieu, Munkhammer and the Confederation of Swedish Enterprise are clearly part of the same Swedish neoliberal network (an ideological kinship that is obvious from a quick perusal of websites).

The article cites two other Swedish sources. The economist Assar Lindbeck is casually framed – without any supporting evidence – as 'one of the world's leading economists' and paraphrased as believing that 'the future of Sweden's economic system is in doubt'. The final source is former prime minister Carl Bildt, who is quoted as emphasising 'the need to look at the economic challenges [as distinct from the *socio-economic* challenges] facing some of the older European economies'. The text makes no allusion to any specific political affiliation between Lindbeck and Bildt, though, as Ryner (2002: 13) observes, 'Lindbeck is an influential advocate of neo-liberal reform in Sweden, who played a prominent role in the policy formation of the Conservative-led coalition government headed by Carl Bildt in the early 1990s'.

The key point to distil from the analysis of sources is that they can all be understood as either explicitly avowing, or being implicitly aligned with, a neoliberal agenda. They are resourced, in turn, to bolster Coleman's own assessment of the Swedish model, which, like his representation of the 'Irish left', assumes a prototypically neoliberal disposition. The article locates its assessment in terms of a culturally essentialist logic which hypothetically asserts that '*if* Sweden's economic system has brought benefits to that country, it is perhaps because it has up to now been consistent with something *deeply rooted* in the Nordic character'. Affirming the findings of a 1993 global study, which 'found that Swedes were more inclined' towards collectivism, and are less assertive as individuals, compared with other nations, Coleman asserts:

> It rings true that the Swedes have up to now been more collectivist in outlook: The name of its economic system, volkshemma (people's home), evokes the image of a village group sitting around a fire in a communal wooden lodge, protected from the harsh Nordic winter outside.

To unpack the ideologically coherent nature of Coleman's analysis, it is useful to reference Laclau and Mouffe's (1985) notion of a discursive 'logic of equivalence'. They describe the latter as a logic of 'sameness and simplification' (p. 130) which endeavours to cement relations between the different elements that give structural coherence to a discourse; or, in this case, *project* a structural coherence onto a discourse that is othered. Hence, in the particular text, one can discern a logic of equivalence between the 'Swedish model' and: an antiquated 'collectivism'; a 'collectivist and communal approach to welfare'; 'an opportunity to free ride'; 'politicians … expand[ing] the size of government in order to increase their own power' (the staple, self-interested figure of rational-choice theory); 'frustrating obstacle[s] to meritocracy'; and a 'system of centralised bargaining … [that] is coming under pressure'. The implication of these logically structured associations is that they construct an imagined reader who, again reminiscent of Hayek's prototypical neoliberal subject, strongly disidentifies with a collectivist logic and its insidious effects on politicians and the wider citizenry. The preferred subject position is antithetically constructed through cementing the discursive associations between 'individualised approaches to work', 'young people's changing values', 'technological change', 'meritocracy' and a 'future' that transcends, while perhaps also learning something from, the antiquated concerns of the Swedish model. Thus, the reader is encouraged to identify with a set of signifying links which, in the overall context of the article, are implicitly linked to a status quo affirmation of the culturally distinct Irish model as better and more modern than the Swedish alternative.

So, one might ask, what has been the point of this close textual reading? It certainly indicates journalistic enthusiasm for a neoliberal agenda in the *Irish Times*, but what conclusions can we reach from the analysis of a single, carelessly constructed text? My analysis should be read as emblematic of how the ideology of the 'sensible centre' (Louw, 2005: 76) that implicitly informs the 'objective' coding of journalism is now routinely embedded in neoliberal assumptions. Furthermore, it can be read as a barometer of the shifting corporate and brand identity of the *Irish Times*, which, as several commentators have observed, has moved more discernibly to the 'right' in recent times (Browne, 2006).

The logic of this necessarily euphemised shift needs to be situated within a wider 'journalistic field' logic. Because of the *Irish Times*' putative 'left liberal' image (see Phelan, 2005), the consistent articulation of an overtly neoliberal identity would clearly undermine the paper's credibility among a significant part of its readership (see the discussion of 'letters to the editor' below). Thus, if the paper is to articulate a neoliberal identity, it simultaneously needs to avoid being institutionally 'colonised' as such, in much the same way that a social democratic identity, embedded in neoliberal discourses, has a strategic need to keep asserting itself as 'social democratic'. This, then, is to reinforce my earlier observation that neo-liberalised identities are also fragmented identities, and to deduce on the basis of my close analysis of a single *Irish Times* text that the paper is 'neo-liberal' would be to deny the heterogeneous nature of the paper's identity and the capacity of journalistic voices within it to interrogate a neoliberal logic. At the same time, to conclude that this heterogeneity amounts to some utopian 'free market in ideas' would be similarly trite, for, as my cumulative analysis has shown, some ideas have a much greater common-sense authority than others when it comes to journalism's mundane, yet deeply political, construction of reality.

Conclusion

The production and representational practices of Irish journalism are the sites of a latent struggle over the hegemonic form and content of political discourse. Contrary to certain common-sense notions, Irish journalism does not merely 'reflect' the world of the (post) Celtic Tiger, but also works to discursively constitute it (Hall, 1996). This may strike some readers as prosaic affirmation of what we can already intuit about the relationship between media and politics. But, if that is the case, I would maintain that we have yet to see a public sphere discourse that satisfactorily politicises these insights. In this respect, it is perhaps telling that, of the three intertextually linked letters published in the aftermath of the *Irish Times'* feature spread on Sweden (all of which expressed a pro-Swedish stance, consistent with the paper's imagined readership), none made any critical reference to the Coleman article. Two specifically reproached Gurdgiev and, as if exemplifying how the media analysis of the 'expert' academic may not cohere with the sense-making practices of readers, the third asserted that 'it was refreshing to read the articles by Marc Coleman and Paul Sweeney on Sweden's economy' (Moran, 2005).

Finally, while I have not had space to consider transformative possibilities in this chapter, I have tried to imbue my analysis with antidotes to political fatalism. Neoliberalism, for all its paradigmatic power and authority, is not some monolithic force, but discursively constructed in ways that rely on the naturalisation of certain signifying associations, some of which may even sound comforting and progressive (Harvey, 2005). That 'it' is naturalised and embedded in the banal practices and increasingly mediatised lives of many of us is certainly one of its strengths. But this gives it a (formally) fragmented and contingent character that is also the potential basis of neoliberalism's hegemonic dissolution. The social world can be represented differently, though this is to invoke a politics of possibility that will need material and institutional correlates. The productive power of media institutions is particularly important in this respect, especially if we are to imagine an Irish future that is genuinely 'other' than neoliberal.

Notes

I would like to thank Lincoln Dahlberg, Ralph Footring, Katie Leach and the editors for their feedback on earlier drafts of this chapter.

1 I am not trying to suggest that the two 'ideal types' of neoliberal discourse are wholly discrete or that the analytical distinction cannot be easily problematised. The distinction is best seen as a useful framework for making *preliminary* sense of the political differences that are articulated within a paradigm of broad ideological sameness.
2 'Discourse' is interchangeably used here to refer to discourse in general and particular discourses.
3 See Allen (2003) for an interrogation of this dominant reading.
4 For example, see the analysis of John Bruton's rhetoric in Phelan (2007a).
5 Although I do not have space for such a discussion in this chapter, Bourdieu's field theory offers a very useful conceptual framework for examining how the Irish journalistic field has been reconstituted as a consequence of the neoliberal turn (Benson and Neveu, 2005).

6 This focus on neoliberalism as the 'cause' of Irish media change involves a considerable degree of simplification, as media change should be understood as 'overdetermined' and hence not reducible to a neoliberal logic.

7 See *Irish Independent*, '*Irish Times* buys property website MyHome.ie', *Irish Independent*, 28 July 2006. Available at www.unison.ie/irish_independent/ (accessed July 2006).

8 The company is indexed as Eircom here, though the name was changed from Telecom Éireann only after the privatisation.

9 The analysis of Eircom editorials summarised here is presented at length in Phelan (2007b).

10 Originally known as *The Cork Examiner*, the paper was rebranded as *The Examiner* in 1996, only to be rebranded again as the *Irish Examiner* in 2000. The paper is referred to here by the latter title only.

11 This notion is, for instance, found in the well known propaganda model advanced by Herman and Chomsky (1994).

12 All italicised emphases, unless indicated otherwise, are those of the author.

13 The various summit-related articles discussed here were published in the 15, 16 and 18 March 2002 editions of both papers.

14 TINA denotes 'there is no alternative'.

15 It also echoes the kind of reductive labelling that structures the identity of the 'left-liberal' 'other' in US neoconservative political discourse.

16 A Google search indicates that Munkhammar would have been more precisely described as a member of the Stockholm-based think-tank Timbro (www.timbro.se). The latter is an affiliate member of the confusingly named Stockholm Network, which is actually a pan-European network of free-market think-tanks run by a London-based limited company (see www.stockholm-network.org).

17 Personal e-mail communication with Marc Coleman, 6 September 2006.

18 See Johnny Munkhammar's website, www.munkhammar.org (accessed 1 September 2006).

6

Republic of Ireland PLC – testing the limits of marketisation

RODDY FLYNN

On 26 December 1999, Chelsea Football Club created a first when they fielded the first ever entirely non-British starting eleven in an English Premier League game. Six years later, Arsenal would take this to its logical conclusion when manager Arsène Wenger named a complete sixteen-man panel of 'foreigners'.[1] Both matches sparked a degree of UK press comment but, although some commentators suggested that it boded ill for the English national team, no reference was made to the manner in which they confirmed a break in the link between the constitution of individual teams and the specific locations to which – notionally at least – those teams were connected. This absence of comment tacitly acknowledged the extent to which professional football teams had long ago abandoned any pretence that individual players owed any organic allegiance to the specific geographical locations their teams represented. When Tottenham Hotspur decided to list on the London Stock Exchange as a public limited company (PLC) in the mid-1980s (a lead quickly followed by a phalanx of other major UK teams) the club was merely making explicit the commercialisation of English soccer.

The same understanding has not generally been true of national teams such as the Republic of Ireland, however. It is commonly understood that players wearing the green shirt of the Republic of Ireland – Jack Charlton's creative exploitation of FIFA rules to recruit second- and third-generation Irishmen notwithstanding – do so out of commitment to the nation rather than for pecuniary ends.[2] In that sense, the Irish national soccer team was, at least until the early years of the twenty-first century, popularly understood to be a primarily cultural institution rather than one subject to the vagaries of the market.

However, the notion that international soccer was virtually a public good was shattered in July 2002 when the Football Association of Ireland (FAI) announced that it had pulled out of talks with RTÉ, the public television station, relating to the sale of broadcast rights for the Republic of Ireland's forthcoming competitive and friendly matches and was instead selling them exclusively to British Sky Broadcasting (BSkyB). Since BSkyB was a subscription broadcaster, Irish viewers were threatened with the prospect of having to become subscribers to the Sky satellite television package to watch the games, at a time when fewer than one in six Irish homes subscribed to such services. At a stroke, something hitherto unproblematically regarded as a national event was suddenly demonstrated to be a commodity, available to the highest bidder via the market.

Given that the deal was announced the day before the publication of the long-awaited Ansbacher report into large-scale tax evasion, it might have been anticipated that the story would quickly have been sidelined. In the event, however, the sale of the matches became perhaps the key political issue of that summer, remaining on the front pages for the months of July and into August. A variety of institutions, including RTÉ, BSkyB, the FAI – and indirectly the Irish Rugby Football Union (IRFU) and the Gaelic Athletic Association (GAA) – the European Commission and the Irish government became embroiled in what became a debate about the limits of state power in the face of the neoliberal project to subject all areas to the rigours of the market. The story demonstrated for Irish citizens in a stark fashion the implications of changes in the broader Irish broadcasting environment and, indeed, in the political economy of culture in Ireland. Nonetheless, the narrative also demonstrates how public pressure can counter what often appear to be immutable laws governing the operation of the free market.

The broadcasting environment

Although BSkyB's acquisition of the Republic of Ireland matches in 2002 was greeted as 'a bolt from the blue' (in the words of Minister for Communications, Dermot Ahern), in many respects it was the logical – indeed, arguably inevitable – conclusion of the deregulation of Irish and European broadcasting in the last decades of the twentieth century. From the 1920s to the 1980s, spectrum scarcity saw European broadcasting concentrated in the hands of a small number of state-owned broadcasters. However, the introduction of cable, 'direct to home' (DTH) satellite broadcasting and digital broadcasting undermined the scarcity rationale for state control of broadcasting, and so European broadcasting markets were gradually 'liberalised'. In Ireland, the 1988 Radio and Television Act paved the way for the creation first of TV3 and more recently Channel 6 (since renamed 3e) and Setanta Sports. At a European level, the passage of the Television Without Frontiers (TWF) directive in 1989 further liberalised national markets by, among other things, prohibiting individual EU member states from blocking broadcasts from other members into their territories.

The advent of new market entrants fundamentally altered the market for broadcast content, including sports rights. Until the 1980s, the relative abundance of sports content as compared with the strictly limited number of broadcasters had conspired to ensure that the owners of sports rights were unable to exploit the full commercial potential of their 'product'. Writing in 1997, however, Cowie and Williams noted that:

> the industry is moving from a situation where spectrum is scarce, and hence where programme content has to compete for scarce 'retail' outlets, to the reverse situation where abundant spectrum competes for (relatively scarce) content. (Cowie and Williams 1997: 620)

In Europe, and in the UK in particular, the major beneficiaries of this shift were the rights holders for professional soccer. Until the early 1990s, the BBC and ITV had actively colluded to avoid an expensive bidding war for English soccer rights. Thus, in 1986, the BBC/ITV duopoly paid only £6.2 million to the Football Association to acquire two years of First Division (now Premier League) rights. When BSkyB entered the market in 1992, however, it offered £191.5 million to secure five years' worth of matches. Even this figure was dwarfed by the £670 million and £1.1 billion BSkyB bid to retain those rights in 1997 and 2000, respectively (Teather, 2000; Cave and Crandell, 2001). In 2006, the English League secured £1.7 billion for six packages of games sold to BSkyB and Irish-based subscription broadcaster Setanta (Oliver, 2006).

The impact of these changes was not immediately felt in Ireland. In part this was due to the attractiveness of the product. Prior to 1988 the Republic of Ireland had never qualified for a major international championship. However, after qualifying for the 1988 European Championships, the team went on to qualify for the 1990, 1994 and 2002 World Cup final competitions, engendering a massive increase in public interest and support (Free, 2005). This was partially reflected in the terms of deals between the FAI and RTÉ: although the value of a four-year deal signed in September 1994 was never published, a joint FAI/RTÉ statement described the sum involved as 'a significant increase on the previous sum, and substantial' (Thornley, 1994). That it was not more substantial still was a reflection of the fact that, by European standards, RTÉ's television monopoly status was unusually long-lived. Despite the 1988 Radio and Television Act, it was not until 1998 that TV3 took to the air. The absence of competition was reflected in the casual nature of the pre-2002 deals between RTÉ and the FAI. Even the 1994 deal committed RTÉ to covering only one competitive game in either the World Cup or European Championship qualifying series (although in practice RTÉ tacitly conceded the value of the Republic of Ireland's games by broadcasting virtually every one played). More overt acknowledgement of the value of such rights came only in 1996, when, motivated in part by speculation that BSkyB was considering bidding to secure exclusive broadcasting rights to all Ireland's home games, RTÉ re-entered negotiations with the FAI. The result was a six-year deal – the biggest hitherto negotiated by RTÉ Sport – entitling RTÉ to cover all home games played by the Republic of Ireland, competitive or otherwise, until 2002 (Byrne, 1996).

However, when the station re-entered negotiations with the FAI in 2002, it initially bid only €1.6 million for the Republic of Ireland's 2002–6 games, *less* than it had paid in 1996. Although RTÉ attempted to justify this on the grounds that the value of sports rights was on the decline (pointing to the collapse of the ITV OnDigital deal with the Nationwide League in the UK), the parlous state of the station's finances must have been a factor. Successive government refusals to countenance an increase in the licence fee had made the station increasingly reliant on commercial revenues. At the same time, RTÉ faced hitherto unknown levels of competition in the advertising market as more and more UK-based channels offered Irish advertisers local opt-outs during advertisement breaks, which allowed them to target advertisements at Irish audiences. In consequence, RTÉ recorded a deficit of €70 million in 2001 (Radio Telifís Éireann Authority, 2002: 50). Thus, when BSkyB made a counter-bid of €7.5 million for the Republic of Ireland rights, RTÉ was blown out of the water.

Public reaction to the BSkyB deal

The scale of the public response to the deal was truly unprecedented, in part because the deal was without precedent. The Consumer Association of Ireland announced that it had received thousands of calls of complaint. For an entire week the deal became a mainstay of Joe Duffy's *Liveline* phone-in show on RTÉ's Radio 1; it was the subject of opinion and editorial pieces in the *Irish Times* and *Irish Independent* and became a mainstay of letters pages in the national press. Eleven days after the story broke, columnist Vincent Browne lamented that:

> Yet again yesterday morning *The Irish Times* led the newspaper with the
> FAI/Sky story, having done so on several days previously. It has not been

alone. Most other newspapers and news programmes have focused on little else. All of a sudden something to do with fairness has crept on to the national agenda. (Browne, 2002: 12)

The strength of the reaction owed much to the extent to which, as Free (2005) argues, the 1990s had seen the Republic of Ireland soccer team become a symbol not merely of Irish independence and legitimacy but also of a 'more mature national identity unhindered by inward-looking cultural nationalism or British colonialism's psychic legacy'. Indeed, the success of the team was frequently invoked as mirroring and symbolising the economic boom of the 1990s (Free, 2005). Such symbolism was reflected in the specific nature of the public response to the BSkyB deal: letters to the national press at least tacitly invoked a sense that a public good, indeed a national asset, had been sold for a mess of potage to a broadcaster which, though part of a transnational corporation, was popularly understood as British:

> Sir, – The FAI deserves hearty congratulations for its tireless promotion of the interests of its only remaining fans – Sky Television and publicans with a satellite dish.... the FAI has now decided that Ireland's football team is merely a commodity to be sold to the highest bidder. (John Walsh, 2002: 13)

> Sir – The news that the FAI has sold the TV rights to screen live home games to Sky demonstrates an appalling lack of consideration for the unflinching loyalty of the Green Army [of supporters]. It is yet another example of fiscal gain superseding all other consideration. (Aidan Walsh, 2002: 25)

> Sir, – ... The other insult to the Irish people is that we will have to pay a foreign company to watch our national team. (Smyth, 2002: 27)

In effect, the FAI/BSkyB deal made manifest in a manner that was universally comprehensible the extent to which all aspects of Irish society were now potentially subject to the logic of the market. The language used by economically conservative commentators like Kevin Myers implied a common-sense understanding that it had always been thus:

> It is this simple. The laws of commerce cannot be suspended without consequence for the commercial activities concerned. However, certain people who have lived outside the laws of commerce and who are used to monopoly powers ... think that you can re-label something that is in essence hugely commercial as a cultural event and thereby remove it from the realm of market forces, making it free to the consumer at the point of supply. (Myers, 2002: 15)

Although no Irish political party overtly identifies itself as neoliberal (with the possible exception of the Progressive Democrats), the eagerness of the Irish state to compete in the globalised economy has meant that, since the 1980s, that ideology has informed the *de facto* policies of virtually all Irish administrations. Yet, despite the liberalisation of, for example, the broadcasting, telecommunications and aviation sectors, it is arguable that many Irish citizens were only distantly conscious of neoliberalism as an influence on their lives. This could no longer be said to be true after the FAI/BSkyB deal: the letters pages of the national press in the weeks after the deal bore witness to the extent to which the deal had stamped this new dispensation on the public consciousness:

> Sir, – I am stunned by how contemptuous the FAI spokespeople are about criticism of their deal with Rupert Murdoch's Sky empire. But this is globalisation at work, a process from which Ireland has profited, and which is now leading to public services being commodified and sold to the highest bidder....
>
> ... the FAI has given us a useful yellow card about the remorseless economic forces driving globalisation, as exemplified by the World Trade Organisation, and especially by the extension of the GATS agreement [Global Agreement on Trade in Services], which are creating a world where it is becoming more difficult to protect key public services from the clutches of multinational companies concerned only to maximise profits. (Tynan, 2002: 13)

So profound indeed was the re-orientation of the public's understanding of the national team – 'perhaps *The Irish Times* would be good enough to publish the weekly FAI results on its business pages' (Ryan, 2002) – that early suggestions for resisting the deal could conceive of doing so only by adopting the stance of the consumer. Within days, letters columns were filled with calls to strike at the FAI's finances by boycotting future internationals. Some letters offered a remarkably nuanced rationale for such action. Recognising that a football match is not solely constituted by the presence of two opposing teams but rather that the presence of supporters at matches 'may contribute to the commodity's actual production' (Free and Hughson, 2006: 88), supporters threatened to withdraw their 'embedded expressive labour' (Willis, 2000: 55):

> The only way to make the FAI realise what a monumental mistake it has made is to boycott of the games that have been sold to Sky. Mr Murdoch's minions won't be too interested in the rights to matches played in an empty stadium. (O'Reilly, 2002: 13)

However, other correspondents maintained the stance of the citizen:

> Globalisation may be an unstoppable process, but there is no reason it cannot be managed in the public interest if we insist that public services,

such as the public broadcasting of major events, are protected … we do have a choice. We live in a democracy. There is no such thing as a done deal if it is clearly not in the public interest. (Tynan, 2002: 13)

Protected events

Ironically, such a perspective found support from a source more commonly associated with a market outlook, the European Commission. Although the 1989 TWF directive focused on removing artificial obstacles to audio-visual trade within the EU, its 1997 sequel (TWF II) was influenced by the stance adopted by the EU over the General Agreement on Tariffs and Trade (GATT) in the 1993 negotiations on the audiovisual sector: cultural products cannot simply be treated as commodities (Miller, 1996). The commercial implications of the shift whereby the market for sports rights increasingly favoured sellers rather than buyers had not gone unnoticed at either a national or a supranational level. As early as 1990, the Conservative government in the UK had introduced lists of protected events[3] which could not be screened on a pay-per-view basis. The UK Broadcasting Act in 1996 had extended the prohibition to subscription channels, essentially insisting that 'listed events' be screened on a free-to-air basis. In a similar vein, article 3a of the 1997 TWF II directive stated that:

> Each Member State may take measures in accordance with Community law to ensure that broadcasters under its jurisdiction do not broadcast on an exclusive basis events which are regarded by that Member State as being of major importance for society in such a way as to deprive a substantial proportion of the public in that Member State of the possibility of following such events via live coverage or deferred coverage on free television. (European Council, 1997)

In effect, the article permitted member states to insist that specific cultural or sporting events be broadcast to their citizens on a free-to-air basis. Furthermore, it enjoined member states to ensure that broadcasters in their jurisdiction did not exercise exclusive rights so as to deprive the public in another member state of the possibility of watching on a free-to-air basis events designated by that other member state.

As of summer 2002, five countries had submitted lists of protected events to the European Commission – Germany, Italy, the UK, Austria and Denmark – and a further three – the Netherlands, Belgium and France – had notified the Commission of their intention to adopt similar lists (Commission of the European Communities, 2003a: 11–12). The size and variety of lists varied from country to country: the UK listed nineteen separate events, while Germany listed just five. Virtually all the lists included the Olympics and soccer's World Cup and European Championship. Indeed, the bulk of the events listed were of a sporting nature, although in Italy and Austria several musical events were also included.

It was the existence of the TWF directive that ensured that the FAI/BSkyB story stayed on the front pages of the national press. In the immediate aftermath of the deal's announcement, the Irish state sought to frame the story as purely a matter for the FAI, BSkyB and RTÉ. Thus the recently appointed Minister for Communications, Dermot Ahern, could describe the deal as a 'devastating blow', while for Taoiseach Bertie Ahern it was 'disenfranchising' Irish fans. Apparently finally washing the state's hands of the affair, Minister for Arts and Sports, John O'Donoghue, glumly described the deal as 'done and dusted' (McDonagh and McKenna, 2002). However, as the days passed, not only did the existence of article 3a become public knowledge, but it also became clear that the article had been transposed into Irish law via the 1999 Broadcasting (Major Events Television Coverage) Bill by the same Fianna Fáil/Progressive Democrat coalition which mutely watched the FAI/BSkyB deal unfold. Introduced by then Minister for Arts and Culture, Síle de Valera, the short bill won broad support from all parties in the Dáil and passed uncontroversially into law in autumn 1999. It was assumed that de Valera's next act would be to prepare a list of protected events, as the legislation required. Indeed, at the final stage of the bill in the Dáil she expressed hope that consultations with rights holders would be complete within two months of the passage of the bill.[4] Yet in the nearly three years between the passing of the legislation and the announcement of the FAI/BSkyB deal, no list was drawn up, despite recurrent warnings of the consequences of not doing so. In 1998, 2000 and again in February 2002, for example, Irish viewers were unable to watch Ireland's rugby matches against England in the Six Nations Rugby Championship as a result of a five-year (1998–2002) deal between the English Rugby Football Union and BSkyB.

Inevitably, the question of why the state had delayed so long on drawing up a list was raised. The state's answer was politically novel: it criticised its own legislation with a series of assertions about its limitations. These were:

- that the legislation was 'legally risky';
- that it was impossible to designate entire tournaments under the legislation;
- that the consent of sporting or cultural rights holders such as the FAI was required before 'their' events could be listed;
- that lists drawn up in other European countries had been rowed back on;
- that to list events under the legislation would effectively force sporting

organisations to sell their television rights to RTÉ, thus undermining their bargaining position when striking deals on those rights.

However, these assertions proved to be either false or irrelevant and actively ignored the relevant legislation. The point about the inability to designate entire tournaments stood out: nothing in the Irish legislation, the EU directive or actual practice in other countries could be remotely construed in such a manner. The first assertion describing the legislation as legally risky was clearly a red herring – no legislative proposition is ever entirely without such ambiguity. It was true that the list had been rowed back in one other country – Denmark. However, this was not the result of any legal difficulty: on 1 January 2002, a new conservative Danish government had simply revoked the list drawn up by its socialist predecessor on the grounds that it 'considered that the arrangement in question was not compatible with free competition on the market' (Ministry of Culture (Denmark), 2003: 1).

Given this, public attention came to focus on the government's assertions, first, that the consent of rights holders was required before an event could be listed and, second, that listed events would effectively have to be sold to RTÉ, thus undermining the bargaining position of rights holders in striking deals on those rights. As regards the first assertion, although the 1999 act did require the Minister for Communications to 'make reasonable efforts' to consult with the organisers of any event which was being considered for designation, the Minister was not obliged to have their approval. Indeed, to suggest that this was the case imposed an interpretation on the legislation diametrically opposed to its original intention.

This point was related to the government's argument that listing would undermine the financial bargaining position of sporting organisations. This was accurate but it was also the sole and explicit intent of both article 3a and the 1999 Irish legislation: to ensure that sporting organisations could not place their own financial interests above the right of citizens to watch national cultural events. Introducing the act in 1999, Síle de Valera stressed that her intent was 'to protect the major cultural and sporting events from pay-per-view':

> There is the danger that, if market forces are left to themselves without some level of co-ordinated control by the member states of the European Union, a small number of companies will dominate the market for major sports and cultural events that are of interest to the general public leading to restrictions on access to television coverage of such events on those who cannot afford to pay. (*Seanad Debates*, vol. 160, 3 November 1999: 1119)

She explicitly acknowledged that event organisers would have concerns, but noted that 'it must be recognised that the citizen has rights too, and these must be safeguarded' (Mac Carthaigh, 1999: 53). In short, it was abundantly clear that the 1999 Irish legislation would fundamentally alter the value of listed events: in effect, they would no longer be subject to the free market.

Unsurprisingly, therefore, when de Valera began her negotiations with the FAI, IRFU and GAA, she encountered outright hostility and threats of legal action (Siggins, 2002). Specifically, the organisations expressed concern that, just at the point when achieving a market value for their event was in prospect, listing under the legislation would compel them to sell their rights to RTÉ. Thus, while the GAA's President, Sean McCague, insisted that his organisation would never sell games to a subscription broadcaster, he also explained that 'their objections were based on the commercial reality that if the GAA was tied by law to one broadcaster, it would seriously undermine its bargaining rights' (Breheny, 2002). In this respect, the *Irish Times* also quoted letters to Síle de Valera from the IRFU's Chief Executive, Philip Browne, suggesting that RTÉ had been guilty of 'ruthless exploitation' of its monopoly status (Hennessy, 2002).

Notionally, at least, McCague and Browne's references to 'one broadcaster' and RTÉ's monopoly were misleading since, by 2002, a second free-to-air broadcaster – TV3 – had been on air for four years. In practice, however, the comments reflected the reality that TV3's reliance on imported programming had left the market for Irish material scarcely altered (Flynn, 2003: 167–8).[5] Surprisingly, Dermot Ahern tacitly conceded this point when he suggested that the position of the sporting organisations was based on 'very valid reasons from a competition point of view', adding that 'you can't pass a law that takes property rights away from people' (Siggins, 2002).

However, such obfuscatory references to property rights aside, the repeated stress on the wishes of the rights holders suggested that the state could not reconcile the theoretical commitment to the rights of citizens as expressed in the Broadcasting (Major Events Television Coverage) Act 1999 with an almost instinctive faith in the invisible hand of the market. In a revealing aside four days after the deal was announced and made in the context of dismissing the idea that the state could buy out the BSkyB deal, Bertie Ahern expressed the view that the FAI/BSkyB agreement was 'a commercial deal', that is, that it was inviolate, regardless of its impact on citizens.

Nonetheless, as the days passed after the announcement of the deal, debate within the public sphere increasingly came to focus on the state's failure to act. As public pressure mounted, the *Irish Times* and RTÉ carried interviews with a senior European Commission official attached to the Education and Culture Directorate who suggested that a list could be drawn up and enforced retrospectively going forward. Suddenly, the government found it politically necessary to reconsider the extent to which the deal was indeed 'done'.

In passing, one should note that, given the prior existence of the FAI/BSkyB deal, such a retrospective designation might well have been 'legally risky'. Although article 3a of the TWF II directive allows governments to draw up lists, it notes that they should do so '*in due and effective time*' (emphasis added). (In this respect, it is not entirely clear that the Commission official contacted by RTÉ and the *Irish Times* understood that a contract had actually been signed between the FAI and BSkyB.) Such retrospective designation would also appear to clash with the Irish constitution's stout defence of property rights.[6] Nonetheless, faced with ongoing public pressure and doubtless taking cognisance of the fact that, for the next four years, supporters would be reminded of the government's culpability every time a game was played, the state adopted the role of the white knight belatedly rescuing Irish fans. Hence on 13 July 2002, days after his Minister for Sports' 'done and dusted' comment, the Taoiseach presented the government's new line:

> We are the sovereign government and there is legislation and an EU directive and it is quite clear. We cannot sit around and disenfranchise a large part of the population from seeing matches they are allowed to see. (Quoted in Flynn, 2002)

Yet the manner in which the government actually sought to turn the deal around suggests that the state was well aware of the very real legal risk in attempting to render the FAI/BSkyB deal effectively null and void. Nonetheless, the lengths to which it was prepared to go to retrieve the games suggested a very pragmatic concern about the longer-term political impact of allowing the deal to stand.

The government followed the announcement of its determination to wrest back the games for Irish citizens by calling a series of private meetings with the major sporting organisations informing them of their intent to designate some of their games. Veiled references were made to the Attorney-General's view that the state had some 'legal options' regarding the deal. Predictably, the organisations objected to any suggestion that deals might be undone by lists that had not been in existence when the original contracts were signed. Nonetheless, in October 2002, after months of consultation, the Irish government published a list of designated events, which included Republic's home and away games in the soccer European Championship and World Cup qualifying rounds, the All-Ireland hurling and football finals, the Irish Derby and the Irish Grand National.

Amending legislation

That the listing of events followed meetings with the *sporting* organisations was puzzling, since both article 3a of the TWF II directive and the 1999 Irish legislation refer to the power of member states/governments to dictate to *broadcasting* organisations with regard to designated events. Given this, why meet the rights holders? The answer came with a contemporaneous announcement of an amendment to the 1999 Irish legislation specifically designed to address the games covered by the FAI/BSkyB deal. That amendment appeared in April 2003 as the Broadcasting (Major Events Television Coverage) (Amendment) Act. The second article of the new legislation covered the question of retrospection:

> This Act applies to a designated event which is designated before or after the passing of this Act … whether *or not any agreement or arrangement has been entered into* between the event organiser and a broadcaster in respect of the acquisition by the broadcaster of the rights to the event. (Emphasis added)

However, the most significant change came with article 4, which now read:

> Where an event has been designated … and if … the *event organiser* has not made an agreement or arrangement with a qualifying broadcaster to enable it to provide coverage on free television services with the state … a qualifying broadcaster may apply to the High Court … for an order directing the *event organiser* to give rights to the qualifying broadcaster to provide such coverage. (Emphasis added)

In short, the amendment shifted the focus of the exercise of the state's authority from broadcasting organisations to rights holders. In effect, while the 1999 legislation would have brought the state into direct confrontation with BSkyB, the 2003 amendment set up a showdown with the FAI. However, in so doing, the 2003 amendment appears to exceed the authority granted to member states by article 3a, which refers only to the exercise of authority over broadcasters.

Indeed, it remains unclear whether the European Commission itself was aware of this shift in focus when it gave approval to the Irish list (as it would do early in 2003). In Ireland's notification to the Commission, published in the EU's *Official Journal* in April 2003, no reference was made to the 2003 amendment act. Instead, the Commission's approval was sought by reference to a list identified as having been drawn up under the 1999 legislation (Commission of the European Communities, 2003b). Yet it was the 2003 legislation which obliged the FAI to renegotiate its BSkyB deal and to ensure that the Republic of Ireland's European Championship qualifying games were screened by a free-to-air broadcaster – RTÉ, which eventually paid out €2.3 million for the rights (Malone, 2003). Rights to live coverage of Ireland's other home games remained the exclusive preserve of BSkyB, with fans allowed to view deferred coverage on TV3.

If the European Commission's July 2002 assertion that Ireland's existing (1999) legislation permitted retrospection was correct, the question arises as to the need for the 2003 amendment. One possible explanation is that it offered the Irish state a means of retrieving (some of) the Irish games at an acceptable political cost. That any administration might be reluctant to confront directly an organ of News International such as BSkyB hardly needs stating. Offending the FAI – a body already the villain of the piece in the public eye – was therefore a pragmatic strategy, especially given that parallel negotiations between the Irish government and the FAI relating to the building of a national stadium offered the government a certain degree of leverage in negotiating the retrospective designation of events.

However, the state offered a more explicit statement of the rationale behind the 2003 amendment in a document submitted to the European Commission in summer 2003 as part of a review of the TWF directive (Commission of the European Communities, 2003a). The Irish state's submission argued for a radical reinterpretation of article 2 of the TWF directive, which denies member states the right to restrict retransmission on their territory of television broadcasts from other member states. The Irish submission noted that, in the era of cross-border broadcasting, the:

> ability of some Member States to have meaningful regulation at a national level will be eroded unless the Directive is revised to provide that services directed primarily at a given Member State are subject to the regulation of that Member State. Ireland suggests that this should be achieved by determining a competent jurisdiction for each individual broadcasting service, instead of focussing on broadcasters. (Department of Communications, Marine and Natural Resources, 2003)

In short, the Irish submission argued that if a UK-registered company established a station explicitly targeting the Irish market, then it should be regulated by the Irish state, not a British regulator. As such, the Irish submission suggested a reversal of one of the original directive's most fundamental tenets – that individual states should not have the power to regulate broadcasting services that were considered acceptable under another state's broadcasting regime.

This point forms the context for the Irish submission on article 3a, which also offers some clarification for the content of the 2003 legislation:

> a UK broadcaster only requires the consent of the Independent Television Commission [ITC] to purchase exclusive rights to an event after an event has been formally designated in another Member State. Thus according

to the ITC code, it was possible for BSkyB to enter into a contract for exclusive live rights for Ireland's qualifying games in the Football World Cup and European Championship games without the consent of the ITC. However the subsequent designation of the events by Ireland did not, it would appear, require BSkyB to seek the approval of the ITC as the contract had already been entered into. There was therefore no retrospective effect.

In order to ensure that these games were made available to Irish free-to-air broadcasters, Ireland enacted new legislative provisions which imposed obligations on sports event organisers to make broadcasting rights available to qualifying broadcasters subject to the payment of reasonable market rates. (Department of Communications, Marine and Natural Resources, 2003)

The reference to the ITC is at the crux of the matter. As a UK-registered broadcaster, BSkyB was subject to the Independent Television Commission. Clearly, the Irish government had little faith in the ITC's ability or willingness to pursue BSkyB, despite previous cases where the ITC had gone to bat on behalf of another member state.[7]

This reluctance seems likely to have been prompted by concern over the legality of retrospective designation. Article 3a's stress on drawing up a list in a timely fashion is reflected in the British Broadcasting Act 1996, section 101 of which was amended to effect article 3a. Subsection 4 of section 101 noted that designations of events would 'not have effect where the television programme providing the first service is exercising rights acquired *before* the commencement of this section' (emphasis added); that is, retrospective designation of events was not permitted.

The 2003 amendment, although it stated that it would give 'further effect to article 3a', appears actively to contravene aspects of that article, by permitting retrospection and focusing on the obligations of event organisers rather than broadcasters. Indeed, it is difficult not to sympathise with the Irish sporting organisations for the position such stopgap legislation has placed them in. As both the FAI and IRFU pointed out with regard to the 2003 amendment in their own submissions to the European Commission[8] on the TWF directive:

> there is no certainty from the point of view of anybody dealing with the Association in relation to contractual arrangements we conclude in the future for the broadcasting of our matches. At any stage in the future the Minister can create a new classification for matches other than qualification matches that we organise which would then retrospectively impact on any contractual arrangements we had already made in respect of those matches. From a commercial point of view this creates an unacceptable level of certainty for any broadcasters we may be dealing with. (Football Association of Ireland, 2003; also Irish Rugby Football Union, 2003)

Despite this, one might think that such concerns were more theoretical than real. The 2003 Broadcasting (Major Events Television Coverage) (Amendment) Act was essentially a piece of 'stroke politics', designed to retrieve a situation which had already eluded existing legislation.

It might have been assumed that, having been caught out once, the state would avoid future difficulties by listing potentially important events in good time. However, this has not proved to be the case. In September 2006, Ireland hosted the Ryder Cup, golf's premiere international event. A combination of the failure to list the event and a long-standing deal between BSkyB and the European golf tour meant that the tournament was not available to Irish viewers on a free-to-air basis. On 31 December 2005, interviewed on Setanta Sports, Taoiseach Bertie Ahern raised a flag by announcing that 'We're trying to organise free-to-air for the Ryder Cup' (Hennessy, 2006) and he subsequently instructed the Minister for Communications, Noel Dempsey, to review the list of protected events. In theory, Dempsey could have retrospectively listed the Ryder Cup under the 2003 legislation but, given the relatively low level of public interest in golf – as compared with soccer – the political will to raise BSkyB's hackles a second time by pursuing the matter did not materialise. Such examples were always likely to recur and in summer 2006, for instance, BSkyB secured exclusive rights to Rugby's Heineken Cup for the 2006/7 season. Thus, Irish free-to-air viewers were denied the opportunity to watch live broadcasts of Munster's attempts to retain the European championship they won in 2006.

Conclusion

These failures notwithstanding, it can be argued that the entrance of the neoliberal discourse into the sporting 'arena' occasioned by the BSkyB deal created an emancipatory impulse for political change rarely evident in Ireland. This was not merely because of the popularity of soccer, the playing and watching of which, as Pierre Bourdieu has argued, demands relatively little 'interpretative capital' (Bourdieu, 1999; cited in Sugden and Tomlinson, 2002: 65), but also because the games in question revolved around the national team in an era when 'sports events have become the most important, regular manifestations of ... national culture' (Rowe, 2004: 96). Thus the deal demonstrated the potentially negative consequences of the breathless sprint to embrace the logic of the market not merely to all citizens, but to citizens who consciously conceived of themselves as members of 'the nation'.

The consequence of this should have been obvious to any observer of the commercialisation of neighbouring sporting contexts (i.e. those

familiar to Irish citizens). Hudson (2001), for example, has discussed how
the acquisition of English Premier League rights by Sky in the 1990s saw:

> A discourse that had previously been dominated by the need for the state
> to control the hooliganism perceived to be attached to football fandom ...
> replaced with a discourse centred around traditional social policy concerns
> such as the need to ensure access, equity and fairness.

Similarly, Rowe (2004) has demonstrated how the series of sports broadcaster bankruptcies in the late 1990s and early years of the twenty-first
century (Kirch in Germany, ITV Digital in the UK, Telepiu and Stream in
Italy) contributed to a 'detectable turning of the tide in the affairs of sports
TV after several years of discursive dominance by neoclassical economic
philosophy' (Rowe, 2004: 106). The subsequent experience of European
soccer has continued to bring home to viewers of the European Champions League the ongoing negative financial consequences of the increasing
marketisation of the game. The *Journal of Sports Economics* dedicated the
entirety of its first 2006 edition to the question of whether European soccer
was experiencing a financial crisis. Although discounting the presence of a
generalised crisis, it did identify as 'the root cause of the financial crises in
some European countries ... *the increasing amount of income entering the
game, from TV and other sources*' (emphasis added) (Lago *et al.*, 2006: 7).
Furthermore, the article also concluded that those countries wherein 'the
ability of clubs to operate as profit-maximizing businesses has been limited
either by regulation or voluntarily' (France, Germany and Spain) were in
a far healthier state than those (the UK and Italy) where 'the scope for
adopting commercial objectives has been greater'.

Inevitably, the destructive impact of these market pressures has
engendered intensely local responses: in 1996, Rupert Murdoch attempted
to circumvent rival Kerry Packer's control of rugby league broadcasting
rights (which were available on a free-to-air basis) in Australia by establishing a breakaway Super League, which would be available exclusively
via pay television. Australia was already notable for having introduced
in 1994 'anti-siphoning' legislation designed to prevent popular sports
programming from migrating to pay television (thus anticipating article
3a of the TWF directive by three years). However, Murdoch's efforts
not only encountered (ultimately insurmountable) legal obstacles but
also prompted 'highly localised resistance' in the form of Aussies for the
Australian Rugby League and the Stop Murdoch Committee (Rowe,
1996: 577). Something similar occurred in Ireland in the wake of the
BSkyB deal, when supporters of both the national and domestic league
teams linked up to establish Irish Fans United, which lobbied for its
reversal (O'Brien, 2002).

However, perhaps the most exciting transformative effect to emerge from the events of summer 2002 was the manner in which the neoliberal presumptions of Irish political discourse were exposed and became the target of public ire. The combined effect of organised groups like Irish Fans United and the more spontaneous outpourings in the public sphere was to impose a discourse of citizenship rights rather than market access on the debate around the national team's games. Once that discursive shift occurred, the state found itself with no choice but to take some action to retrieve the games.

It has had further effects as well: in the short term, the highlighting of RTÉ's precarious financial position led the state to accede to the largest television licence fee increase since 1996, placing the national broadcaster (and notionally, at least, public service broadcaster) on a much firmer financial footing. Furthermore, although European Commissioner Viviane Reding dismissed Dermot Ahern's 2003 suggestion that the basic premise of TWF be reversed, it was salutary to witness the first official questioning by the Irish state of the rationale underlying that directive.

However, the most exciting thing to emerge from the BSkyB deal and its aftermath is the simple reminder that citizens can effectively exercise their political will outside the limited and constrained circumstances of national plebiscites. Having witnessed this with regard to the – for some – rather trivial subject of watching television, the possibility is raised that political activism in other fields may ultimately see inspiration from the playing field itself.

Notes

1 The eleven players who start for a team on the field, plus five substitutes who may be brought on during the course of play.
2 Jack Charlton was at the time the manager and coach of the Irish national team, responsible for the selection of players. Eligibility criteria for those players are set by the Fédération Internationale de Football Association (FIFA, the International Federation of Association Football).
3 These included England cricket test matches, the Grand National and Derby, the Olympic Games, Wimbledon finals and the FA cup final and the FIFA World Cup.
4 Síle de Valera in *Dáil Éireann*, vol. 509, p. 315, 13 October 1999, during debate on Broadcasting (Major Events Television Coverage) Bill, 1999: report and final stages.
5 In correspondence with Síle de Valera leaked to the *Sunday Independent*, IRFU President Philip Brown wrote: 'Unfortunately the arrival of TV3 has done nothing to increase competition … this company has shown no willingness to make a meaningful investment in rugby through coverage of the domestic game and money for payment of rights fees'. See 'Gaelic and rugby chiefs look to join FAI in TV sell-off', *Sunday Independent*, 14 July 2002 (available at www.independent.ie/national-news/gaelic-and-rugby-chiefs-look-to-join-fai-in-tv-selloff-502109.html).

6 During the final stage of the Dáil debate on the 1999 legislation in October of that year, Síle de Valera herself, in response to a question, stated: 'There can be no retrospection'. See *Dáil Debates*, vol. 509, 13 October 1999, p. 321.

7 In June 2000, TVDanmark, a Danish subscription broadcaster, outbid two Danish public broadcasters to secure exclusive rights five Danish World Cup qualifying matches. Although designated events under Danish legislation, the fact that TVDanmark was registered in the UK meant that it fell to the British Independent Television Commission (now Ofcom) to force TVDanmark to restore the games to a Danish free-to-air broadcaster. *Lord Hoffman, Regina* v. *Independent Television Commission, Ex Parte TVDanmark 1 Ltd*, House of Lords, 25 July 2001.

8 Interestingly, the Satellite and Cable Broadcasters' Group (which included BSkyB) also made a submission to the Commission but made no reference to article 3a or the Irish events.

Part III
Social control

7

Rebel spirits?
From reaction to regulation

MICHAEL CRONIN

In 1937, Professor Denis Valentine Morris, the holder of the Chair of Obstetrics and Gynaecology at University College Galway, visited his friend Halliday Sutherland, the Scottish doctor and writer, in his house in Kensington, London. The Professor's question was simple. Would Sutherland write a book about Ireland? The Scottish author's response was equally to the point, 'No one can write a book about Ireland without getting into trouble' (Sutherland, 1956: 1). He might have added that getting into trouble, indeed, was part of what it was to be Irish, in the eyes of many, including the Irish themselves. In 2005, when the maker of Paddy whiskey embarked on a new advertising campaign in Ireland for its product, the choice of a mischievous red-head in the form of television presenter Hector Ó hEochagáin appeared to sit easily with the statement 'Rebel Spirit'. A post-colonial cussedness may be a flattering image for native and newcomer alike – from the nod and the wink and 'I'll see you right' to Dublin as the new Rio – but this chapter will explore the ways in which a relentless culture of coercion and regulation in contemporary Ireland has made the reality of the myth more tenuous than ever. The most troubling thing about Ireland is increasingly how 'trouble' itself is defined.

As human settlements evolved from family or tribal-based structures to the more abstracted and extended structures of society, there was a fundamental shift in who or what individuals looked to for protection. Whereas at one stage they might have looked to other kinsfolk or members of the immediate community for help, as the emancipated individual of modernity emerged and mobility and large-scale urbanisation became increasingly widespread, communal ties became less important than a more contractual relationship between the individual and society. Here, the state offers protection in exchange for the subjection of the citizen to its laws and the state's right to exercise a legal monopoly on violence. However, it is crucial to distinguish between what Robert Castel calls 'civil protection' and 'social protection' (Castel, 2003: 5). Civil protection relates to those basic freedoms offered by a society under the rule of law and which guarantees the protection of people and property. Social protection, on the other hand, involves making provision for risks that can gravely affect the circumstances of citizens, such as accidents, illness, unemployment, impoverished old age or educational disadvantage.

One of the signal achievements of progressive movements and labour organisations in the nineteenth and twentieth centuries was to ensure that a person's autonomy was not based solely on the possession of property. If French revolutionaries and the United Irishmen were preoccupied with the rights of property, it was less because they were innately reactionary and more because, in the society of the time, property represented some form of protection for the individual from want and coercion. The advent of social protection, however, through legislative reform and the creation of the welfare state, meant that 'men of no property' were to be judged equal citizens and to benefit from the full range of civil and social protection offered by society (in the case of women, this was to happen more slowly). It is precisely, of course, social protection which is a privileged target of neoliberalism, through the privatisation of health, education, pension provision and public services, and it is arguably this sundering of civil and social protection which leads to the transition from the 'social state' to the 'garrison state' in contemporary Ireland (Giroux, 2002). David Garland, in *The Culture of Control: Crime and Social Order in Contemporary Society*, notes that, in many modern societies in recent decades:

> there has been a marked shift of emphasis from the welfare to the penal modality…. The penal mode, as well as becoming more prominent, has become more punitive, more expressive, more security-minded…. The welfare mode as well as becoming more muted, has become more conditional, more offence-centred, more risk conscious. (Garland, 2001: 175)

What we might then ask is a series of questions in specific relation to the Irish case:

- How has the shift to the garrison state and the penal modality manifested itself?
- What provoked this change?
- And how might society retrieve a duty of care and protection which is not punitive and exclusionary?

In advancing an analysis of a new culture of rabid regulation in Ireland, it is necessary for the sake of demonstration to separate out the realms of the public and private, even if, in reality, the two are inextricably linked.

The penal state

Some 5,000 police were deployed for the occasion and 2,500 troops were mobilised. An entire wing of Cloverhill Prison for up to 100 prisoners was cleared of inmates and held in a state of preparedness. Provisions were made for special sittings at the Prison Courthouse. Accident and emergency services in the city hospitals complained that there would not be enough beds and staff to meet demand. Water cannons from the Police Service of Northern Ireland were proudly displayed. The Garda Representative Association complained that not enough armed Gardai would be present to meet the threat (Lally, 2004a; see also Humphreys, 2004; Lally, 2004b).

One of the largest security operations in the history of the Irish state, on the occasion on the accession of the ten new member states to the European Union on 1 May 2004, finally ended in a sodden farce, a group of fewer than twenty demonstrators, much the worse for drink, throwing cider cans at police in full riot gear. In 2005, a photograph prominently displayed on the front page of a national newspaper showed a Tiananmen-like column of armoured personnel carriers on their way to an anti-war demonstration outside Shannon airport, though the demonstrators numbered only a few hundred. The question might be asked as to why such conspicuous and excessive displays of military and police power are necessary when the real threat to state security is so minimal?

One answer might be that intelligence and security services have a vested interest in fear. P. J. Stone, the head of the Garda Representative Association, in advance of the May Day demonstration in 2004, claimed:

> One never wants to presume that any situation will get out of hand. But so much preparation needs to be carried out that it boggles the mind as to how we can prevent it, especially if so many people arrive here fully intent on committing violence to highlight their cause in the streets of the capital. (Lally, 2004a)

The scale of the preparation becomes incontrovertible evidence of the threat, and the size of the threat demands in turn even more punitive measures, such as the frontline presence of armed police. The beauty of fear is that it is a win–win situation for the bodies appointed to combat it. If something happens, citizens can be told that it was fortunate that the security forces were in an adequate state of preparedness; if nothing

happens, they can be informed it was due to the competence of the same
forces that nothing materialised. In the circular logic of self-justification,
the demand for more powers and more resources tends to infinity, as
nobody (least of all security correspondents, the stenographers of state
security speak) is prepared or allowed to challenge the self-serving rhetoric
of risk inflation. However, in considering public displays of coercive might,
it is worth examining a deeper connection between the emergence of the
garrison state and the nature of economic life in late modern Ireland.

Michael Casey, a former chief economist with the Central Bank of Ireland, has noted that as much as 80 per cent of Irish manufactured output
comes from multinational companies located in Ireland. A relatively small
number of foreign companies account for over 60 per cent of Ireland's
merchandise exports (Casey, 2006). In 2003 alone, US investment in
Ireland was two and half times greater than its investment in the People's
Republic of China (O'Clery, 2004). Casey's conclusion was:

> there are probably about 10 or 12 multinational companies in Ireland that
> could exercise extraordinary leverage over the Irish government. If any one
> of these companies pulled out of Ireland, the economic consequences for
> employment and growth would be so severe that any government would
> probably fall. (Casey, 2006)

Ireland is a classic beneficiary of the initial post-Fordist switch from con-
gested, high-cost centres of production to the decentralised, networked
nodes of activity in the informational economy (Castells, 1996). The
attractions of Ireland as a location for multinational corporations are
well rehearsed: a well educated, English-speaking workforce; generous tax
breaks; a pro-business environment; and access to the markets of the European Union. One of the characteristics of the informational economy is, of
course, extreme mobility and the ability of corporations to shift activities
to the most lucrative locations. As the primary concern of corporations is
maximising profits for shareholders, even if a company is productive and
profitable, there is no guarantee that the operation will be maintained if
higher profits can be obtained elsewhere (Sennett, 2006: 37–40).

The stark reality of corporate choice was articulated by a general manager
and vice-president at the Hewlett-Packard technology campus at Leixlip,
County Kildare. Interviewed in the context of a collection of photographs
produced by Mark Curran, the manager refused to divulge his full name
but was not reticent about expressing some inconvenient truths:

> It all depends on who puts the next grant on the table.... No multinational
> has any attachment to Ireland or Singapore, or China or India. It is busi-
> ness, right? And if there is no business reason to be in Ireland, we will leave
> tomorrow.

Low corporation tax, a 'cooperative' government and the ability to dispense with trade unions made Ireland attractive, said the manager, but now China was 'looking good' (McKay, 2006). The manager's credo at one level gives lie to the notion that the nation state has no role to play in a global economy. It is both purveyor (of grants, tax breaks) and punisher (of unionisation). At another level, however, what is being stated is a central article of faith of corporate capital, that loyalty lies with shareholders and not with the workers or citizens of the country whose flag happens to be flying in the car park. Ultimately, then, the economic fortunes of a country will be decided beyond that country's borders, which limits the ability of states to intervene in a national economy, even more so if they are part of a supranational structure such as the European Union, with its own particular set of regulations and constraints.

The dilemma for governments is a credibility deficit. How is it possible to maintain legitimacy if key areas of people's lives are susceptible to the unaccountable decisions of international pension fund managers or the fiat of the European Central Bank and are no longer the sole remit of the nation state? One way is to extract maximum benefit and publicity from one of the remaining prerogatives of national governments, the penal mode, the absolute right to discipline and punish. As Zygmunt Bauman points out:

> The citizen's concerns with personal well-being have thereby shifted away from the treacherous ground of market-promoted *précarité* on to which state governments have neither the capacity nor the will to tread, and towards a safer and much more tele-photogenic area, where the awesome might and steely resolution of the rulers can be effectively displayed for public admiration. (Bauman, 2004: 54)

The dramatic display of military force in Shannon or the elaborate staging of police power for the May Day 2004 demonstration showed that the state was still in control or, rather, that what the state remained in control of was control itself. As social protection is surrendered to the market, from the corporatisation of higher education to the privatisation of pension provision, the only secure refuge for an increasingly insecure citizenry is the media-friendly spectacle of civil protection.

As stated above, the nation state is not wholly without influence in the economic arena and an important dimension to the mutation from social state to garrison state is the link between profit and punishment. Ghassan Hage points to the need the global/transcendental corporation has for the facilitative and coercive functions of states, as opposed to the redistributive ideals of nations: 'National and sub-national (such as State or provincial) governments all over the world are transformed from being primarily managers of a national society to being the managers of the aesthetics of investment space' (Hage, 2003: 19). The over-riding preoccupation for national governments is how in the global economy to make one location more attractive than another to transcendental capital. Where capital chooses to land is determined in part by the careful cultivation of image, relating to quality-of-life issues such as desirability of urban environments, leisure opportunities and a supportive infrastructure for multi-ethnic workforces. The frenzy of attention surrounding the Ryder Cup in Ireland in 2006 staged in the exclusive K Club was not only a photo-opportunity for the indigenous bourgeois to strut their successful stuff but also, more importantly, a function of the aesthetics of investment space.

Putting greens and green-field sites have more than grass in common. Presenting a country as an attractive place to play is also to project it as a desirable place to work, hence the inextricable link between tourism promotion and economic development (Urry, 1990: 156; Cronin and O'Connor, 2003: 1–18). However, state intervention is not only to manage the socio-economic aesthetic, but must equally prove itself capable of policing the interests of transcendental capital. The importance of the sustained police presence in the Bellanaboy area of County Mayo in protests surrounding the construction of the Corrib gas pipeline lay as much in the signal sent out to foreign investors such as Shell and Statoil as it did in the direct intimidation of local community activists. The state was prepared to devote considerable resources to protecting the investments of multinational firms, even though these were directly at variance with the rights of the local community and the greater national interest (O'Toole, 2005b). As Hage observes, 'the aesthetics of globalisation is the aesthetics of zero tolerance' (Hage, 2003: 20). What rapidly becomes intolerable to the garrison state is tolerance itself. What is adjudged best practice in the neoliberal global order is the conspicuous and speedy ability of 'cooperative government' to intervene on behalf of the powerful. The nation may do for citizens, but only the state will cut ice with shareholders.

Deregulation

On 14 October 2005, Patrick Joseph Walsh died in Monaghan General Hospital. He need not have died. Surgical intervention would have saved his life but there was a rule that no surgery could be carried out in the hospital after 5 p.m. Walsh was the victim not of medical malpractice but of a regulatory culture which rendered null and void the Hippocratic injunction to save lives. Commenting on the case a number of days later, Eddie Holt made the following observation:

The prevailing relationship between doctors and lawyers adds to a lack of trust throughout the society. Whether it is as a cause of or result of a general erosion of trust can be debated but it is certainly pivotal. Mary Harney's concern [as Progressive Democrat (PD) leader] that 'community values' – dependent on trust – are under pressure is absurd seeing as PD policies – rules, rules, rules – contribute hugely to making it so. (Holt, 2005)

Holt's identification of the Progressive Democrats as the villains of the piece is somewhat ironic in that being 'closer to Boston than to Berlin' was to mean, among other things, fewer rules, not more, less state, not more. As the ardent champions of 'deregulation' in everything from electricity supply to public transport services, the party, along with its coalition partner, Fianna Fáil, presented itself as the architect of the state which would wage war on the state, freeing our infant souls from the evil ministrations of the demonised nanny of the neoliberal imaginary. Here we come, however, to one of the central paradoxes of the systems put in place by apologists of the free market. Nicholas Boyle, in his analysis of the Thatcher era and its Blairite legacy in Britain, noted that although the British Tories, like the US Republicans, made much of the fact that they would reduce the role of government, in fact the opposite happened. Not only did government not shrink, but it continued to expand continuously throughout the whole Thatcherite period:

By extending the role of money in British society, by insisting that tradi-tionally defined services, benefits and injuries should be given arithmetical cash value, Thatcherism necessarily extended the role of the state. Public spending as a proportion of the GNP may have remained more or less static, but the production of public paper, of statutes and statutory instru-ments grew uncontrollably. (Boyle, 1998: 42)

Regulatory inflation is a necessary rather than accidental consequence of the global operations of corporate capital. These global operations are possible only because states are there to define and protect property (physical and intellectual), ensure contracts are honoured, resolve contractual disputes, act as a guarantor for the currency and, in some instances, fix basic interest rates. Hence, one of the most visible outcomes of deregulation is relentless and unwavering regulation. It is this structural paradox which unsettles a business community eager to support the cheerleaders of privatisation but which is then aghast to find more, not less, state intrusion in its affairs.

Seán Fitzpatrick, the former chairman of Anglo Irish Bank, a financial institution with business interests worldwide, observed balefully that one of the most worrying elements in the Irish business environment was the 'move towards more and more regulation' and that 'the pronounced moves towards greater control and regulation could squeeze the life out of an economy that has thrived on intuition, imagination and a spirit of adventure' (Fitzpatrick, 2005). Part of that 'imagination and a spirit of adventure' for many Irish and foreign banks involved, of course, imaginative and innovative ways of defrauding the Revenue Commissioners of millions of euros through the use of offshore accounts. However, if merchant bankers are alarmed at the unforeseen outcome of the neoliberal crusade against 'big government', citizens have even more cause to be worried at the coercive over-reach of the penal state.

When civil liberties are eroded, it is almost invariably done in the name of liberty. The ritual defence of corporal punishment was that it was 'for your own good' and this has now become the justification of every measure that seeks to diminish still further the freedoms that are available to citizens. When political posters are banned in Dublin City, the measure is not enacted through a bald piece of Stalinist or McCarthyite legislation decreeing an end to un-Irish activities but is given effect through the Litter Acts. Political posters constitute 'litter' but the rampant visual pollution of private-sector advertising which has defigured large areas of the city does not. When journalists are legally prevented from covering the all-too-human stories of refugees and asylum seekers coming to Ireland, the decision is presented not as a serious violation of the public's right to know about the circumstances of refugees coming to the country or as a cynical move to prevent the emergence of understanding or compassion (the problem for the penal state with our common humanity) but as protecting the privacy of refugees and asylum seekers. Privacy and privation are a useful couplet for those engaged in the war on the unwanted.

A particularly striking example of the regulatory drive of the penal state was the data retention legislation introduced by the avowed enemy of nanny statism, Michael McDowell, in 2005, when he was leader of the Progressive Democrats and Minister for Justice, Equality and Law Reform. Under this legislation, phone, mobile and fax data must be retained by companies and service providers for three years, one of the most draconian regimes in the world. The Minister for Justice's defence of the legislation was that it was designed to protect ordinary citizens from paedophiles, terrorists and serious criminals. Surrendering the freedom to privacy was a small price to pay for the greater freedom from fear of external threats. Access to the data was to be strictly controlled and specifically limited to investigations for the most serious criminal and terrorist offences. Within a year of the enactment of the legislation, the Data Protection Commissioner, Billy Hawkes, revealed the true nature of the operations of the legislation. In the end, no restrictions with respect to access were introduced into the legislation, so that the police were able to access hundreds of call records, for even the most minor suspected offences. Hawkes pointed out that the 'legislation gives the opportunity to access records of perfectly innocent people' (see Lillington, 2006). Such was the scale of the invasion of privacy proposed by the champion of the market that even the private sector felt compelled to respond using the language of public rights and civil liberties. Chris Horn, co-founder and vice-chairman of Iona Technologies, acknowledged that law-enforcement agencies had legitimate concerns about tackling crime and protecting citizens, but 'Our society also has a right to protect itself from unwarranted personal intrusion by agencies of this state and other states' (Lillington, 2006).

To have suggested a decade ago that Ireland would be, among other things, a country where political posters were banned in its capital city, where it would be an offence to report on the cases of refugees coming to the country, and where the police would have unlimited access to telecommunications data held on citizens would have invited charges of political scaremongering and irresponsible comparisons with repressive regimes worldwide. However, all these measures, and they are simply a number of examples, have come to be. What they have in common is that they all purport to protect the individual from a threat – litter, intrusive journalists, terrorism, crime, paedophilia – whereas increasingly the greatest threat to individuals may come in fact from their protectors, the allegedly reluctant agents of the omnipresent penal state.

Individualism

The energy efficiency campaign launched in 2006 by the Department of Communications, Marine and Natural Resources went under the heading 'Power of One'. What may be true for energy saving is conspicuously less so for civil society. The Power of One is the Power of None. Marcel Gauchet has pointed to one of the paradoxes of the social state: the fact that it has been one of the most powerful contributory factors to the rise of individualism. Because the social state made provision for the needs of individuals in their formative years (education) or in periods of difficulty or distress (unemployment benefit, healthcare, pensions), the individual became less dependent on immediate familial and communal networks and, thus, the autonomous individual of a specific kind of modernity emerged (Gauchet, 1991: 33–57). There are no individuals without a society to support them and if, according to a former British prime minister, there was no such thing as society, there would be no such thing as individuals either. Only social provision allows individuals to function and exist outside the traditional life-support systems of kinship arrangements. Privatisation, deregulation and the systematic dismantling of the public sector in the name of 'individual choice' leave individuals with no choice but to demand not less but more state protection, precisely because the neoliberal dissociation of civil and social protection diminishes individual autonomy rather than enhances it. Robert Castel argues that, in modern societies:

> Because such importance is attached to individuals who feel, at the same time, fragile and vulnerable, they demand of the state they be protected. Thus, the 'demand for more State' appears to be much stronger in modern societies than in previous societies where various forms of protection-subjection were available through membership of groups situated at various levels below that of the sovereign. (Castel, 2003: 22) [My translation]

The individual in late modern societies is more needy and demanding than ever, if only because of a largely unacknowledged anxiety that the social state which brought him or her into existence is being ritually undermined.

Bodies

One of the classic sites for state control and the development of regimes of control and punishment has been the body (Foucault, 1977). In post-independence Ireland, for example, women's bodies were a notorious target for the coercive projects of church and state. Thinking about the body in contemporary Ireland, therefore, is also a way of reflecting not only on how cultures of regulation refer to a changing notion of self but also on how a particular kind of socio-economic aesthetic has come to colonise people's deepest fears. The Catholic Primate of All Ireland, Archbishop Seán Brady, in an interview claimed that increased secularisation and the marginalisation of religion had led to a 'growing coarseness and aggression' in Irish life (McGarry, 2006). As a representative of a church which, in the pre-secular decades, when religion was central to Irish life, practised widespread 'coarseness and aggression' through the punitive disciplinary regime of the schools and institutions under its control, Archbishop Brady would seem to be ill-placed to lecture citizens on civility. However, there is a sense in which the penal state owes part of its prominence and power to the decline of religion, its erstwhile rival in the public sphere in Ireland.

In the same week that the Catholic Primate of All Ireland made sombre pronouncements about the malign influence of satirical television puppets Podge and Rodge,[1] a major national newspaper carried an article entitled 'Dark chocolate may relieve symptoms of ME' (Edwards, 2006). The article was in a regular supplement which ran to eight full pages. A weekly supplement on, for example, 'Faith and Doctrine', would appear unimaginable in contemporary Ireland but one on 'Health' seems unexceptionable. In traditional Catholic belief, the ultimate court was the afterlife. There, misdemeanours were duly punished and virtue rewarded. The body may have been the temple of the Holy Ghost but only the merchants of the Temple, those who championed the pleasures of the flesh, greatly cared about its fate. For the godly and the good, it was a vessel, a stepping stone, not a destination. In a secular society, there are, of course, no afters. There is no life after life. Rewards and punishments cannot be deferred beyond the grave. And the ultimate punishment, in a sense, is the grave itself. When readers of the supplement are faced with headlines such as 'Irish men ignoring weight risks, cancer society study finds' (Labanyi, 2005), or 'Taking a dramatic approach to dealing with suicide' (Bracken, 2005), or 'Learning to keep a lid on your temper' (Edwards, 2005), they realise that hell is indeed on earth and that rewards and punishments are liberally distributed in the present rather than the hereafter.

The ultimate punishment for a life not lived, according to the teachings of the health supplement, is not so much in the afterlife as in the end to life. In the black and white prose of the wayside pulpit, smokers, like sinners of yore, are reminded of the torments that await them before they go to a certain death. An important impulse for secularisation and a crucial backdrop to lifestyle journalism in the print and broadcast media is the Enlightenment notion of the self-fashioning subject. In casting off the nets of faith and fatherland, modern individuals shape their own destiny, make their own decisions, decide on their own future (Taylor, 1989). In more recent times, the body itself has been annexed to the project of self. The routine fantasies of the television show *Nip and Tuck* are to do with a desire to make the material body conform through the surgeon's scalpel to an ideal selfhood, where the words of longing are made flesh. The problem of authority still remains, however. The Enlightenment solution was to replace the deity with nature. What was natural was good and unnatural bad. In contemporary Ireland, it is the secular state rather than the post-Tridentine Church which is invoked to outlaw the ungoodly rather than the ungodly. In this respect, it is striking that the form of episcopal authoritarianism practised by Primate John Charles McQuaid[2] was exercised with such consummate ease by Michael McDowell. As the fragile, embodied self becomes more and more fretful, increasingly abandoned to the flexibilised short-termism of new forms of economic organisation and tutored endlessly in the print media, on talk radio and documentary television about the cruel and ingenious ways in which physical and mental illness is visited upon others, the demand for protection rises towards infinity. The two main beneficiaries of this demand are, not surprisingly, the private sector and the penal state.

The privatisation of health insurance and pension schemes and the increasing individualisation rather than mutualisation of social risks means that what is potentially bad for people is always good for business. In other words, the greater the inflation of risk and the more that individuals feel they need to insure themselves against them, the greater will be their outlay on a range of private financial products designed, ironically, to protect them from the savage consequences of the uncertain future ushered in by the privatising zeal and ecological destructiveness of neoliberal corporate capital. If the financial services sector, along with, as we saw earlier, the state's intelligence services, has a vested interest in fear, then the medico-pharmaceutical sector (as detailed in chapter 9) is equally driven by distress. The more risks to personal health and well-being that can be identified, the greater will be the range of medical services and pharmaceutical products which can be supplied to paying customers, anxious to bankroll their way out of despair.

A new clerisy

The penal state and a predatory private sector have little purchase on reality, however, if their actions in a society governed by the rule of law are not guaranteed, in a sense, by the law itself. It is therefore instructive to look at how, in contemporary Ireland, status and financial rewards in the liberal professions are substantially directed towards the legal profession. If a son in Holy Orders decades ago was a tangible symbol of social advancement in Ireland, the conspicuously high-entry requirements for any Irish third-level course offering law as a component subject point to the redistribution of symbolic capital, as a new, dark-suited clerisy of regulation, the legal profession, takes over from an erstwhile theocratic elite. In the 1990s, the number of solicitors practising in Ireland grew at a cumulative rate of 62 per cent, which represented nearly six times the rate of increase in the general population. In 2005 in the Republic of Ireland, there was one general practitioner for every 2,000 people but one solicitor for every 712. In terms of overall numbers, there were 2,500 family doctors and 6,000 solicitors. If the approximately 1,300 barristers are factored into the equation, there were almost three times as many members of the legal profession as there were general practitioners (O'Toole, 2005a). The former and current presidents of the country were prominent members of the same profession. And, as Fintan O'Toole pointed out, so were half the members of the then serving Cabinet:

> Brian Cowen, Dermot Ahern, Willie O'Dea and John O'Donoghue have all been professional solicitors; Michael McDowell is a barrister; and Mary

Hanafin studied law. The tribunals of inquiry have given lawyers a new hold on the political process, as well as a new source of wealth. The consequences of the most intimate tragedies – the break-up of marriages – are now largely determined by lawyers. Almost every subject that requires investigation (from medical scandals to clerical sex abuse) is automatically handed over to a lawyer. No State board is complete without at least one member of the profession. (O'Toole, 2005a)

It is, in a sense, only to be expected that if regulation and coercion are to be dominant features of a new political order then a new clergy will be drawn from the ranks of those schooled in the arts of discipline and punishment. Again, as the social state recedes from public life, then individual citizens are left with litigation as the sole means of vindicating various rights, assuming, of course, that they have in fact the means to do this, which is by no means a foregone conclusion, given the systematic underfunding of the Legal Aid Board. The culture of litigation means a further shrinkage of collective life and an increase in individual vulnerability as everything from running schoolboy soccer teams to free outdoor concerts becomes plagued by the spectre of costly and disputatious lawsuits.

One of the difficulties in challenging the prevailing cult of coercion in Ireland is that what parties on the left and right agree on is the need for more regulation. Those on the left see regulation as a way of combating Haughey-era gombeenism and bringing appropriate standards into the way the affairs of the state and business are conducted; and those on the right see it as a way of controlling dissidence and threats to established rights and privileges. So when politicians from various parties enter into debate, they tend to want to outbid each other in a kind of regulatory frenzy, the only difference lying principally in whom or what they want regulated. This debate is, at one level, perfectly legitimate, and any functioning democracy will properly want to sanction certain forms of behaviour and encourage others. However, there is a sense in which the regulatory auctions, from a progressive standpoint, prevent the emergence of a more radical form of transformative politics, a politics grounded in addressing the causes rather than the symptoms of widespread social unease. The relentless drive towards regulation on the part of the penal state is ultimately self-defeating, of course, because, as Hage notes, the 'search for zero vulnerability produces a gaze that sees threats everywhere and ends up reproducing the vulnerability it is supposedly trying to overcome' (Hage, 2003: 135–6). Elias Canetti pointed out in *The Human Province* that order seeks to be total, but in the end:

[it] depends on so little. A hair, literally a hair, lying where it shouldn't, can separate order from disorder. Everything that does not belong where it is, is hostile. Even the tiniest thing is disturbing: a man of total order would

have to scour his realm with a microscope, and even then a remnant of potential nervousness will remain in him. (Canetti, 1986: 115)

As we saw above with the increasingly cavalier and intrusive use of data retention legislation in Ireland, the agents of order indeed perceive new threats everywhere, so that legislation which is supposed to be used in only very restricted circumstances ends up encompassing a much wider usage.

In describing an alternative future for Irish society, the most fundamental move must be to reconnect the social and the civil. Projects of 'active citizenship' are doomed if they reduce citizenship to good works, volunteering as a sticking plaster for social wounds. Confident, active citizens emerge against a background of constructive social protections which support and sustain the capacity of societies to distribute hope, lay the framework for trust and create confidence in the future. The uncoupling of economic causes and civic consequences leads only to moral hectoring and the dubious compromise of charity. Reinstating the public and the social means also the courage of a new political ontology, one which realistically assesses risks and examines ways in which they can be collectively managed by a society rather than being left to be exploited by self-serving elites. One of the most urgent tasks of a new generation of 'rebel spirits' is to contest a culture of risk that institutionalises fear, insecurity and paranoia, and whose agents and beneficiaries are, in many respects, the greatest troublemakers of all.

Notes

1 Podge and Rodge are the names of two characters who first appeared on an adult puppet show on Irish television, *A Scare at Bedtime*.
2 John Charles McQuaid was Archbishop of Dublin from 1940 to 1973. He was noted for his traditional doctrinal views and a markedly conservative view of the role of the Church in Irish society.

8

Irish education, mercantile transformations and a deeply discharged public sphere

DENIS O'SULLIVAN

The meaning of education in state discourse has fundamentally changed from what it was as recently as the early 1960s. In 1962, the Council of Education, considered at the time as an organ of the Department of Education, proclaimed the aim of schooling to be 'the formation of God-fearing and responsible citizens' (Council of Education, 1962: 88). In an earlier report on the primary school, it had singled out for special mention, along with 'the other moral virtues', 'purity, patience [and] temperance' (Council of Education, 1954: 132). By 1990, however, the major national advisory body on social and economic matters, the National Economic and Social Council (NESC), was arguing that 'the principles of consumer representation, participation and accountability' should be reflected in educational management and decision-making structures and that 'performance indicators' should be established as a mechanism for assessing the effectiveness of the education system (NESC, 1990: 313–14).

This represents a change in what education was unquestionably assumed to be about and, relatedly, the use of a different repertoire of concepts, words, appeals and justifications in speaking about the educational process and in making recommendations for practice. Such a characterisation of change captures what is meant by the construction of a paradigm, an interpretive framework we use to make sense of our world. Here, it is argued that the cultural transformation experienced within Irish education over the past half century can be best characterised as a transition from a theocentric to a mercantile policy paradigm, from one which had God at its centre to one with trade/exchange at its core. This is not an abstract or remote matter of 'merely' thinking or talking differently about education. The transition to a mercantile paradigm has far-reaching and deep implications for systemic aspects of the institution of education, and can be observed in the plasticity of educational aims, schools/colleges assuming commercial/service dimensions, contractual pedagogical relationships, quantifiable evaluation, vigilant users, professional regulation, the erosion of trust and a managerial state (O'Sullivan, 2005).

In describing this ongoing development, expansion and penetration of mercantile orientations, this chapter discusses a number of recent controversies and episodes: the secondary teachers' dispute of 2000/1, 'free fees' at third level (higher education) and proposals for their reintroduction in 2003, the establishment of the Teaching Council, the reconstitution of professionalism, and the policy response to inequality, disadvantage and difference. Efforts to have such substantive issues analysed in this cultural politics manner, let alone challenged, are impeded by the deeply discharged nature of the educational public sphere. Nonetheless, it will be argued that any hope of transformation must reside in the cultivation of a public sphere that is intense and diverse, and capable of accommodating a generative politics of possible educational futures.

Detraditionalisation

As the theocentric paradigm of education experienced disruption from the 1960s, new ways of thinking and communicating about education were given space to develop. In this, the cultural deployment of the study *Investment in Education* (Survey Team, 1965) was pivotal. While the new discourse projected itself as a feature of the modernisation of Irish education and society, it is more appropriately understood as a process of detraditionalisation that deployed modernist themes and subjectivities. From this, five strands of meaning-making about education (described as 'texts') can be identified and continue to evolve: commercial, managerial, vocational, consumer and market. These are considered as manifestations of the cultural resources that, through their interplay, construct the mercantile paradigm. Intertextuality, a term developed by Julia Kristeva (1981), is used to describe this process. At the core of the theory of intertextuality is the assumption that a text cannot exist in a self-sufficient way or as a closed system. It draws attention to the interplay between texts and specifically to the manner in which meanings, in their circulation, negate, challenge, interrogate, parody, support, transpose or otherwise interrelate. In the mercantile transitions described here, two patterns of intertextuality – complementary and predatory – are diagnosed.

Eroding education's exceptionalism

The centrality of trade/exchange in the institutional understanding of education cannot be revealed by a sealed reading of these commercial, managerial, vocational, consumer and market texts on their own. It is the cultural transformation produced and revealed by their interplay that represents the realisation of the mercantile paradigm, rather than the sum of them. This takes the form of a complementary intertextuality, in which mutually supporting, validating and symbiotic texts realise meanings that range beyond what they textually produce individually.

It is easier to understand this dynamic by beginning with the inter-dependency of the consumer and market texts. To act as a consumer requires the existence of some version of an education market. To be able to make choices in how one educates one's children, it is necessary that there be diversity in the nature of the education provided by schools and colleges, together with an absence of prohibition in accessing them. Conversely, the existence of an education market presents parents (and pupils) with choices, and positions them as consumers, obliging them to judge and choose.

But consumer and market texts do not merely sustain one another in a fixed loop. They also mutually intensify and systematise each other. If seen in paradigmatic terms in relation to people and systems in education, they exhibit a tendency to merge around interconnecting points of conceptualis-ation, propositions and subjectivities. In the process, other themes are recruited from within the cultural tapestry of which both texts are a part and from which they have been analytically extracted. Obvious examples are rights and consumer discourse from other social sites besides educa-tion, themes of risk and its regulation, together with associated legislation and structures of monitoring, protocols and agencies relating to the use of services. A range of practices and issues – from the weight of school bags to the publication of school league tables – provide a material presence for the consumer/market conceptualisation, which is sustained, normalised and expanded in the process. Specifically, the 'exceptionalism' claimed for education, in opposition to treating it in trade/exchange terms along with other varieties of transfers in social life, is undermined.

The commercial and managerial texts operate in a similar dynamic in relation to the social setting in which educational transfers take place. A common sequence in discourse is where contesting one invokes the other. Teachers who might express the view, for instance, that specific proposals for change, derived from the commercial world, are inappropriate where educational relationships and contexts are involved, are often materially repositioned and culturally signified as problems themselves – fearing change, unadaptable, resisting modernisation – requiring managerial intervention in the form of re-skilling courses, programmes on 'coping with the challenges of change' and general staff development days. Skilbeck (2001: 114) exhibits this discursive pattern when he attributes nostalgia and false memory to those academics who unfavourably contrast the use of management and business procedures in universities with collegial-style forms of decision making traditionally associated with universities. Richard Bruton, as Fine Gael spokesman on education, provided a more explicit example in the *Irish Times Education and Living Supplement*. Sensing that 'quality management concepts are viewed by many within the education system as something threatening rather than something fulfilling', he moved not to reconsider the practices themselves in the light of the professional judgement of teachers, but rather advised that any application of such concepts in schools should involve 'strong personal development policies' to enlist the support of teachers (Bruton, 1998).

One of the effects of the managerial text is the conceptualisation of teachers as resources, in a manner that increases its compatibility with commercial texts and renders unremarkable themes relating to the recording, monitoring and auditing of teachers' work. This is further confirmed and extended by the vocational text, in which the service provided by schools – as end product of tradable qualifications or as process of engagement between teacher and pupil – becomes instrumental and technical, amenable to quantification. Health and safety, equality and educational welfare legislation is invoked in a process that normalises the manner in which teachers and pupils, and teachers and teachers relate to one another through the construction of protocols, prohibitions and designation of 'best practice'. The role of trust in the pedagogical relationship is dissipated, professional judgement, even teacher agency itself, becomes circumscribed and vocation is recast as dedication to one's attributed role. Education's claims to be unique among service providers are stripped away. This signals a defining point of transition in the cultural transformation of education as it comes to be successfully thematised in terms of trade/exchange. Within discourse about education, this conceptualisation can now circulate without special pleading, and has the potential to engage individual subjectivities and to experience expansion throughout culture and society.

Teacher resistance and its response

The teachers' unions had the power to resist, and at least delay, the material implications of the mercantile paradigm. For its part, the mercantile paradigm lacked a distinctive discourse and designated authoritative agents. Its associative status experienced difficulty in making the transition from the atomistic to the collective, because of the absence of a discourse of mobilisation that would confirm common sentiment and perception. It needed a dedicated language, a collective existence and a monumental work or social project to frame it coherently. To date, the secondary teachers' dispute with the government in 2000–1 provided it with the best single episode of favourable circumstances for its realisation and development as a paradigm. Apart from the salary claim involved and the related issues of teachers' working conditions, the policy conflict that characterised the dispute was the opposition by the Association of Secondary Teachers Ireland (ASTI) to the application of benchmarking procedures to the work of schools, on the basis that it industrialised education and was unsuited to the nature of the educational process and the professional character of the teacher's role. Yet, the public response was to repeatedly challenge the 'exceptionalism' of schools and teaching. Common arguments included: stress was now a feature of all kinds of work where, unlike teaching, it included the fear of redundancy; the multiple nature of the teacher's role paralleled the expectation of multi-skilling in the post-Fordist workplace; teaching was substantially a repetitive exercise in which similar lessons were given year after year; the equivalent of 'under-performing' teachers in industry and commerce would not be tolerated; and teachers should be open to evaluation, as were other workers. As one prominent journalist (Browne, 2000) argued, if society is satisfied to measure the achievement of pupils with the Leaving Certificate, which has career-determining implications, why should it be considered improper or impossible similarly to assess, measure and compare their schools and their teachers?

This was not an uncontested interpretation. Apart from challenges from teachers and the general public, there were differences within the policy-making process itself, between parent bodies, for instance, on the construction and publication of 'league tables' of schools. Yet, it seemed clear that, in the heightened conflict and discourse of this long-running dispute, a wide range of individuals, from government, media and employers' organisations, as well as those who were parents and private-sector employees, came to recognise themselves as belonging to a like-minded social configuration in their conceptualisation of schooling, teaching and learning within a framework of trade/exchange experienced by them in their social and occupational lives. Ironically, what was widely seen, even in hindsight (Oliver, 2003), as the inflexible, defensive and embittered 'hard done by' stance of teachers during the dispute would have confirmed the appropriateness of the mercantile conceptualisation. The diagnosis in this stance of a differentiation of interest, a maximising of individual benefit and a flexible commitment would have underscored for those who saw themselves as consumers of an educational service the need for protocols to regulate and ensure predictability and equilibrium in exchanges between teachers and parents and pupils. Whatever the merits of the teachers' objections to benchmarking, the nature of their campaign would have confirmed for many the need for some such regulation of the exchanges involved in their work. This had the potential to be a cultural flashpoint, allowing the more vigorous and enthusiastic 'believers' to make explicit and name the basis of this shared conceptualisation. This potential has yet to be fully realised: it is the rare intellectual who seeks to frame it within theorised parameters and, apart from the print media's now routine practice of publishing rankings of schools, there is no significant social project that explicitly proclaims itself as seeking to advocate a mercantile reconstruction of education. A mercantile paradigm exists more collectively than it did. But it is lived rather than named in its infusion of what have become unremarkable practices and expectations in the relationship between education and its public.

Change without advocacy

This adverts to a distinguishing feature of the Irish experience of replacing a theocentric with a mercantile paradigm, in that, unlike cultural transformations of a similar scale in other education systems, it happened largely without advocacy. While there have been calls for the separation of church and state and criticism of the power, even monopoly, of the church in Irish education, it would be difficult to find an example of support for the specific cultural and material shift that is identified here as the emergence of the mercantile paradigm. To use our nearest neighbour as a foil, there has been no equivalent of the Black Papers on education, Callaghan's Ruskin speech, Thatcher, Hayek or the Education Reform Act. The international policy debate following Chubb and Moe's (1990) research on markets and schooling in the United States, in which they argued not for school reform but for a pulling back from direct democratic control and the creation of private schools or market-based and autonomous public schools, did not extend to Ireland.

'New right' education policy never transferred to Ireland as a model for macro-educational policy. Yet, many of the themes of new right educational discourse – consumer rights, performance indicators, devolved budgets, private investment in education, enterprise, corporate linkages, new forms of school management, quality and efficiency – were successfully inserted into Irish educational discourse and experienced varying levels of expansion and development. But, in their representation, they were never explicitly linked in pursuit of a neoliberal restructuring of education. Whatever receptivity there might have been for new right thinking to become a participant in the cultural politics of Irish education was systematically undermined by its representation as a construct of 'Thatcherism'. In the local construction of 'Thatcherism', it was successfully positioned to mean cutbacks, anti-education and anti-teacher policies, low standards of pupil achievement, indiscipline, teacher shortages and low morale, but also arrogance, anti-Irishness and empire. Any theme that could be semantically linked to 'Thatcherism' was suspect.

Such is the enduring exclusionary power of 'Thatcherism' that, throughout the 1990s and beyond, discourse and propositions relating to enterprise as a school subject, the publication of the examination results of individual schools, school and teacher evaluation, performance indicators and benchmarking reveal how their advocates were obliged to resort to disclaimers and special pleading, credit-building techniques, dilution and alteration of terminology in an effort to establish them as themes in policy discourse. It would be wrong to infer from this that the cultural politics of Irish education was hostile to the underlying principle of new right educational thinking. As used in Irish discourse on education, 'Thatcherism' related to propositions for practice rather than the neoliberal conceptualisation of people, society, motivation and prosperity, together with their associated legitimatory armoury. Thus, when we look at the detail of the deployment of 'Thatcherism' for new right thinking, we find that what were being protected and culturally ring-fenced were teachers' interests and working conditions rather than some overall principle of education. In terms of the process described as 'policy borrowing' (Finegold *et al.*, 1992), this draws attention to the manner in which 'cautionary texts' from experiences elsewhere are deployed as filtering mechanisms in regulating the entry of new ideas.

Governance and populism

Substantially, the consequence was that, unlike in England, in Ireland the transformation took a cultural form independently of social and political movements in education broadly referred to as the new right. The dominance of the mercantile paradigm is not without its material implications for the governance of education, a problem for the state in Ireland as in England. This has taken the form of representative and populist demands for action relating to ineffective teachers, grievance mechanisms for parents and pupils, and evaluative information about school standards and efficiency, and their quality of service, such as the length and organisation of the school year and the timing of parent–teacher meetings. New structures of control and regulation relating to the higher-education sector, including processes of accreditation, certification and quality assurance, are already in place. Local education committees were proposed and rejected; a policy of allocating some of the functions of the Department of Education – such as examinations, educational welfare and special education – to separate agencies has featured in both green and white papers on education and has been pursued. Whole-school evaluation is being advanced as the means of regulating, at a remove, practices in individual classrooms, the most challenging of tasks in the governance of education. The power of teachers in Irish education is such – their representation on the National Council for Curriculum and Assessment (NCCA), review bodies and the Teaching Council is a manifestation of this (Granville, 2004; Sugrue, 2004) – that these structures and mechanisms of control are less developed and less threatening to teachers than they are in England. However, as the mercantile paradigm continues to expand, populist demands for the regulatory and disciplinary procedures routine in other relationships of trade/exchange to be applied to schools will not alone strengthen whatever inclinations the state may have in this regard, but will oblige it to act as the auditor and guarantor of standards and efficiency in what remains a quasi-market in education.

Already, the Teaching Council (2007), established by the Teaching Council Act 2001 and the Teaching Council Amendment Act 2006, is proceeding with the formulation of a code of professional conduct for teachers indicating standards of teaching, knowledge, skill and competence. This facilitates the diversification of teacher subjectivities and their institutional allocation, with professionalism realised within the deliberations of the Council and teachers' rights and working conditions allocated to union-type practices. This allows teachers to speak with two voices, to enunciate divergent texts and adopt disparate positions, when dealing with controversial topics such as under-performing teachers. Teacher associations may find it difficult to back away from this without considerable loss of face and effectiveness, particularly as they vie with the state in their efforts to mobilise populist sentiment. This routinely follows the discourse of partnership. For example, in March 2007 the Irish National Teachers' Organisation (INTO) appealed for the support of parents on that most populist of issues, class size, in a nationwide pre-election campaign. With a more sophisticated public, this practice becomes increasingly ambivalent: a more comprehensive common front with parents opposing education cutbacks in the 1980s is still spoken of in teaching circles as having let the genie (of parent power and diluted professional autonomy) out of the bottle. Early in the INTO's campaign on class size, and much to its annoyance, the Department of Education and Science Inspectorate (2006) published an evaluation of a sample of final-year student teachers in primary schools which found more than a third to be fair or weak in their general work in the classroom, a finding that was accentuated by the media. The Minister protested that the timing of its release was coincidental.

While it would be too glib to predict that Irish education is set to experience Thatcherism in the absence of Thatcher, it does seem likely that the cultural shift represented by the mercantile paradigm will produce real material consequences in new modes of governance in education. But if it is valid to describe Thatcherism as 'authoritarian populism' (Hall, 1980), in Ireland the new forces of regulation and control are being ushered in by means of a managerial populism in which the state, positioned (or self-positioned) as the agent of popular sentiment, will approach its task in a technical-managerial rather than an explicitly ideological-interventionist role. The introduction of the 'free fees' initiative for third-level education by Niamh Bhreathnach, Labour Minister for Education, in 1995 followed this pattern. Despite retrospective efforts by the Minister's programme manager at the time (Wrynn, 2003) to represent it as a social-democratic intervention, it was transparently motivated by the politics of electoral calculation following the anxiety of government politicians in the light of the recommendation of the De Buitléir report (Advisory Committee on Third-Level Student Support, 1993) on third-level student support that assets as well as income should be considered in the assessment of eligibility. This report was presented to the Minister in November 1993 but not published until the announcement of the 'free fees' initiative in February 1995. Subsequently, the efforts of Education Minister Noel Dempsey in 2003 to reopen this debate, raising issues of equity and fairness in terms of access and student support, followed a similar pattern in falling to the power of political acquiescence in the face of anticipated popular outrage.

Compromising the modern

Even as the mercantile paradigm was being structured, it was assuming the role of predator of its cultural progenitors. It would succeed in modifying, diluting and narrowing dimensions of Irish cultural production, such as those relating to civil society, social morality, citizenship and democracy. This was facilitated by the fact that, as well as sharing some key features, the mercantile and the modern appear to use a common language – choice, individual freedom, achievement, reason – and yet realise different meanings. The predatory intertextuality that ensued will be illuminated by reference to the culture wars surrounding equality and difference. A core modernist theme is that of equality as a principle for the allocation of educational resources and opportunities, which seeks to break the dominance of inherited status and facilitate its replacement with a status that is achieved through individual talent and effort.

While initiatives aimed at furthering equality of educational opportunity have existed since the 1960s, efforts to combat socio-economic disadvantage have become a more specific feature of state education policy since the 1980s. The range of interventions is extensive and varied and, in terms of formal policy statements, characterised by a change of focus from inequalities in access and participation to the underdevelopment of talent and potential. Yet, when one examines the policy issues that the principle of educational equality generates, one finds a basic focus on an individual's opportunity to access and participate in specific educational levels. Repeatedly, equality is seen in terms of equity in the progression of pupils through the educational system and is presented as a theme of official discourse in a manner that is informed by the mercantile paradigm, or at least neutral towards it. 'Achievement' has gained in attention since the 1980s, but it came to refer to how far one progressed rather than how one performed in relation to one's peers. Insofar as there has been attention to issues of achievement in equality discourse, it has been understood in terms of the 'distant other' (O'Sullivan, 2005), those pupils at the extremes of low achievement who, since the 1980s, have been constituted as the educationally disadvantaged. It continues to be remarkable that so little public discourse about equality in education addresses the full extent of social class differences in achievement at all levels, as revealed by Clancy (2001) and his successors (O'Connell *et al.*, 2006). A key factor in this omission is the suppression of social class inequality in achievement as a theme, by the construction of disadvantage in terms of low achievers requiring improvement and inclusion within a more acceptable achievement range. Despite the efforts of radical egalitarians (Lynch, 1999) and the Christian communitarianism of the Conference of Religious of Ireland (CORI) (see O'Sullivan, 2005), it continues to be difficult for 'equality' to attain a cultural form, such as a principle that encompasses collective issues of social justice, that cannot be accommodated by the mercantile paradigm or co-opted by it.

Early debate from the 1960s on equality of educational opportunity was in the context of the human capital paradigm. In the 1990s, with the growth in the economy, a more contemporary variant of human capital theory surfaced in influential national and international reports (Gleeson, 2000). According to this, the demands on education have become more comprehensive, no longer merely requiring that those with talent would be recognised and developed, but that all pupils should be adequately trained for the increasingly higher technological demands of modern industry. Consistent with this, concern for low-achieving/early school-leavers is repeatedly represented in terms of their experience in the labour market. As the annual school-leaver surveys reveal (Gorby *et al.*, 2003), the association between increasing educational attainment and greater labour market success became more pronounced since the surveys began in 1980, and particularly so over the past decade. However, variations in employment rates across those with different levels of educational credentials are repeatedly treated in a manner that elides the distinction between employability and employment chances.

In employability discourse, low-achieving/early school-leavers are represented in mercantile terms and specifically so in relation to their violation of its conventions of social engagement and subjectivity. Rather than consider these findings as examples of the hiring practices of Irish employers, they have been treated as indicators of the capacity of young people to fulfil the requirements of available positions. The issue is constructed as a problem of labour market preparation and readiness. Low-achieving/early school-leavers are positioned as deviant participants in a mercantile world. Not only are they considered to be deficient in the skills and knowledge that would render them employable, but their subjectivities are suspect in their potential to disrupt the processes of trade/exchange. Their disposition towards the labour market – unmotivated by its opportunities, unwilling to compete on its terms, unable to segregate their self-interests from the alienating tendencies of the school–labour-market nexus – serves as an exemplar of an alternative and disturbing understanding of social and economic exchange. Policies aimed at extending participation in education and improving credentials are represented as having the potential to reduce unemployment and social welfare spending, and supply competent workers to the labour force. Bringing those who leave school early with minimal or no qualifications to higher levels of achievement is therefore seen as benefiting all, through the raising of the skill levels of the labour force and through the reduction of unemployment and the costs of social welfare. Less publicly, 'social inclusion' objectives in relation to low-achieving/early school-leavers at once confirm the virtue of the social system from which they are assumed to be 'excluded' and seek to co-opt their culturally destabilising potential. This does not involve the direct suppression of citizenship themes, which have been even more formalised in new curricular areas, through the dominance of labour market preparation understood in mercantile terms. What happens is more subtle, penetrating and silently non-discursive, as citizenship itself comes to be reconceptualised around the entitlements and expectations of individuals to mercantile competencies and subjectivities.

An analysis of the scholarly and policy discourse which informs the rationale of programmes targeting the disadvantaged 'distant other' reveals how difficult it has been for it to move beyond an understanding of the person that is predominantly psychologistic and atomistic. This individualism, aetiological, ontological and methodological in nature and consistent with the mercantile paradigm, persists alongside the acknowledgement of complex, social, economic and cultural influences on disadvantage. Yet, people are projected in a psychologistic/atomistic fashion, devoid substantially of a social and, particularly, of a cultural dimension. They could be social isolates were it not for the acknowledgement of families and communities, which nonetheless remain 'black box' and aggregated rather than relational constructs. Culture is understood in the thin rather than the 'thick' sense (Geertz, 1975), as a veneer of values, attitudes and characteristic practices. At most, the recognition of an intersubjective life, cultural patterns and their pervasiveness in identity and habitus, local social structures, even norms, reference or peer groups, but particularly the structural positioning of people, is limited.

There is no recognition of the collective experience of disadvantage or its structural dimension, be it at local community or school level. A consequence of the psychologistic/atomistic view of disadvantage is that disadvantaged areas are seen as geographical entities that contain a concentration of disadvantaged pupils. The importance of area is administrative rather than structural, collective or cultural. Recent interventions (e.g. 'Delivering Equality of Opportunity in Schools', DEIS; Department of Education and Science, 2005) acknowledge that schools with a high concentration of disadvantaged pupils are facing accentuated difficulties because of this, and it is in this regard that norms and peer groups are likely to be invoked. But the accommodation of the 'social context' dimension is framed in terms of resource allocation within a theory of intervention rather than of disadvantage. It is not construed as a feature of social action, as a force within a pupil's habitus, which is more routinely relegated to a less immediate and even remote sphere of influence.

This finds affinities with a positivistic/empiricist orientation to the understanding of educational disadvantage, giving priority in intervention and evaluation to what appears most immediately visible, tangible and 'real'. As a corollary, there is, for the purpose of intervention, a distancing of those structural and cultural factors which cannot be as readily differentiated, isolated and measured as can indicators of the specific cognitive and behavioural skills and abilities of individuals. There can even seem to be an incredulity as to their existence. Sociologists have not succeeded in inserting into policy discourse an understanding of social structure at a level other than macro change, which tends to further confirm its 'remote' conceptualisation. Indeed, the methodology of much of the more prominent policy-related sociological research in Ireland itself embodies assumptions about the relationship between the individual and the social that do little to challenge or offer alternatives to the psychologistic/ atomistic understanding of disadvantage or the mercantile paradigm itself (Nolan *et al.*, 2000).

Difference

An early assertion of difference in contemporary Irish education from the 1970s has been the multi-denominational school movement now operating under the umbrella of Educate Together. The re-emergence of Irish-medium schools since the 1980s under Gaelscoileanna (the National Organisation for Irish-Medium Schools) can also be considered in terms of the construction of difference – in this case, the classification of linguistic communities within Irish society. Along with the multi-denominational initiatives, the Gaelscoileanna movement represented a modernist inter- vention in relation to doxic objectives of Irish education – religious formation and linguistic revival – but it did so in the manner in which it embraced the Irish language as the chosen heritage rather than as an ascribed and inescapably essentialised indicator of Irishness. The multi- denominational schools were facilitating parents with an understanding of education other than the theocentric and providing a lived expression of it in the manner in which they educated their children. The Gaelscoileanna movement allowed parents to engage anew with the distinct position of Irish within society and education, but according to an interpretation of cultural identity that stressed the active and selective engagement of people with their past, as distinct from an objectification of identity in terms of historical and external forces.

When situated in their changing cultural context, modernist dimen- sions of both school types can themselves be seen to be vulnerable. A significant mercantile threat to the modernism of multi-denominational and Irish-medium schools, and indeed to their distinct defining rationale, is its capacity to culturally re-signify them as manifestations of post-Fordist production, as initiatives in educational provision that respond to the requirements of specialist configurations of differentiated and discrimin- ating consumers in the form of niche markets. In such a reinterpretation, they come to be represented as boutique schools, brands with discerning appeal, distinguishable from high-street Fordist products, attractive to mercantile subjectivities that take self-confirmation from being active and discerning consumers and doing so in a public and visible manner, at once experiencing and declaring one's mercantile credentials. Schools may seek to resist these threats to their modernist principles through induction and ongoing educational programmes for parents and achieve some success in this regard. But no organisation can insulate itself from social and cultural change. As Catholic schools have experientially accommodated in their ethos and practices to the erosion of the theocentric regulation of lifestyle since the 1960s, in a similar process of cultural penetration multi-denominational and Irish-medium schools were to experience being chosen by parents because of the fact, whatever of the nature, of their difference and its alignment with mercantile subjectivities of market alertness, judgement and activism.

Contestation and a deeply discharged public sphere

Because mercantile transformations in Irish education involve the cultural realm, contestation must begin with a recognition of the centrality of the politics of meaning-making and the relationship between educational understanding and action. This requires the circulation of concepts, languages and discourses with a significant level of publicness that successfully delineates, names and interprets this realm of cultural politics in all its diversity as it applies to education. Without this, the transitions diagnosed in this chapter remain hidden, silenced, evaded or superficially understood. This addresses the construct of the public sphere, routinely identified with Habermas's (1989) original model of private individuals coming together as equals to discuss matters of public concern, but which has benefited from substantial and disparate development (Calhoun, 1992; Crossley and Roberts, 2004). Here, the public sphere is understood as a socio-cultural realm that requires evaluation of the nature of its dynamics in terms of the resources and knowledge it makes available for democratic deliberation. Bourdieu is considered to have conducted such a project, but one that is faithful to Habermas's assumptions about the truth-determining capacity of critical theory (Crossley, 2004). In this chapter, the critical discourse prescribed for Irish educational policy issues comes 'without guarantees' (Giddens, 1994: 21).

The most tangible manifestation of the character of the public sphere is to be found in public discourse on education – the reporting and consideration of educational issues available to the general public through the print and broadcasting media. What this reveals is not encouraging. The early Bernstein (1971) would have found much to illuminate his restricted speech code – simple sentence structure, limited use of qualifications, 'sympathetic circularity' in appeals to emotion and personalism and, most characteristically, particularistic, context-specific meanings. A wide range of constructs, such as inclusion, disadvantage, partnership, access and parent power, are routinely deployed without a recognition of their contested nature as concepts (Gallie, 1955). Manifestations of Heidegger's (1962) 'idle talk' – communication as the passing on of a commodity (rather than the consideration, negotiation or reworking of meanings), a dominance of recipe knowledge, the closing off of further analysis of the issue in hand, an anti-intellectualism (the assumption that everything is instantly knowable, and what is not is of no more than remote significance for our lives) and the need for novelty – are commonplace.

None of this can be justified or explained by the obvious need for the mass media to be understood by its public. A comparison with media treatment of legal, commercial, financial and medical matters reveals these characteristics to be less prevalent than in the representation of educational topics. Nor is this restricted discourse exclusively or primarily the responsibility of the mass media. The nature of policy and scholarly discourse is also at issue. Such is the populist orientation of the state to society that, rather than involve people in a generative process for change, there is a refusal to challenge them through the presentation of different possibilities for the future development of education. As for the academic treatment of education, it provides sufficient 'franchised discourses', uncritical circulation of imported ideas that have achieved popularity elsewhere, to prove too attractive as novelty to the mass media.

A pervasive weakness of Irish education policy discourse is its failure to theorise the nature of educational change in recent times. Despite the frenetic policy activity of the 1990s, which includes policy documents, voluminous submissions, highly publicised consultation and an unprecedented raft of legislation, educational discourse within the public sphere continues to betray an inadequacy of conceptualisation and language to engage with the fundamental shifts in meaning and practice diagnosed in this chapter. The institutional dimensions of the educational public sphere, the social arrangements, protocols and settings established to generate knowledge, policy and prescriptions for educational change, such as councils, fora, centres, departments and projects, reveal the absence of a dedicated institutional setting for the consideration of such issues as mercantile transitions as a feature of social and educational change. When social change does come to be considered in the institutional settings that do exist, it is by way of bullet-pointed introductions or context-setting for some aspect of their mission – curriculum, assessment, employability, social welfare, and economic productivity and efficiency. What should be a dynamic complex of relationships involving both social and cultural dimensions of the public sphere in effect operates as a 'restrictive equilibrium' of ideas and people, in which challenging policies or penetrating ideas are neither transmitted nor received. Foucault's (1980) power/knowledge nexus is allowed to remain intact in the production and communication of educational knowledge: what gets said reflects the power relationships; states of knowing constitute an entitlement to power. This mutuality of tactical self-restraint reveals itself in the most routine and visible of practices – submissions from advisory bodies and interest groups, state policy initiatives, terms of reference for projects/committees of inquiry, selection of chairpersons, commissioning, bidding for and presenting research, and the selective media coverage of educational issues. This 'restrictive equilibrium' not only excludes challenging proposals for policy change but also, more pervasively, refuses the use of a more penetrating level of educational discourse.

Within the state itself, the effect is to subjugate significant resources and voices in the form of research and support staff (ranging across the inspectorate, examinations commission, school and staff development and curriculum change), who have been introduced to a more discriminating language of educational practice as part of their postgraduate education studies (Department of Education and Science, 2007). The consequence is a deeply discharged public sphere that requires more than the cultural equivalent of routine charging, such is its limited and limiting resources in terms of a conceptual literacy of education and an awareness of difference in the range of possible educational futures. When it repels stimulus, it is most likely to be doing no more than failing to recognise meaningfulness by reference to its restrictive interpretive world of particularistic speech, uncontested concepts and 'idle talk'.

There is a challenge here for established academics who engage with the state's process of policy deliberation. As scholars, with a civic duty to scrutinise issues of public concern and enjoying the protection of legislation, they need to show leadership in disrupting this 'restrictive equilibrium', they need to assert the relevance of the resources within educational studies and provide a space for the submerged discourses and voices to surface and participate in the recharging of the educational public sphere. A final suggestion, which cannot be developed here, is that an even greater potential for intervention may well lie outside the conventional fields of educational discourse and include such generative sources as flashpoint controversy, judicial spectacle, transgressive performance and genres such as e-communication and satire.

9

Pharmaceuticals, progress and psychiatric contention in early twenty-first century Ireland

ORLA O'DONOVAN

Intensifying expectations about the possibility of controlling health and suffering by means of biomedical techniques and technologies, together with the commodification of more and more aspects of life, are just some of the forces inciting new and expanded biomedical markets throughout the globe. This chapter considers the recent dramatic expansion of one such market in the Irish context, the market for the pharmaceutical industry's products, in the form of drugs and drug promotion messages. In contrast to radical critiques of the biomedical enterprise, such as Ivan Illich's (1976) brilliantly thought-provoking treatise that mooted the clinical and cultural harm associated with the 'pharmaceutical invasion', the construction of this shift in consumption by the pharmaceutical industry, one of the most profitable sectors in the global capitalist economy, as both desirable and inevitable is discussed. The Irish pharmaceutical industry's discourses reiterate the ubiquitous narratives of progress of conventional histories of biomedicine and, in line with the nauseating norm of 'othering' Ireland's past as a European backwater, they emphasise that drug consumption in Ireland is now set to catch up with that in the rest of western Europe.

I discuss how the industry constructs transformed drug consumption patterns and attitudes towards pharmaceuticals as markers of the 'advanced' society that Ireland has recently become. How this transformation in consumption has also been encouraged by Irish state pharmaceutical policies is briefly considered, policies that impose few restrictions on the public subsidisation of medicines and that prioritise the speedy licensing of drugs for sale on the Irish market over measures to maximise drug safety. The contributions of many patients' organisations in Ireland to the extension of pharmacocentric frames of understanding health are also addressed.

Before concluding, the chapter considers a current, albeit a minority one, in the mental health movement in Ireland that contests the pharmaceutical industry's prescriptions for progress and the common-sense belief in respect of pharmaceutical consumption that 'more is better'.

New and expanding biomedical markets

Irrespective of one's response to Illich's controversial thesis that the biomedical–industrial complex is a counterproductive institution, it would be hard to deny that, during the three decades since his *Limits to Medicine* was first published, medicalisation, the expansion of the biomedical jurisdiction beyond its former boundaries, has continued apace. Though complex and contextually embedded, medicalisation is evident internationally in the proliferation of new disease entities, health identities and – as a consequence of the intimate relations between biomedicine and the generation of wealth – capitalist biomedical markets. There is a propensity for commentators to position the pharmaceutical industry as *the* catalyst of medicalisation, but others argue, as did Illich, that this is an oversimplification (Metzl and Herzig, 2007). Instead, pharmaceutical marketing tends to intensify and exploit existing hopes and expectations about health and illness; it seeks 'to understand the desires of potential consumers, to affiliate those with their products, and to link these with the habits needed to use those products' (Rose, 2007: 702). Cognisant of trends in biomedicine and of the pervasiveness in late modernity of discourses on 'risk', which assume something can be done to avert future misfortune, the concept of medicalisation has been extended and growing attention is being paid to the biomedicalisation of risk and the pharmaceuticalisation of biomedicine (Lupton, 2000; Klawiter, 2002). In the current era of 'consumerist medicine' (Pickstone, 2000), not only are we witnessing the emergence of novel biomedical markets enabled by new technologies and the blurring of 'health' and 'lifestyle' products, such as bio-banking and an ever-expanding range of cosmetic surgeries for an increasingly 'plastic body', but older markets, such as private hospital care and health insurance, are also expanding, due to neoliberal inducements for individuals to assume responsibility for their own healthcare. Of all the flourishing biomedical capitalist industries, the market for pharmaceuticals is arguably the most lucrative.

By the 1980s, there was abundant evidence that pharmaceuticals were consumed heavily throughout the world, including in many so-called 'third world' societies (van der Geest *et al.*, 1996). Since then, medicine consumption has further escalated, not least because of the growing market for so-called 'lifestyle drugs'. These drugs are used in the treatment of newly biomedicalised conditions, such as sexual dysfunction, obesity and social anxiety disorder (Lexchin, 2001). The expansion of the market for pharmaceuticals has also been attributed in part to the growing emphasis on new forms of preventive medicine, which redefine healthy people as risky subjects (Klawiter, 2002). This involves a break from the idea that sick people can be distinguished from healthy ones and its replacement with the idea that we can all be placed along a health risk continuum.

Growing drug consumption has been particularly evident in the United States, whose healthcare system in the eyes of Irish officialdom provides the model to be emulated (Wren, 2003). In the United States, sales of prescription drugs were fairly stable between 1960 and 1980, but in the period 1980 to 2000 they tripled and by 2004 had reached over $200 billion per annum (Angell, 2004). Not surprisingly, this growth in spending on medicines coincided with the emergence of the pharmaceutical industry as one of the most profitable sectors in the global capitalist economy. In 2001, the pharmaceutical industry was deemed the most profitable sector of the US corporate world by *Fortune* magazine, 'making this decade the third in which the industry has been at or near the top in all the magazine's measures of profitability' (Gottlieb, 2002). The industry ranked fifth in the most profitable corporations in the United States in 2005. As well as being highly globalised in terms of production and distribution, merger following merger has resulted in the pharmaceutical industry being highly concentrated in a shrinking number of giant companies. Consequently, as noted by Denis O'Hearn and Stephen McCloskey (2008: 14), this 'makes these companies very powerful globally, but it also means that they can have strong and even distorting social and economic effects in the regions where they operate'. Pfizer emerged as the drug company with the highest revenue in 2005, with profits exceeding $8 billion. With production plants in Ireland since the 1970s, Pfizer is one of the eighty-three foreign-owned pharmaceutical companies with bases in Ireland (IPHA, 2005). Taxation and other policies designed to make Ireland an attractive location for transnational corporate investment clearly succeeded in luring the pharmaceutical industry. These policies also produced such economic dependency on the industry that, by 2005, 44 per cent of the country's annual exports were products of the pharmaceutical industry (IPHA, 2005).

While expenditure on medicines in Ireland is lower than in many other western European countries, dramatic increases in Irish spending on drugs have occurred in recent years. This is evident in the drug outlays of the pharmaceutical industry's biggest customer, the state. Between 1993 and 2005, public expenditure on drugs grew from €211 million to €1,367 million (Barry *et al.*, 2008). Commentators in the National Centre for Pharmacoeconomics attribute the rise in public expenditure on drugs in Ireland to two main factors: the 'product mix', that is, the prescribing of new and more costly drugs; and the 'volume effect', that is, the increasing number of items prescribed and the number of tablets per prescription (Barry *et al.*, 2008). In Ireland, there has been a staggering growth in the prescribing of medicines to people eligible for free drugs under the General Medical Scheme (GMS). Between 1995 and 2005, there was a doubling in the number of items prescribed to GMS patients, even though the number of people eligible for free drugs under the GMS fell by over 9 per cent during this period. Also, over the same period, there was a 390 per cent increase in the number of prescription forms for six items and a 780 per cent growth in the number of prescription forms for seven or more items. The cost to the state of drugs per GMS patient grew by a factor of 4.5 during the decade (Barry *et al.*, 2008).

Many of the top publicly subsidised drugs in Ireland are contested medical technologies whose clinical effectiveness is the subject of dispute. For example, in 2004, clinical nutritional products were the second most expensive medication reimbursed under the GMS and cost the state more than €25.9 million (Barry *et al.*, 2008). However, a 2004 review conducted by the National Medicines Information Centre found that the clinical evidence supporting their use was poor. Another example is a drug used in the treatment of Alzheimer's disease. Donepezil (Aricept) was number 18 in the top 100 drugs in terms of expenditure under the GMS in 2004. In that year, over 61,000 prescriptions for the drug were issued, at a cost to the GMS in excess of €7 million.[1] However, this and other anti-dementia drugs have been the source of considerable scientific disagreement; many reviews of clinical trial data have concluded that the scientific basis for recommending the drug is questionable, but this has been challenged by the manufacturers of the drugs and by patients' organisations. As will be discussed below, psychiatric drugs are the source of considerable contention. One such drug, olanzapine (Zyprexa), which is widely used in the treatment of schizophrenia and certain forms of depression, was the sixth most costly drug to the GMS in 2005 (Barry *et al.*, 2008).

Growth in the consumption of drugs has been matched by increasing consumption of marketing messages produced by the pharmaceutical industry. Previously, its marketing was largely directed at the prescribers of drugs, but increasingly it is targeted at the general public. Our encounters with the messages and logos of drug companies are no longer confined to the packaging on their medicines: we meet them on our television screens, on T-shirts at charity events, on leaflets and 'gifts' distributed at meetings arranged by patients' organisations, in doctors' waiting rooms, on health websites and even in 'health education' materials distributed to our children at school. In 2002 in the United States alone, the industry spent almost $21 billion on drug promotion, including over $2.6 billion on direct-to-consumer advertising (Norris *et al.*, 2005). Direct-to-consumer advertising of prescription medicines is banned in Ireland and the rest of the EU, but drug companies seek other ways to 'inform' potential consumers of their products. They spend increasing amounts of money on 'disease awareness campaigns' that encourage people to seek medical advice in relation to specific conditions. Expenditure on advertising in Ireland by the industry tripled between 2004 and 2005, and Pfizer was the biggest spender, promoting drugs used in the treatment of cholesterol, overactive bladder and Alzheimer's disease (Labanyi, 2006).

The industry has become increasingly involved in the provision of 'health information' purportedly designed to empower the consumers of medicines. A 2005 survey of 112 patients' and health advocacy organisations in Ireland found that almost half of them had received some form of sponsorship from the pharmaceutical industry, and the most frequently cited purpose of the sponsorship was 'patient education' (O'Donovan, 2007). The health information website www.irishhealth.com provides an illustration of cooperation between drug companies and patients' organisations. In 2007 the website offered a number of 'health clinics' for specific conditions. The clinic on epilepsy was provided in association with Brainwave, the Irish Epilepsy Association, and was 'supported by an educational grant from Pfizer'. Similarly, the asthma clinic was provided in association with the Asthma Society of Ireland and was sponsored by Merck Sharp & Dohme. A 2005 school-based health education initiative involving a partnership between the industry and statutory educational bodies was the 'Way2Go' programme, sponsored by Pfizer, which involved the distribution of workbooks and videos to all secondary schools. In 2004 this same company also sponsored, and had its logo displayed on, a health programme, *The Health Squad*, broadcast on Ireland's public television station, RTÉ.

The inference promoted by the pharmaceutical industry is that increasing consumption of drugs is unequivocally to the benefit of people's health. Likewise, industry-sponsored 'information' initiatives are widely constructed as responses to an increasingly astute public who now eschew passive patient-hood. However, even within biomedical circles, these inferences are deemed by some to be deeply flawed. Marcia Angell (2004), former editor of the *New England Journal of Medicine*, argues that the pharmaceutical industry is not especially innovative, and that most of the array of supposedly 'new' medicines launched on the market in recent years are either of dubious value or are 'me too' drugs, versions of which are already on the market. This is illustrated by data on new drugs approved by the US Food and Drug Administration (FDA) between 1998 and 2002. Of the 415 new drugs approved, 77 per cent were classified by the FDA as no better than the medicines already available.

Such pseudo 'new' drugs, however, are patented and thus more lucrative for the industry than older, cheaper and generic versions. Furthermore, Angell contends, health information sponsored by drug companies is simply a disguised form of promotion by an industry that has become largely a marketing machine. Others, such as the Australian-based non-governmental organisation (NGO) Healthy Skepticism, try to stem the over-consumption of medicines by attempting to counter the effects of industry marketing. The ideas of Illich inspire many of these efforts, such as the fight against 'disease mongering', a term used to capture the selling of sickness that widens the boundaries of illness to include aspects of ordinary life and that grows the markets for those who sell and deliver treatments (Moynihan and Henry, 2006). Others point to the harm caused when marketing triumphs over the science of drug safety, as in the case of the rofecoxib (Vioxx) drug disaster, the arthritis drug withdrawn from the global market in 2004 following its implication in thousands of deaths (Mintzes, 2005). Though not extensively publicised, some members of the Irish medical establishment have also expressed concern about the over-consumption of some medicines, such as antidepressants (Houston, 2005). Others, such as the chairperson of the Irish College of General Practitioners (Labanyi, 2006), have pointed to the 'creeping commercialis-ation' of drug information provided to the public evident in the growing frequency and reach of the industry's 'thinly-veiled marketing tools'.

Progress and pharmaceutical consumption

In epidemiology, the medical science concerned with studying the health and illness of populations that allegedly provides the 'evidence base' for public health interventions, there has been an 'unmitigated devotion' to epidemiological transition theory (Avilés, 2001: 166). This theory, other-wise referred to as epidemiological evolution, shares the foundational assumptions of the modernisation theory of international development; it understands the history of health in individual societies as a universal and natural 'phased Europeanised or Americanised process of development, beneficial for all, towards which all nations converge' (Avilés, 2001: 166). The motor of progress that impels the transition to the most highly evolved type of society is largely biomedical progress and especially the application new disease-prevention technologies. This doctrine of development has been criticised on many fronts – for its silence about matters such as health inequalities, its ignoring of the global processes of capital accumulation that result in the poor of 'first world' countries receiving 'third world' healthcare, and its questionable empirical evidence base. Despite profound criticism, epidemiological transition theory continues to be a vibrant discourse of development.

'Epidemiological evolution' is a term used repeatedly by the Irish Pharmaceutical Healthcare Association (IPHA), the body that represents the interests of the globalised pharmaceutical industry in Ireland, to explain in part the mounting expenditure on pharmaceuticals that has occurred in recent decades. It appears again and again in the IPHA's submissions to the Irish government, which seek to counter concerns about the rising public medicines bill and to foster a 'new perspective on health expenditure' (IPHA, 2002a: 4). This new perspective is one that accepts the 'realities' that medicines expenditure will continue to escalate in coming years, and that this is both desirable and inevitable. Increased expenditure on and consumption of medicines is inevitable, we are told, because Ireland has the disease profile of an epidemiologically evolved society. The medicalisation of 'conditions' such as obesity and the pharmaceuticalisation of their treatment underpin this logic. Explaining why the state's medicine bill is going up every year, the IPHA (2003a: 1) highlights the increasing incidence of chronic and non-communicable diseases 'such as asthma, diabetes and obesity which are generally quite costly to treat'. Two other features of 'developed' societies are also cited to explain rising drug costs, namely an ageing population and rising patient expectations. Not only is it taken as self-evident that old age equates with greater drug consumption, but also that patients with high expectations in relation to their health demand access to more and more drugs. These are the 'expert patients' of consumerist medicine, who have access to multiple online sources of information and whose 'rising expectations inevitably have knock-on effects on health care demand, use and cost' (IPHA, 2003b: 3).

Despite the low level of innovation in the pharmaceutical industry in recent years, industry narratives are replete with references to biomedical 'advances'. Increased expenditure on medicine, according to the industry, is desirable, as it makes the fruits of biomedical progress available to Irish citizens and this constitutes 'an investment in the future prosperity of Irish society' (IPHA, 2002b: 4). We are told that many of the new drugs likely to be available from 'advances' in biomedicine are preventive and early-intervention treatments; this means 'increasingly, health policy makers will be confronted with the need to spend more money now to achieve long-term gains' (IPHA, 2002b: 4). The importance of moving beyond curative to pharmaceuticalised preventive medicine is emphasised because

'We now live in a world where if a condition is diagnosed early, it can often be quickly, effectively and efficiently treated using modern medicines, medical interventions and behaviour modification' (IPHA, 2004a: 5). Echoing the emphasis placed on the application of new medical technologies to promote progress in the field of healthcare in epidemiological transition theory, the IPHA asserts that 'A willingness to reconfigure the health system to take advantage of advances in medicine and technology … offers the opportunity to develop a world class health service' (IPHA, 2004a: 3). A prerequisite for further progress in healthcare, therefore, is recognition of the growing centrality of drugs in determining health.

Not surprisingly, the IPHA argues that recent health reform measures to curb escalating drug expenditure by the state, such as those recommended in the 2003 Brennan Report (Commission on Financial Management and Control Systems in the Health System, 2003), are misguided and would stymie progress in the Irish health service. In fact, increased expenditure on medicines is advocated as a means to save on overall healthcare and welfare spending. Psychiatric medicines used in the treatment of schizophrenia and depression are singled out as examples, whereby 'using newer, so-called "expensive" medicines, patient quality of life is improved, hospital stays are shortened and net savings' can be made (IPHA, 2002b: 6). Furthermore, in one response to the recommendations of the Brennan Report, a reminder of the Irish economy's reliance on the industry is issued:

> It would be a matter of concern for the research based pharmaceutical industry, which has invested over €12 billion in the Irish economy and which provides employment to over 20,000 people, should a system be introduced which would favour *old* products over *new* products and make it difficult to develop a market for *potentially* better products with enhanced efficacy, safety and/or quality profiles. (IPHA, 2003a, emphasis added)

The Brennan Commission's proposals to restrict the public subsidisation of drugs where equally effective but cheaper versions are available are not in the best interests of patients, according to the IPHA (2003a) – they would have negative repercussions on 'poorer patients' access to the full range of modern medicines'. Such concern on the part of the industry with patients' access to medicines sits uncomfortably with the pricing and intellectual property rights policies favoured by the globalised industry, which, for example, have resulted in millions of the world's poor being denied access to AIDS medicines, as highlighted by the work of organisations such as Médecins Sans Frontières ('t Hoen, 2002; Downes, 2008).

An additional argument repeatedly advanced by the industry for why the mounting consumption of medicines should be celebrated is the relatively low level of drug consumption in Ireland, compared with that in some other member states of the EU and the Organisation for Economic Co-operation and Development (OECD). The assumed desirability, if not inevitability, of convergence with western European and OECD norms is evident in industry statements which note that the growth in medicine expenditure 'has to be seen in the context of the fact that Irish spending on pharmaceuticals is starting from a low base. According to comparative data for 2003 Ireland had the lowest expenditure per capita on medicines in Western Europe' (IPHA, 2006a: 15). In the IPHA's annual publications that chart *Healthcare Facts and Figures*, Ireland's relatively low consumption of and spending on medicines are constructed as Ireland lagging behind. Reminiscent of 'league tables' of indicators of 'development', which repeatedly positioned Ireland at the bottom prior to its economic transformation during the 1990s, low levels of drug consumption are assumed to be a reflection of the underdevelopment of provision for public health. The country is, however, regarded as being in the process of catching up: 'Irish consumption of medicines remains amongst the lowest in Western Europe. Growth in the Irish market has to be viewed against this background and against the ever increasing sums being invested to improve public health' (IPHA, 2004b: 23). The rebranding of Ireland as the Celtic Tiger was celebrated in industry discourses and the country's economic transformation was presented as enabling Ireland to advance towards the drug consumption levels of its western European neighbours. Indeed, in a presentation available for download from the IPHA's website entitled 'From Bust to Boom: The Story of the Pharmaceutical Industry in Ireland', the Association congratulates itself for the crucial role it played in transforming Ireland from 'the poorest of the rich' into 'Europe's shining light'.[2]

According to the industry, concern with promoting patient safety together with demands from patients are impelling the growth of consumption of industry-sponsored 'health literacy' messages directed at members of the public. What critics have described as thinly veiled marketing exercises, the industry frames as educational initiatives aimed at enhancing patient compliance. A key cause of adverse side-effects of medicines, according to the IPHA, is patients' incorrect use of them and, in recognition of this, 'IPHA member companies are proactively working to improve compliance' through initiatives such as the publication of patient information booklets and sponsorship of patients' associations (IPHA, 2006b: 5). (This industry construct of the 'recalcitrant patient' stands in contrast to its 'expert patient' construct.) Blurring of the boundaries between the marketing of drugs and the provision of health information is also evident in the industry's claim that a further important aspect of 'contributing to the correct use of medicines relates to the advertising and promotion of medicines by the pharmaceutical industry' (IPHA, 2006b: 5). At EU level, the industry is currently attempting to have the ban on direct-to-consumer advertising of prescription medicines lifted, arguing that it stymies the industry's role in the provision of health information. The IPHA has supported previous efforts to remove the ban, arguing that advertising of prescription medicines educates patients and improves compliance (Bowers, 2001).

The pharmaceutical industry's celebration of Irish people's mounting consumption of drugs and industry-sponsored 'health messages' as evidence of Ireland's 'development' has been endorsed by pharmaceutical policy and also by many patients' organisations. Elsewhere I have discussed in detail how medicines regulation policy in Ireland has followed a neoliberal, pharma-friendly course and has in recent years been largely informed by the logic of market competition (O'Donovan, 2008). Here, let me illustrate this by noting the prioritisation of speedy drug licensing, which enables more and more drugs to be sold on the Irish market, over measures to generate drug safety information. If we examine the history of drug regulation in Ireland, two shifts in the definition of the role of the state in protecting the public from unsafe medicines can be discerned. First, the state shifted from a Pontius Pilate 'it's nothing to do with us' official attitude at the time of the thalidomide drug disaster to the establishment in 1966 of the National Drugs Advisory Board (NDAB) and a severely under-resourced and consequently largely ineffective regulatory system. Despite its shortcomings, the NDAB's primary function was pharmacovigilance, that is, monitoring reports of suspected negative side-effects of medicines, or adverse drug reactions.

The second major shift in medicines regulatory policy involved the establishment of the Irish Medicines Board (IMB) in 1995, which constituted a move to an industry-funded drug regulation system principally concerned with the industry priority of speedy drug licensing, which enables the marketing of pharmaceuticals as quickly as possible. This second resituating of the state involved a new mode of regulation, a shift from 'hands-off' regulation to regulation for 'competition'. The replacement of the NDAB with the IMB constituted a significant and unhealthy reorientation of the Irish drug regulation system and a prioritisation of speedy pre-marketing assessments of drugs over post-marketing pharmacovigilance. Even though pharmacovigilance generates superior drug safety information, it is very much the 'poor relation' of product authorisation in the current drug regulation system. The limitations of pre-marketing clinical trials are clearly evident in the fact that, for 50 per cent of new drugs, serious adverse drug reactions are detected following market approval (Roughhead and Lexchin, 2006). While pharmacovigilance never rose to the top of the agenda for drug regulation policy, the industry's priority of accelerating the product authorisation process did. By January 2002, the backlog of product authorisation applications had been reduced to 327, from 2,097 in 1986. In 1999, the median time for new product authorisations was 73 weeks. By 2004, it was down to 34 weeks. As a result of this increased 'efficiency', by March 2007 there were 7,914 products on the IMB's list of authorised medicines for human use on the Irish market.

What is remarkable about the prioritisation of the backlog issue is the virtual absence of evidence of critical questioning among policy-makers about its causes or consequences for public health. Apart from a few exceptions, the explosion in the number of (mainly 'me too') drugs queuing up to go on the Irish market and the dramatic escalation of public spending on health have not been questioned. An examination of the parliamentary debates around the time of the establishment of the IMB reveals that the backlog was almost invariably discussed with reference to the importance of the pharmaceutical industry to the Irish economy and the industry's disquiet about the delays in getting its products onto the Irish market. By and large, the equation of more drugs with better health was accepted.

As in many other parts of the world, there has been a mushrooming of patients' organisations in Ireland in recent years. A 2005 study of these organisations' modes of engagement with pharmaceutical corporations found evidence of a strong and growing cultural tendency to frame these corporations as allies in their quests for better health (O'Donovan, 2007). While there is little evidence to support the thesis that patients' organisations are unwittingly manipulated into being industry 'fronts', many of them encourage the investment of hope in pharmaceutical innovation and play a role in expanding the markets for pharmaceuticals. As noted above, almost half of the organisations surveyed in 2005 reported they had received pharmaceutical industry sponsorship, mainly for 'patient education'. Many patients' organisations are involved in 'disease awareness campaigns' that promote pharmaceutical treatments. An example is the Alzheimer Society of Ireland's public education campaign, sponsored by Pfizer, which received a special award in 2006 from the Institute of Advertising Practitioners in Ireland. It is worth noting that Alzheimer's disease has only comparatively recently gained recognition as a disease entity; in the United States it was transformed from being a rarely applied medical diagnosis in the early 1970s to being characterised as the fourth or fifth leading cause of death by the late 1980s (Fox, 1989). The Alzheimer Society of Ireland's educational campaign promoted the idea that early diagnosis and treatment with anti-dementia drugs, as well as other activities, can stave off the 'loss of self' that is understood to be a feature of the late stage of the disease. To use the campaign's slogan, the medications are promoted as a potential means to help 'keep you being you'. These medications are among the contested medications mentioned above. Unlike Ireland, in

Britain and elsewhere, the conclusion that anti-dementia drugs are largely ineffective and a waste of money has been reached by public bodies and there are restrictions on their public subsidisation. However, the Alzheimer Society of Ireland is among the many organisations involved internationally in opposing such drug subsidisation decisions and contesting the science underpinning them. In sum, the pharmaceutical industry has not been alone in acclaiming and contributing to recent transformations in the consumption of drugs and pharmaceutical marketing messages in Ireland, and in circulating the associated expectations and promises.

Psychiatric contention

Turning to political mobilising around other health conditions, and drawing on Nick Crossley's (2006) argument that social movements are best understood as 'fields of contention', a term that avoids the tendency to see social movements as culturally static and uniform 'things', I suggest that an emerging current within the mental health field of contention in contemporary Ireland contests the widespread belief that mounting pharmaceutical consumption is unequivocally to the benefit of people's health.

Consistent with portrayals of the NGO sector in general in Ireland that point to the overwhelming predominance of conventional and consensualist political strategies, social movement organisations in the mental health field in Ireland have been characterised as being professionally dominated and deferential towards orthodox psychiatric frames of understanding. Ewen Speed (2002) argues there has been an absence of a user-led movement, as mental health service users have not organised by and for themselves in any significant way. His analysis of two movement organisations led him to conclude that, in addition to propagating biomedical interpretations of mental 'illness', they endorsed state consumerist discourses and the recasting of the mental health service user as a consumer. That said, in recent years there has been a propagation of the psychiatric 'survivor' identity, associated with the establishment of new organisations in the field, such as the user-led Irish Advocacy Network and the Cork Advocacy Network, founded in 1999 and 2001 respectively. A more recent analysis of the 'culture of action' of one of the organisations considered by Speed, Aware – Helping to Defeat Depression (one of the largest mental health organisations in Ireland), notes that it frames depression as an illness that can be effectively treated with pharmaceuticals, but is under-treated owing to lack of public understanding of its disease status and stigmatisation (O'Donovan, 2007). Similar to the Alzheimer Society of Ireland, Aware is a player in the mental health field that has been entwined with pharmaceutical manufacturers in the dissemination of health narratives that encourage greater consumption of drugs. Every year, the organisation has a 'depression awareness week' involving a mass media campaign, which in the past was sponsored by a drug company that manufactures antidepressants. However, recent years have witnessed a shift in the organisation's mode of engagement with the pharmaceutical industry, and drug company sponsorship is no longer a feature of its annual awareness campaign or of the online 'depression clinic' with which it is associated. The chief executive of Aware explained that the organisation's increasing wariness of collaboration with the industry in awareness-raising activities stemmed from experiences of 'sharp practice' on the part of the industry that increasingly expects 'a bang for its buck', but also concerns that strong links with the industry would undermine Aware's image in the eyes of the public, on whom it relies heavily for funds (O'Donovan, 2007). At a seminar held in December 2005 at which the chief executive of Aware outlined the rationale for her growing ambivalence in regard to collaboration with industry in raising awareness of depression, actors from some other patients' organisations recounted how similar rethinking of the wisdom of cooperation with industry was taking place within their organisations. Therefore, while there is evidence of a growing cultural tendency in patients' organisations in Ireland (and internationally) to frame pharmaceutical corporations as partners in their quests for better health, such partnerships are being critically questioned by actors within some organisations. These relationships are not inevitable and, once formed, do not necessarily endure.

Resistance at a more profound level to the supposed inevitability and desirability of mounting consumption of the pharmaceutical industry's products is evident in an emergent network of 'survivors', (post)psychiatrists and other individuals in the mental health field of contention. This loose network is very much part of a minority current, or undercurrent, and, unlike the professionalised NGOs that populate the mental health field, its public visibility waxes and wanes. In an effort to give a flavour of the counter-narratives articulated by this network, here I will focus on just one episode that I observed, a presentation in October 2006 to a government committee, the Joint Committee on Health and Children's Sub-committee on the Adverse Side Effects of Pharmaceuticals. First of all, let me provide some background to the establishment of this committee, which in itself was an outcome of the lobbying activities of members of the network.

Following the death of her husband in 2003 in what she regards as an antidepressant drug-induced suicide, Nuria O'Mahony began a campaign for stricter state regulation of antidepressants and, more generally, for greater public awareness of the potential harmful effects of pharmaceuticals. This can be seen to be part of a broader campaign, as antidepressants have been a source of ongoing and considerable psychiatric contention internationally (Medawar and Hardon, 2004). Nuria O'Mahony succeeded in publicising her grievances in the Irish mass media, and in building alliances with critical psychiatrists and psychiatric 'survivors'. For example, an article in the *Irish Times* published on 28 June 2005 detailed changes in pharmaceutical policy called for by O'Mahony, including greater monitoring of the prescribing of antidepressants, public access to information about their potential adverse effects, and public access to full clinical trial data. This is a very different kind of patient 'health information' to that advocated by the industry. She called for the establishment of a new drug licensing authority, which would be wholly publicly funded rather than deriving its income from fees paid by pharmaceutical corporations. The article reported the endorsement of O'Mahony's campaign by Pat Bracken, a consultant psychiatrist, who added, 'As medical practitioners, I feel we need to become more aware of how corporate interests can sometimes dominate agendas within medicine, in a way that isn't necessarily always in the best interest of patients'. A practising psychiatrist in the Irish public mental health service, Bracken is an advocate of 'postpsychiatry'. As detailed in his co-authored book *Postpsychiatry – Mental Health in a Postmodern World*, this entails an abandonment of the modernist enterprise of psychiatry, which is rooted in a technical and individualised framing of madness and emotional problems as illnesses that require professional intervention (Bracken and Thomas, 2005). Akin to the ideas of Illich, postpsychiatry reflects a concern to understand the limitations of psychiatric interventions. Bracken is also a critic of the close links between academic psychiatry and the pharmaceutical industry, and the commercialisation of drug research.

Nuria O'Mahony's resolute campaign, which included public petitioning and the deluging of politicians with e-mails, succeeded in prompting the establishment in 2006 of the Oireachtas Sub-committee on the Adverse Side Effects of Pharmaceuticals. Although the limitations of parliamentary initiatives such as the public consultations undertaken by the Oireachtas Sub-committee have to be acknowledged, its establishment nonetheless reflected official recognition that the adverse side-effects of pharmaceuticals may be a public problem, and it provided a public platform for O'Mahony and her allies to articulate their counter-cultural concerns about trends in pharmaceutical consumption in Ireland. When O'Mahony addressed the Sub-committee, she was accompanied by four others, three of whom had been involved in the Cork Advocacy Network. These health activists also had formal links with globalising mental health movement organisations, such as Mind Freedom International. Two of them had published personal narratives of 'surviving' psychiatry – one in the form of a biography (Maddock and Maddock, 2006) and the other through poetry (McCarthy, 2005) – and another was a psychiatrist who had been involved in disseminating ideas that challenge pharmacocentric understandings of mental health, including the co-authoring of a book entitled *Depression. An Emotion Not a Disease* (Corry and Tubridy, 2005), establishing an online discussion forum called Depression Dialogues and assisting with the organisation of a public conference addressed by the author of one of the 'sacred texts' of the international mental health movement, Peter Breggin, author of *Toxic Psychiatry* (1991). In other words, the parliamentary field was just one among many in which members of this network articulated their opposition to orthodox ideas about the role of pharmaceuticals in promoting health.

Both the communicative style and the arguments put forward by the group ran contrary to the norm. Using song recordings and enactment of the stupefying effects of some psychiatric medicines, combined with the mobilisation of experiential and 'expert' knowledge, they spoke about the harm, devastation and deaths being caused by the inappropriate medicalisation of depression.[3] The disease status of depression was contested and so too was the science that underpins its treatment with pharmaceuticals. Orthodox psychiatry's claims to know and cure depression were disputed. The increasing 'automatism' whereby antidepressants are becoming the routine answer to a widening array of depressive symptoms was problematised, as were the pharmaceutical industry's 'weapons of mass seduction' targeted at doctors and members of the public. Contrary to pharmaceutical industry discourses that emphasise poor patient compliance in explaining adverse drug reactions, the members of the group argued that adverse drug reactions are largely attributable to inappropriate prescribing of medicines and the inadequacy of existing measures to ensure drug safety. Antidepressants were taken as a case in point to highlight what were deemed to be the failings in the state's regulatory approach in respect of drug trials and the licensing of medicines more generally, and the pharmaceutical industry's 'unhealthy influence'.

The transformative potential of networks of individuals such as this one is unclear, but what is indisputable is that they generate a dissensus in the mental health field and beyond, and enable the articulation of health narratives about drug consumption that run counter to those propagated by the pharmaceutical industry.

Conclusion

Ireland in the early twenty-first century has clearly provided the political economy and cultural conditions that are conducive to growing markets for pharmaceutical drugs and marketing messages. Considering the evidence of the dramatic increase in expenditure on pharmaceuticals presented in this chapter, it would seem that the pharmaceutical industry understands very well the desires, hopes and expectations of Irish doctors and 'consumers'. Echoing the assumptions of modernisation theory, the pharmaceutical industry's discourses explain recent changes in Irish drug consumption patterns as an inevitable and desirable convergence with trends in other 'advanced' societies. The Irish state has demonstrated a willingness to foot the bill for the prescribing of significantly greater quantities of drugs, many of which are 'new' and costly, and has been responsive to industry pressure to speed up the licensing process to enable companies to have accelerated access to the Irish market. Recently proposed measures to curb public pharmaceutical spending have met with industry efforts to foster a 'new perspective' on health expenditure, one that recognises the 'reality' of the growing centrality of pharmaceuticals in determining health and the necessity of increased pharmaceutical expenditure to attain a 'world class' health service.

The cultural effects of patients' organisations in Ireland can be seen to be complex and contradictory in regard to pharmaceutical consumption, although many of the large ones encourage the further expansion of the market for drugs. The struggles of an informal network of mental health activists involved in psychiatric contention considered here provide an example of health activism in Ireland, albeit a minority current, which questions the hegemony about the inevitability and desirability of mounting pharmaceutical consumption. In addition to challenging drug-based mental healthcare, this network promotes an alternative form of 'health intelligence' to that pushed by the pharmaceutical industry in which patient compliance is paramount. Moreover, these struggles constitute an effort to circumscribe the growing preoccupation with the pursuit of biomedically defined health and normality. They spur us to think about the reasonable limits of drug therapies and to imagine alternatives to what is conventionally passed off as progress in the field of healthcare.

Notes

1 Communication from Michael Barry, Director of the National Centre for Pharmaco-economics, 7 September 2006.
2 Presentation available at www.ipha.ie/htm/mediacentre/download/presentations/From_Bust_to_Boom.ppt (accessed 19 March 2007).
3 A full transcript of the group's presentation is available at http://debates.oireachtas.ie/DDebate.aspx?F=HEP20061017.xml&Node=H3#H3 (accessed 19 March 2007).

Part IV
Power and politics

10

Celtic, Christian and cosmopolitan: 'migrants' and the mediation of exceptional globalisation

GAVAN TITLEY

> Our country today is vibrant, cosmopolitan and filled with energy, and with our own distinctive national character, and our international relations are playing an important part in our maturing as a nation and deepening our understanding of our place in the world. (President Mary McAleese, St Patrick's Day message to the Irish abroad, 17 March 2006)

Signs taken for wonders

Ireland is now cosmopolitan. It is not always clear what this most troubled of concepts means, but it is certainly, as the opening quotation from President McAleese attests, a pliant addition to the fridge magnet poetry of collective representation. 'Cosmopolitanism' accommodates both trajectories of transformative thought and euphemistic banality. Its prevalent use in the mediated claims of public figures, agencies and institutions in Ireland about Ireland may amount to little more than performative self-regard, or to a corroboration of its most superficial accents. Yet as Gerard Delanty has observed, while 'cosmopolitanism does not simply refer to cases or situations that are called by those involved in them cosmopolitan … this dimension of cosmopolitan self-description is by no means irrelevant' (Delanty, 2006: 40). A cosmopolitan Ireland – notwithstanding the term's elusiveness – suggests important forms of socio-cultural transformation. Such self-descriptions implicitly make claims and, in activating a term which is shaped by multiple philosophies of openness and solidarity, they invite forms of immanent critique.

The 'vibrant', energetic, 'cosmopolitan' nation of the opening quotation not only recalls the conceit of the Celtic Tiger era that Irish society has organically harnessed the possibilities of global capitalism through astute management, self-confidence and openness (Kirby *et al.*, 2002; Coulter, 2003; Fagan, 2003) but also suggests that cosmopolitanism has emerged as a cultural dividend of globalism. In particular, 'cosmopolitan Ireland' connotes the presence of people who have migrated to Ireland, people who are always – in the liberal, multicultural imagination – vibrant and colourful, but who nonetheless confirm an organic cosmopolitanism while contributing to it. Thus, the widespread observation that 'Ireland is now cosmopolitan' is more than a description of the socio-cultural diversity of global capitalist societies, and of an Ireland attempting to describe its relatively recent and relatively significant inward migration. It is a projection of socio-cultural transformation, manifestly for the better, and anchored in the world openness and inclusivity of the host society.

The focus of this chapter is on cosmopolitanism and other narratives of what 'they' say about 'us'. It is all too obvious that these mediated claims to cosmopolitan conversion – a 'makeover' for the nation – can be contested on several grounds, not least the concomitant and less celebrated vision of Ireland as a 'racial' state, following the citizenship referendum of June 2004, which 'created a racialised two-tier system where *jus sanguinis*, or ancestry, hence *race*, becomes the basis and prime criterion for being an Irish citizen' (King O'Riain, 2006: 283). Yet, while cosmopolitanism could be evaluated as a normative claim, as a contentious *state of being*, in Irish terms it is a self-representation produced by ambivalent and unending *becoming*. Much of what is taken to signify a burgeoning cosmopolitanism in Ireland can be more critically understood as 'cosmopolitanisation': the visible results and felt impacts – intended and unintended – of globalising processes (Beck, 2006). The confident claim that 'we are cosmopolitan now', in this framework, becomes a soothing imaginary of progress, coherence and control.

It is not hard to see the attraction of this image in noughties Ireland. The influence of nationalism and right-wing cultural Catholicism has substantially dissipated, and at least a decade of economic growth and consumerism has given rise to widely disseminated visions of a 'new Ireland'. Irishness has become a fluid global brand, its value in the global economy stemming, as Diane Negra argues, from its status as 'politically insulated whiteness'. Similarly, Ireland 'has come to ground a set of consoling fictions about forms of social health that could be recovered amidst dawning perceptions of the losses globalisation inflicts' (Negra, 2006: 12). These fictions are not just for export; as several authors have suggested (Kirby *et al.*, 2002; Coulter, 2003; Keohane and Kuhling, 2004), an important aspect of the Celtic Tiger as a collective representation of transformation was its reliance on notions of Irish exceptionality.

Through a 'cultural reading of economic success' (Kirby, 2002b: 21) it presented a people blessed not only by cost-free globalisation, but also by the collective cultural disposition to harness 'it' (Kirby, 2002b; Coulter, 2003). An important – if far from universally celebrated – measure of this cosmopolitan rebirth has been labour migration to Ireland. Beyond contributing to the 'building boom', expanded services sector and partially forgotten agri-business, people who migrate have been held to contribute to this sense of confident cultural arrival.

Yet cosmopolitan culture, as Gerard Delanty argues, is not a product of the 'inevitable diversity' experienced in national sites through the accelerated mobilities of capital, labour, commodities and information (Delanty, 2006). *Cosmopolitanisation*, despite its unwieldiness, attempts to describe the ambivalences produced by these mobilities, and to examine how intensified economic, political, ecological and human interdependences are interpreted and negotiated. It suggests connexity and risk, and in a broader analysis could focus on a range of interdependences, from how the politics of foreign direct investment aligned Ireland in 'the war on terror', to the economic and cultural implications of Irish investors becoming the landlords of Europe and beyond. Cosmopolitanisation, as Ulrich Beck (2006) suggests, 'befalls us', while cosmopolitanism becomes us. In other words, the claim that 'Ireland is cosmopolitan now' is an interpretation attempting to explain and secure the ambivalences of globalisation, where the signs of cosmopolitanisation are taken for the wonders of cosmopolitanism.

This chapter explores a key aspect of this disputed transformation by examining how people who migrate are appropriated to the ongoing framing and narration of Irish cosmopolitanisation. As with other dominant constructions of life in multinational and multi-ethnic sites, such narratives are never really about migrant lives and experiences (Hage, 1998; Gilroy, 2004) but nevertheless have a performative impact on them. Cosmopolitanism is one such narration, and while superficially more positive, it is as dependent as more repressive discourses on dynamics of appropriation. Programmatic understandings of 'multiculturalism' (Lentin, 2002), of 'integration' (Gray, 2006) and of 'diversity' (Titley and Lentin, 2007) – as well as the racialising reflexes that were refracted in the citizenship referendum of 2004 – mediate understandings of Irishness and Irish society through shifting constructions of 'migrants' as an abstracted subject of commentary and biopolitics.

People who migrate, and different modalities of their labour, identity and collectivities, are discursively organised according to perceptions of the material and symbolic resources they contribute to society. While these typologies of migrant utility are central to economistic discourse in Ireland and elsewhere (Loyal and Allen, 2006), they are compounded in this context by the drive to assert control over ambivalent processes of globalisation. Here, ironically, there is full *integration* for 'migrants', both within the narrative of Irish exceptionality and within ongoing constructions of a globally reflexive national society. Whether it is a cosmopolitan or 'Celtic and Christian'[1] vision, the presence of vibrant, energetic, racialised and appropriated migrant bodies, labour and identity is reified in its elaboration.

But then, as any one of the many life coaches who now therapise our airwaves could attest, it is not really about them, it is so all about us. Loyal and Allen (2006: 213) note that the emergence of 'self–other or us–them processes' must be explained rather than merely described. This shifting 'utility' of migrants must be understood in the context of a self-consciously changed Ireland lacking a spectrum of socio-political visions of what constitutes a 'good society'. What follows is a focus on this limited dimension of the 'migration debate' and its mediated and mediating dynamics. As anxiety increases about the hyper-individualism of consumer society, so 'migrants' must act as a surrogate social fabric by making good their innate responsibility to integrate. As social inequalities and inadequate public services puncture the myth of cost-free globalisation, so a new, racialised category of 'non-EU migrants' and asylum seekers must be seen to be prevented from bleeding the state. As Muslims become the 'threatening global other' required by 'western governments who are committed to the eradication of unmanageable uncertainties in political and cultural life' (Sparks, 2006: 152), a tiny Muslim population in Ireland becomes an object of surveillance and the scrambled construction of non-negotiable cultural sureties. And as it becomes clearer that sustained economic growth will not suffice as a unifying social end, a racialised Irishness has been produced as a placebo.

Cosmopolitanism, cosmopolitanisation and global publics

Prior to examining how these narratives are taking shape in Ireland, it is important to note how cosmopolitanism has re-emerged in recent years as a broad discursive space in discussions of globalisation. This re-emergence spans a vast array of disciplinary boundaries and scales of agency, from its senses in politics as an ideological bulwark against the 'razor-wired camps, national flags and walls of silence that separate us from our fellow human beings' (Vertovec and Cohen, 2002: 22) to its broadly transformative associations with individual and collective efforts; 'globalization is a set of designs to manage the world while cosmopolitanism is a set of projects towards planetary conviviality' (Mignolo, 2000: 721). This renewed exploration, while productive, must contend with the often over-determining senses of cosmopolitanism preferred by varied histories of usage. Its accents of 'root-less' solidarity and enlightened utopianism may position it as hopelessly aspirational, or as a celebration of elite affinities. Yet as Sheldon Pollock and colleagues recognise, 'cosmopolitanism is not some known entity existing in the world, with a clear genealogy from the Stoics to Immanuel Kant, that simply awaits more detailed description at the hands of scholarship' (Pollock *et al.*, 2000: 577). Instead, cosmopolitanism incorporates a set of complex genealogies requiring situated shaping and reinvigoration.

An important strand of this reinvigoration has been attempts to examine how cosmopolitanism emerges, as opposed to delineating cosmo-politan values and politics or describing elite and subaltern cosmopolitan practices. Ulrich Beck's (2006) suggestive notion of cosmopolitanisation is one such possibility, though it demands careful application. His argu-ment builds on the banal acknowledgement that contemporary citizens and institutions – depending on their positionality and power – are con-strained to factor transnational influences and processes into their life worlds. Cosmopolitanisation is immanent in globalised societies because of a complex of economic, political, environmental and cultural processes, from bird flu to neo-imperialism, and emphasises the ambivalence and ambiguity of interdependence:

> The concept cosmopolitanization is designed to draw attention to the fact that the becoming cosmopolitan of reality is also, and even primarily, a function of coerced choices or a side effect of unconscious decisions … my life, my body, my 'individual existence' becomes part of another world, of foreign cultures, religions, histories and global interdependencies, without my realizing or expressly wishing it. (Beck, 2006: 19)

Thus Beck proposes cosmopolitanisation as ambivalent potential, as latent cosmopolitanism. Despite this, he does not centrally engage with the ques-tions he himself poses, such as 'Reality is becoming cosmopolitan … but how does the cosmopolitanization of reality become conscious?' (Beck, 2006: 68). More promising in this regard is Gerard Delanty's (2006) discussion of 'the cosmopolitan imagination' and the constitutive role of 'global publics' in culturally interpenetrated societies. Delanty is inter-ested in how situated ideas of 'post-universalistic' cosmopolitanism can ask normative questions about alternative social formations and visions. Like Beck, his approach suggests that it is partly through social actors being increasingly constrained to interpret and negotiate cosmopolitanisation. Integration into a volatile global economy and a mesh of transnational connections between people, places and nations unsettle established notions of society, and it is 'through the interplay of self, other and world that cosmopolitan processes come into play' (Delanty, 2006: 40–1). In proposing a triangulation which challenges the 'us–them'/'self–other' dichotomies discussed above, Delanty argues that cosmopolitan possibilities emerge from the reflexive awareness of global connectivity:

> Rather than see cosmopolitanism as a particular or singular condition that either exists or does not, a state or goal to be realized, it should instead be seen as a cultural medium of societal transformation that is based on the principle of world openness. (Delanty, 2006: 27)

This principle of world openness is not dispassionately arrived at through ethical reflection, but is instead a product of global surveillance, the awareness that 'the world is watching', as articulated by Taoiseach Bertie Ahern immediately after the 'Love Ulster' riots in Dublin in 2006 (Reid and Lally, 2006). Delanty discusses this form of reflexivity as a product of the 'global public', which is less about defined and embodied audiences than about the recognition that mediated flows of images also mediate everyday life, shaping a shared 'space which is increasingly mutually referential and reinforcive' (Silverstone, 2006: 5). The 'global public', then, is a notion which suggests that 'our' national debates and actions are increasingly aware of debates, incidents and ideologies from 'elsewhere':

> The global public has a major resonance in all communication in the sense that it structures and contextualises much of public discourse.... The global public is inside as well as outside national publics and is the central dynamic in cosmopolitanism, conceived of as an opening of discursive spaces and which has a critical function in shaping the social world … the constitution of the social world in and through globally filtered processes of communication cannot be seen in simple terms of Self and Other, terms which are often attractive illusions for many social scientists and social commentators. (Delanty, 2006: 37)

In Delanty's argument, this nascent sense of global immanence leads to forms of self-problematisation – how the 'world' may evaluate relationships between 'self and other' as played out, for example, in discussions of migration – and hence possibilities for ongoing transformation. Yet this notion of the 'global public' is also ambivalent. As Bella Dicks has argued, powers of display have become centrally important to global competitiveness, and state agencies and national actors have been required to project images that overlap in their appeal to tourists, investors and to an undefined yet powerful sense of global surveillance (Dicks, 2004). Nation states – articulated through the frame of national cultures and iconic places – must present 'legible and coherent' narratives and symbols of particularity and conformity (Dicks, 2004: 17). Politically, states may face disapproval unless they 'display cosmopolitanism upon the global screen' (Urry, 2003: 133), that is, mediate themselves through discourses accepted as cosmopolitan: human rights (cf. Douzinas, 2006), multiculturalism, integration and 'diversity'. In the Irish narrative of exceptional globalisation, the global public has been seen less as an unsettling witness and more as an adoring audience, involved in a dialogic exchange between self-understandings and 'the imaginings and fantasies that others have of us' (Keohane and Kuhling, 2004: 142–3). A 'cosmopolitan Ireland' is an emerging form of self-understanding derived from this sanctioned range of representations, one which informs interested global publics that change is seamless, not unsettling.

To whom it may concern, it's the late hate show

These theoretical dynamics require different forms of illustration; *The Late Late Show*[2] of 13 October 2006 provided an instructive compression of the interplay. Introducing the evening's show before and after RTÉ's *Nine O'Clock News*, the host, Pat Kenny, informed his not insubstantial public that 'tonight we ask, is it time to tell our Muslim immigrants to adapt to our ways, or go home'?[3] It is unclear which homes were being alluded to or, indeed, the legal procedures by which culturally recalcitrant immigrants would be conveyed to them. It transpired that what Kenny had in mind was a 'mature and open' debate on the alarming incidence of *niqabs* and *burqas* on the streets and laneways of Ireland. Inspired by Jack Straw's attempts to induce a similarly mature and open debate in contemporary wartime Britain,[4] this pedagogy of the oppressive is congruent with the trend in Irish public opinion that cautions the newly receptive nation to learn from the fissures of Britain's 'parallel societies' (Titley, 2008). However, the discursive function of the 'covered women' is fully revealed only in the context of the show as a whole.

The show began with Michael Barrymore's ('I lost me and got me back') discussion of marriage breakdown, mid-life coming out, addiction and depression. He was followed by former Miss Ireland Olivia Treacy ('we live in a world that is not kind to the ageing process'), Kerry Katona ('I found out I was bi-polar last year after rehab') and Take That's Gary Barlow ('discovering real life saved me'). Kenny then introduced the Festival Polski ('evidence of a changing society') and as 'something for our Polish viewers' he presented the Polish singer Kayah; she thanked him in Polish, he responded in Irish. However, multiculturalism is not always so mutually enriching. Returning to his earlier foray into biopolitics, Pat Kenny, Yvonne Ridley, Ruth Dudley Edwards and John Waters discussed the radical 'social discomfort' veiled women introduce into our societies. Dudley Edwards in particular felt unsettled enough to accelerate from the pain of her exclusion to the 7 July 2005 bombings in London, while Waters confronted the politically correct taboo that retards debating these issues openly, and presumably maturely, with the 'Islamic community among us'.

The Late Late Show has been theorised as a stealthy agent of Irish modernity (Pettitt, 1999), gradually but relentlessly addressing social taboos through the exposition of personal testimonies and experiences. With this in mind, what preceded the 'covered women' item unwound as a corroborating show-reel of Irish arrival. The vibrant, energetic, cosmopolitan country is now mature, its implied audience nesting in the 'reinvented Ireland of the Celtic Tiger ... based on the creation of a "modern, liberal progressive multicultural image"' (Kirby *et al.*, 2002: 197). Cultural inclusivity is a natural extension of this mediation, as Kenny's sublime moment of 'you show me yours and I'll show you mine multiculturalism' demonstrates. However, with these credentials established, the televisual flow turns to policing the borders of 'our ways and our norms' by embracing the neo-integrationist paradigms occasioned by the 'war on terror' and a purported crisis of immigration, and the euphemistic discussions of culture which attend to (non-white) non-European migrants (Lentin, 2004).

The 'Muslim turn' in *The Late Late Show* example is undoubtedly sensationalist and opportunistic, but this does not explain it. The contention that a 'debate' saturated in the securitisation of racialised identities in wartime Britain – and further mired in what Paul Gilroy (2004) has critiqued as post-empire melancholia – has immediate purchase in Ireland is informed not by an actual consideration of the 'Muslim community among us' but by the meta-communicative need to negotiate 'thresholds of tolerance'. This is not only because Irish commentators who implore us to learn from the mistakes of British multiculturalism seem incapable of appreciating the specificities of the British postcolonial 'multicultural settlement' (Kundnani, 2002), the spectrum of political critique to which multiculturalism is subject in Britain (cf. Gilroy, 2004; Goodhart, 2004) or the complex social networks of transnational and local affiliation invisible to the mandarins of 'community cohesion' (Werbner, 2005). It is because, as Blommaert and Verschueren (1998: 78) perceptively observe:

> The threshold of tolerance is ... [a] concept that defines the conditions under which the all-European tolerance and openness may be cancelled without affecting the basic self-image. The European does not become intolerant, until this threshold is crossed. Just let him or her step back over the same threshold, i.e. just reduce the number of foreigners again, and the good old tolerance will return. In other words, even in moments of intolerance the European is still tolerant at heart, and the observed behaviour is

completely due to the factual circumstances which render it impossible to exercise this essential openness.

It is here that we can begin to see the ambivalences of the self–other–world relations advanced by Delanty; the socially inconsequential issue of 'covered women' in an Irish context is mediated in this fashion, as it allows a pre-sanctioned European intolerance without diminishing our cosmopolitanism on the 'global screen'. In fact, given the incessant construction of Europe's Muslim population as a racial–civilisational anomaly and security threat (Sparks, 2006), it allows a performance of righteous control over cosmopolitanisation's darker ambivalences. The 'beautiful Kayah' is a gendered accessory to the delineation of the threshold of tolerance, and the barely sublimated racial politics cannot be understood without the contrapuntal presence of Poland and its migrants. Kayah allows the fiction of a Polish audience – the global public in the national – integrated within the public ritual of *Late Late Show* viewership, and the performance of mutual appreciation and interculturalism. She is both a witness to our cosmopolitanism and a subject of the dynamics of cosmopolitan appropriation.

Kayah and our Polish viewers are evidence of a 'changing society' because they are held to make material and symbolic contributions to it, not the least of which is their mediated testimony to Irish world openness. In the logic of selective appropriation, they witness the intercultural reasonableness of 'our ways and our norms' – ironically represented here by a parade of fading and mainly British celebrities – and give an alibi to the regretful limits of our tolerance transgressed by the 'covered women' and their internationally proscribed incompatibility. For Irish cosmopolitanism to define its exteriority – 'the outside needed by the inside' – it needs testimony that the borders are actually demanded by those who 'seek exclusion', in behaviour if not in voice. Indeed, in concentrating racial anxieties on permissible targets, the 'veil debate' has become a classic threshold of tolerance. Kevin Myers, for example, has borrowed the argument ventilated in France and the Netherlands that rejecting the veil is nothing more than a rejection of the initial rejection; 'the burqa proclaims its wearer's modesty, and is an insulting and explicit declaration of the immodesty of women who do not wear it' (Myers, 2005; cf. Buruma, 2006).

Yet this abject racialisation is almost beside the point. The discussion is of performative control in a changing society; Muslims are here, to a degree, symbolic of cosmopolitanisation and fantasies of revocable cultural change. This is not to suggest that such mediations do not have a social impact; they not only compound mainstream Islamophobia but also serve to obscure the forms of discrimination Polish workers and dwellers continue to face in Ireland.[5] But even this limited, if rich, example does suggest that the interplay of self–world–other as a cultural medium of transformation does not easily lead to the transformative self-problematisations theorised by Delanty. Nonetheless, this interplay is infused with reflexive attention to a global public, from Kenny's cultural self-authentication through the *cúpla focal* to the eager acceptance of the latest trends in racialisation from Paris, Amsterdam and London (not to mention Bavaria and Flanders).

Appropriation and exclusion in the mediation of Ireland

The Late Late Show example is important only insofar as it illustrates ongoing processes of discursive framing and construction found in wider public debates concerning Ireland as a 'cosmopolitan society'. The strategic appropriation of Kaya and 'our Polish friends' is part of the everyday logic of what Ghassan Hage has described as 'multiculturalism without migrants' (Hage, 1998) or, in more elaborated terms, 'global middle class multi-culturalism' (Hage, 2003). A 'multiculturalism without migrants' clearly does not mean invisibility but, in fact, precisely the opposite: stylised and aestheticised tableaux of difference and diversity – from 'the way we live today' advertisements for the Centra retail chain to 'Ireland Embracing Cultural Diversity' (the National Action Plan Against Racism) – project cultural diversity, though shorn of the baggage of *race* and geometries of power and inequality (Benn Michaels, 2006).

Irish society is far from unique in its consumption of the symbolic meaning of migrants, for example in the stylised multicultural milieu of the Celtic Tiger assembled by advertisers (O'Boyle, 2006). The fusion of migration with the accelerated circulation of commodities and images in an affluent consumer society to create a semiotically diverse environment is perfectly – if unintentionally – captured in the 'Hiberno-Cosmopolitan' of David McWilliams' imagination (2005). The conspicuous hybridity of the 'Hi-Co' is precisely that of global middle-class multiculturalism, marrying the enhanced cultural capital derived from a discerning negotiation of 'diversity' with a heightened if equally stylised appreciation of aspects of Irish culture. This dynamic of appropriation is hardly remarkable in late-capitalist consumer society; however, the range of ways in which 'migrants' are assigned semiotic labour in Irish public discourse is striking. 'Migrants' to Ireland are brandished as witnesses to the fact that 'there are few better places in the world to live' (O'Brien, 2006), as embodiments of the general cultural dynamism of the nation, and occasionally as a mild corrective: the spirituality and organic tendency towards community of 'migrants' may be an antidote to the coarser excesses of the individualism and consumerism widely discussed in the meltdown of the Celtic Tiger (Fitzpatrick, 2006).

The mutuality of appropriation and exclusion displayed in *The Late Late Show* play out in the discursive frameworks employed to narrate and 'manage' migration, where migration acts as a synthesising focus for controlling the ambivalences and anxieties of globalisation. 'Multiculturalism' – a contested and enormously complex site of situated philosophies, policies and practices (Watson, 2000) – is a close relation of cosmopolitanism, not only in its default liberal celebration of 'good migrants' as a form of national Viagra, but in the ways in which it constructs perspectives on socio-cultural change that implicitly avoid the forms of self-problematisation theorised by Delanty. In other words, 'multiculturalism', as downloaded in Irish debate, is often a way of talking about change without really engaging with it. This avoidance is both philosophical and discursive. In conceptual terms, Ronit Lentin's (2002) examination of 'disavowed multiculturalism' has become the touchstone critique of multiculturalism's particularisation in Ireland: dissecting how top-down multiculturalist structures reinsert hegemonic power relations while pretending to dismantle them, and arguing for a 'politics of interrogating' the legacies of Irish emigration and racialised identities to replace soothing discussions about recognising different cultures and respecting cultural difference derived from the 'politics of recognition' (cf. Taylor, 1994).

In practice, however, the prevalence of multiculturalism – or *interculturalism*, as it is frequently rebranded – owes much to its power and possibilities as an 'ideological franchise' (Kirby *et al.*, 2002: 14). The apparent obviousness of what multiculturalism is and what it leads to implies that 'mature and open' debates concerning it are rarely informed by analysis of Irish society, but by arid typologies of 'multiculturalists' and 'integrationists' and pre-digested exchanges of value positions. Thus David Quinn, in an *Irish Independent* article entitled 'Walking over majorities to usher in the minorities' (2007), felt able to assert that 'the meaning of multiculturalism is to give minorities rights at the expense of the majority' with no more empirical evidence than a reference to Muslim taxi drivers at a US airport being allowed to refuse to transport alcohol. As he helpfully instructs:

> Let's make this as down to earth as possible. If a guest comes into your house, you will make every effort to make them feel as welcome as possible. But how would you react if the guest suddenly demanded that you throw out the drinks in the cabinet, remove the holy picture from the mantelpiece, and that your wife covers up her shoulders?

The imagined guest is, inevitably, an imagined Muslim, and this triumph of the imagination avoids discussing the cosmopolitanisation of Ireland in favour of throwing comforting shapes. The ambiguous reflex of the

'global public' is instrumental here; it could be argued that the utility
of multiculturalism as an ideological franchise arises because rejections
of multiculturalism's excesses are widely rehearsed and pre-sanctioned,
and discursively established regardless of the specificities of migration
and dwelling in Ireland. Thus, for all the sound and fury of apparently
foundational clashes, it is again an enactment of narratives of control, the
celebration and rejection of multiculturalism without migrants.

The meta-narrative of control and exceptionality persists in the recent
shift from 'multiculturalism' and 'interculturalism' to the similarly franchised rubric of *integration*. A listener to radio phone-in shows or, indeed,
government-sponsored initiatives on citizenship, witnessing discussions
about the social impact of commuting, urban sprawl, poor public infrastructure, substance abuse and the fear of violent crime, would be forgiven
for being puzzled about the nature of the integrated entity migrants are
expected to integrate with. Yet, once again, this substantive evaluation
is beside the point; it is the mediated logic which is important. As Breda
Gray argues in a critique of 'integration' in policy discourse, the logics of
integration reproduce a comforting relationship between 'tolerant, inclusive nationals' and 'migrants' who are always in need of integration and
thus always already excluded (Gray, 2006). Integration is a more explicitly
mediated and performative discourse, offering, as it does, the cognitive
surety of a social end that will always be just out of reach, while ordering
and classifying forms of presence and the impacts of cosmopolitanisation;
'integration is never achieved but is a promise held out to migrants and
reminds them of their status as matter out of place' (Gray, 2006: 138).

Integration is a discourse calibrated to the demands of what Thomas
De Zengotita (2005: 159) has termed 'the performative politics of a mediated world' or, in more mundane terms, being seen to do something,
enacting control over the uncontrollable. In this instance, as Gray argues
(2006: 139), integration confirms the fantasy that national borders and
populations can be controlled amid the 'speed and globalised nature of
capitalist development' while normalising the classification of 'migrants'
into the 'tolerated and the unacceptable' (Gray, 2006: 137) – the dialectic
Kayah and the 'covered women' were coerced into embodying.

The reproduction of racialised differentiations of migrant utility and
hierarchy is an international process eagerly particularised to Irish governmentality, and one embedded in modernity's will to classify and discipline
ambivalent and irreducible heterogeneity (Bauman, 2000; Goldberg,
2002). Yet such fantasies of control have a specific significance in Ireland,
as evidenced by the teleological particularisation of 'multiculturalism'
and 'integration'. Ireland's need for flexible and mobile migrant labour is
not only generically in conflict with the banal nationalist assumptions of

territorial integrity; this human mobility has come to stand for the risk and uncertainty of *cosmopolitanisation*, while providing political possibilities for asserting control. This assertion has become crucial as the myth of cost-free globalisation – the 'most globalised' yet most particular people – has been eroded in a variety of ways.

The first wave of critiques of the mythology of the Celtic Tiger (Kirby *et al.*, 2002; Coulter and Coleman, 2003; Keohane and Kuhling, 2004) pinpointed the ways in which astute governance and endogenous cultural competence were established as explanatory starting points for the astonishing harnessing of economic globalisation. As Michael O'Sullivan has suggested in a more recent critique, these wonders of design are beginning to be seen as a 'coincidence with external factors' (O'Sullivan, 2006: 1). He notes that 'a profound and underestimated' effect of globalisation has been how it raises people's expectations, particularly when the transformation of society has been attributed to grand design and the 'totemic' strength and confidence of the Celtic Tiger (Keohane and Kuhling, 2004: 144). The gradual erosion of this bullish confidence can be attributed to the lop-sided nature of Irish globalisation, where transformations in infrastructure, in social provision such as health and education and in comparative indices of equality and human development are subjects of internal political criticism and have the potential to shame 'on the global screen' (see O'Sullivan, 2006: 7–10). Moreover, the latency of neoliberal certainties in the orthodox explanations of the Celtic Tiger is increasingly overt in the transfer of fiscal risk from the public to the private, and in the 'increasing privatisation of state enterprises and also in the creeping privatisation of public goods like healthcare and education' (O'Sullivan, 2006: 7).

As Irish 'exceptional globalisation' is rendered increasingly mundane and vulnerable, the importance of narratives of control over cosmopolitanisation – the condition of global interdependence – increases. Migration increasingly offers a widely sanctioned nexus for these performances, and it is in this context that the mediated, performative politics of the citizenship referendum of June 2004 may be understood. The cynical – and as it turns out, unifying – objectification of another quasi-mythic population threatening the threshold of tolerance allowed for a collective purge without, from the perspective of the state, serious socio-economic consequences. The logic of the referendum recognised that 'migrants' are both proof of cosmopolitanisation and symbolic of it, and that non-cosmopolitan 'migrants' – 'covered women', Nigerian mothers, Afghan asylum seekers seeking sanctuary in a cathedral – may generally be subject to increased biopolitical subjugation without attracting opprobrium from 'global publics'. The prevalent mantra of 'simply bringing our citizenship into line with other European countries' tacitly acknowledged this.

The citizenship referendum was a manifestation of what Ghassan Hage describes as the interiorisation of 'border politics'. Refugees, asylum seekers and 'migrants' embody a threat to the nurturing, caring 'motherland' which requires the 'fatherland' – the regulative, authoritative state – to reassert control and assuage currents of risk and vulnerability. Assertions of the 'integrity' of Irish citizenship – dispensed with scant proof of the degree and nature of the threat to its integrity – seem to provide a fatherly discipline, yet are designed to elide why nurture has been withdrawn:

> The more the nation moves into becoming the non-nurturing social reality of neo-liberal policy, the more this hope for a good motherland becomes unrealistic, with no connection to the immediate empirical reality of the subject. That is, rather than the imaginary of the motherland becoming articulated as a reality that needs protecting, it becomes an increasingly hollow imaginary that needs to be protected from reality … the defensive mechanisms of the fatherland are no longer directed towards ordering and protecting the nurturing motherland from internal and external threats; instead their task is to defend a fantasy of the motherland against the reality of the motherland. (Hage, 2003: 96)

The recent vision of Ireland as a racial state defends a fantasy not only of an 'as if ethnicity' (Beck, 2006: 29) but of a people blessed by globalisation, where motherland and fatherland have parented assiduously, where unintended consequences can be controlled and disciplined, and where, ironically, globally mediated notions of a racialised Irishness are re-presented as 'consoling fictions' (Negra, 2006: 3).

Conclusion: beyond exceptionality

At the time of writing, compensatory fantasies distilled from the appropriation and alienation of non-cosmopolitans have proliferated. Enda Kenny, in a well received speech in January 2007 notable for its repressive intent and banal predictability (see note 1), spoke of the need: to manage immigration in a way that 'keeps Ireland safe'; to assure Ireland's global publics that Ireland is not a 'soft touch'; and to advise 'immigrants' of the need to integrate and 'respect our cultural traditions'. His description of Ireland as a 'Celtic and Christian' country was a well calibrated synthesis of the mediated and reflexive dynamics featured in this argument – 'Christian' manages the feat in an Irish context of being both pluralistic and exclusionist, as well as being a dog whistle antonym for the internationally permissible instrumentalisations of Muslims. While the Minister for Justice, Michael McDowell, took issue with Kenny's exclusionary imagery, he was not reliant on mere rhetoric. His election-era proposals on detention centres for the new racial category of 'non-EU migrants'[6] were consistent with his elaborate exploitation of non-cosmopolitans through biopolitical spectacle. Despite falling numbers of asylum seekers since 2005,[7] draft immigration legislation proposed in September 2006 would prohibit marriage for asylum seekers and non-EU nationals without permanent residence to Irish citizens without ministerial approval (Department of Justice, Equality and Law Reform, 2006; see also Whelan, 2007). Thus the integrity of the motherland is defended through postmodern feudalism, acting out fantasies of resolve and control over 'human waste' surplus to the symbolic and material needs of the dominant society.

The argument in this chapter has linked superficial and porous discourses of cosmopolitanism with emerging and overlapping discourses of multiculturalism and integration in Ireland as a way of interrogating how 'migrants' are appropriated to ongoing constructions of Ireland as a society navigating globalisation. This appropriation and instrumentalisation are intensified by the need to control and impose coherence not only on cosmopolitanisation but also on the myth of exceptional globalisation. The public mediation of a compensatory Irish racial home through the citizenship referendum and the obsession with being seen to administer the lives of un-cosmopolitan others has repressive consequences for the lives of many. Yet they are at least partly motivated by, in Hage's terms, defending the fantasy of the motherland against its far more unsteady and vulnerable reality. The unsettling and problematising relations between self–other–world have proven ambivalent.

Nonetheless, the processual notion of cosmopolitanism advanced by Delanty is important in Ireland for its insistence on how the internal transformation of social and cultural phenomena necessitates more reflexive forms of understanding. In other words, the mediated and performative politics under discussion are in and of themselves *recognition and subsequent avoidance of self-problematisation*. As such, they are also cultural mediums that permit contestation, and in their reliance on constantly securing constitutive exteriors they invite forms of deconstruction that are not limited to academic discussion. Prime among these must be the vogue for *integration* – a discourse of longing in a society coming to terms with the consequences of accelerated globalisation and individualisation. Beyond the spectacularised examples of 'parallel societies' in France and Britain which retard Irish discussions, it is widely argued by a range of analysts that people who migrate also integrate, but in situated ways, modalities and rhythms which evade romanticisation and which programmatic notions of integration cannot recognise, and perhaps do not want to (Hage, 1998, 2003; Gilroy, 2004; Werbner, 2005).

It is hard to escape the suggestion that the emerging vogue for 'integration speak' is another evasion: of the need to articulate the kind of society to which 'migrants' are compelled to integrate, and of the degree of integration which is presumed to exist. In the present moment, the uneven globalisation of Irish society and the forms of inequality which narratives of exceptionality can no longer assuage would suggest that 'integration' is vehemently projected onto 'migrants' as a surrogate social fabric, where well rehearsed articulations of 'our ways and our values' are far more comfortable than proffering visions of what an irrevocably multi-ethnic Ireland could look like. The perpetually displaced promise of integration as an ameliorating end state conceals the paucity of competing social visions produced during a period of supposedly creative and dynamic transformation. Contesting these logics of appropriation, which not only speak for members of the dominant society but also speak *of* its apparently settled shape, may be one dimension of the self-problematisation from whence a more meaningful, critical cosmopolitanism may emerge.

For claims of cosmopolitanism to become more than burnishing the national brand for a global public, mediated discussions of migration need to move away from sterile downloads of internationally franchised models of 'multiculturalism' and its conceptual descendants, and from the polite forms of racial politics currently all the rage in 'old Europe'. A transformative cosmopolitanism will emerge only when the possible futures of an increasingly transnational, multi-ethnic and multinational Ireland are shorn of myths of exceptionality and fantasies of control. An easy rhetoric of 'we are cosmopolitan now' suggests transformation; however, cosmopolitanism is dialogic, and depends on 'them' – a diversity irreducible to an emerging cohort of 'community leaders' – being seen not as an accessory or a burden but as here to stay, and as social agents authoring transformations that cannot be merely branded or wished away.

Notes

1 'Celtic and Christian' nation is taken from a speech by Enda Kenny, the leader of the political party Fine Gael. Kenny's speech to a parliamentary party meeting in Dublin on 23 January 2007 attracted attention and comment, much of it disputing the historical and sociological accuracy of the notion, and some comment pointing out that Kenny had intended this as a vision that augured well for Ireland's dealings with 'migrants'. However, in the logic of mediated politics, the point of Kenny's articulation was a performance of control, of an existing coherence protected and guided by political vision. Set in the context of an election-era speech which focused on deportation policy for migrants convicted of crimes and screening for those coming from outside the European Union with criminal records, the function of the 'Celtic and Christian' is to convey unquestioned and thus unquestionable surety.

2 The show under discussion can be viewed at www.rte.ie/tv/latelate/20061013.html.
3 Kenny repeated the question immediately at the start of the show, amending it slightly to 'adapt to our ways and our norms'. In the subsequent discussion, 'going home' was not mentioned or discussed.
4 Jack Straw raised the issue of 'comfort' and communicating with women in *niqab* in a widely discussed column in the *Lancashire Telegraph* of 5 October 2006.
5 In November 2006, for example, the Irish Services, Industrial, Professional and Technical Union (SIPTU) and the Polish trade union Solidarnosc signed a cooperation agreement aimed at tackling continued exploitation of Polish workers in several sectors of the Irish economy. See www.siptu.ie/CampaignsandCurrentIssues/ ExploitationandDisplacement/Name,9457,en.html.
6 In a speech to the Law Society of Ireland on 28 January 2007, the Minister for Justice suggested amending the Immigration and Residence Protection Bill to include provisions for detention centres for asylum seekers from countries deemed to involve 'high-risk' (i.e. groundless) applications. At the time of writing, it is unclear whether or not such a suggestion remains as a passing articulation of control or whether it will be acted upon.
7 According to government statistics reported in the *Irish Times*, asylum applications to Ireland for 2006 were the lowest for almost ten years, a decrease attributed to an overall decrease in asylum applications in the EU as well as to 'the change in citizenship rules for children of foreign nationals'. Despite or perhaps because of this, asylum seekers have re-emerged as the favoured subject of biopolitical control. As well as the detention centres aimed primarily at black African 'migrants' and asylum seekers, the proposed Immigration and Residence Protection Bill contains restrictions on the right to marry of asylum seekers and of all non-EU nationals on temporary or non-renewable residence permits. Marriages to Irish citizens must be given exempted status at the discretion of the Minister for Justice, and being party to a non-exempted marriage is a criminal offence. In a submission, the Irish Human Rights Commission (2006: 12) has argued that such a clear interference with human rights protected under the European Convention would demand the explication of the pressing social aim informing the legislation, and a further justification of how it constitutes a response proportionate to the need: 'A difference in treatment can only be justified where it pursues a legitimate aim, and where the means employed are proportionate to the legitimate aim pursued'. Given that no such justification is elaborated, and in the context of significantly diminished asylum claims, the racialised and performative aspect of the provision becomes more clearly articulated.

11

The politics of redirecting social policy: towards a double movement

MARY MURPHY

This chapter examines the direction of change in recent Irish social policy in the context of Ireland's neoliberal macro environment and elaborates an argument as to how social policy reform could contribute to a democratic and egalitarian Ireland. It argues that a shift to a more positive social policy and more equitable outcomes will require a corresponding shift in power and in the structures of governance. The first section briefly outlines the nature of the Irish social security system (the past) and the next reflects on how Irish income-maintenance policy has developed over the last two decades (the present) in the context of an increasingly neoliberal macro policy. The chapter then reviews the debate prompted by the proposal from the National Economic and Social Council (NESC) for a developmental welfare state (NESC, 2005) and subsequent policy proposals to develop a more active social policy (the future). Having reflected on the likely direction for income-maintenance policy over the next two decades, the chapter argues that the proposed policy direction will not necessarily enhance efficiency or equity but will redefine the concept of citizenship for those on low incomes and particularly for women. A further section examines social policy governance and asks what governance process might make egalitarian outcomes more likely (the politics). The chapter concludes by highlighting what needs to be done to maximise the potential transformative role of civil society.

The past

Irish income-maintenance policy has its roots in nineteenth-century English Poor Law and in the UK National Insurance Act 1908. Post-independence Ireland inherited a mixed welfare system based on means-tested social assistance payments and flat-rate social insurance payments. Both types of payments were characterised by a focus on 'less eligibility', where social welfare rates, in order to preserve work incentives, were set at rates considerably below the lowest subsidence wage of the time. Ireland was distinguished from the UK by the Catholic and nationalist nature of its political culture (reflected in the family focus of the 1937 constitution) and an inability to finance any significant expansion of Irish social security until the 1970s. Catholic social policy principles of self-reliance and subsidiarity fitted well with this ungenerous liberal welfare regime. While the transformative UK Beveridge report of 1942 was debated in Ireland, it was not until the 1960s that economic growth allowed some expansion of Irish social security policy (Cousins, 2005).

It is difficult to locate most national regimes in international welfare-state typologies. Irish income-maintenance policy has been characterised by Titmuss (1956) as a residual laggard welfare regime with a heavy reliance on social assistance means-tested payments. Although it has been fairly critiqued on gender and methodological grounds (Van Hoorhis, 2002), modern debate about comparative welfare regimes still focuses on Esping-Andersen's *The Three Worlds of Welfare Capitalism* (1990) and his typology of liberal, conservative and social democratic welfare regimes. Many argue that Ireland either does not fit into any of Esping-Andersen's ideal types (Cousins, 1995; O'Donnell, 1999; Boyle, 2005) or is a hybrid system (NESC, 2005). Others, while acknowledging the liberal nature of Irish social security, describe Ireland as cross-cutting, due to its corporatism (McLaughlin, 2001), or moving from a conservative to a liberal regime (McCashin, 2004). Castles and Mitchell (1993) stress the importance of culture in an alternative 'families of nations' typology, which includes a fourth 'radical' category to account for Australia and New Zealand. They conclude that Ireland is a hybrid of liberal and radical welfare regime models. Leibfried (1993) developed a fourth, 'Latin rim' category to account for southern European welfare regimes. Because of Irish peripherality and Catholicism and its agricultural economy, he associated Ireland with this Latin rim typology. Therefore, it can be seen that while Ireland's welfare state was clearly influenced by the Anglo-Saxon models of liberal English-speaking regimes, other cultural and political factors also influenced its development.

While Ireland's general welfare state (including health, education, housing and social services) may accurately be described as mixed or hybrid, the social security system has many features associated with a liberal, residual or Anglo-Saxon welfare regime. These include a Poor Law legacy of 'less eligibility', ungenerous social welfare payments associated with low replacement ratios (RRs),[1] an exceptionally high proportion of means-tested payments (NESC, 2005: 98) and flat-rate social insurance payments. Even taking into account both public and private spending on social inclusion, the Organisation for Economic Co-operation and Development (OECD) has found that Ireland is a low spender on social protection, by EU standards (see NESC, 2005: 113). Relative to its wealth, whether measured as gross national product (GNP) or gross domestic product (GDP), Ireland has low levels of social expenditure or transfer effort. Finally, when evidence of welfare outcomes is reviewed, Ireland ranks among the countries with the highest levels of relative poverty and income inequality in the OECD. It is little wonder, therefore, that many classify it as a liberal welfare regime (Pierson, 2001; O'Connor, 2003; Dukelow, 2004; O'Connor, 2005; Murphy, 2006).

Gender, racial and health or disability typologies have also been developed to capture how structural features of social security exclude certain groups from forms of social protection. Awareness of how the social security system directly and indirectly discriminates between different social groups will become more relevant as globalisation and associated pressures produce ever more vulnerabilities and social risks. Lewis (1992) firmly located Ireland as a strong male-breadwinner social security regime, with a household payment structure, low female labour-market participation and weak childcare provisions. Bradshaw and Shaver (1995) associated Ireland with countries that gave generous support to women's care role in the home. As more women enter the labour market, social policy is challenged to play its traditional role of supporting women in the home while enabling greater economic participation of women (Mahon, 2004). The Irish state's ambiguity on this issue is reflected in the slow evolution of a childcare infrastructure and the low level of support for women in the labour market (Coakley, 2005; Murphy and O'Connor, 2008). More recently, the Irish social security regime has begun to display a sharp racial segregation or division, where habitual residents are defined as the only legitimate receivers of welfare, and asylum seekers are segregated from mainstream social security (Geddes, 2003).

Reviewing options for the development of social security raises some central questions. How can Ireland move from a liberal regime that stresses efficiency over equity and results in greater income inequality (Sapir, 2006)? How can Ireland reduce significant class, gender and racial segregation and develop a regime that can produce more equitable outcomes that lessen rather than strengthen social divisions?

The present

There is substantial evidence over the last twenty years of movement from a redistributive welfare state to a productivist reordering of social policy to meet economic needs (Murphy, 2006; Kirby and Murphy, 2008). This is consistent with neoliberalism. From the mid-1990s, the OECD (1994) Jobs Study and the Expert Working Group on the Integration of the Tax and Social Welfare Systems (1996) signalled a strong productivist agenda. The focus on employment as a key driver of competitiveness meant policy has focused on the promotion of work incentives. This is characterised by policy initiatives to reform child income support and family income supplement, to promote individualisation of the tax system, to reduce the value of pay-related social insurance benefits and to tax social benefits. The focus on employment and activation is also characterised by an increased investment in education, training and active labour market measures and a debate about how to promote a more active social policy which not only promotes employment but in fact obliges people to work. The development of Irish social security is increasingly characterised by a new regulatory approach, by the privatisation of pensions and by new public management-inspired changes in social security delivery (all features of a more neoliberal policy approach). All of this points to a more efficient regime.

Real levels of expenditure grew substantially over the same period, almost doubling in real terms, from €2,918 million in 1985 to €6,714 million in 2000 and €11,291 million in 2004. Real increases in social welfare payments have contributed to reductions in the proportion of people living in deprivation-based consistent poverty (living below 60 per cent of median disposable income and experiencing enforced deprivation) from 15 per cent in 1997 (Government of Ireland, 1997) to 6 per cent in 2005 (Government of Ireland, 2007). However, welfare effort, defined as social welfare expenditure as a percentage of GNP, halved from 14.6 per cent of GNP in 1985 to 7.8 per cent in 2000, before rising to 9.2 per cent in 2004.[2] Demographic factors and a substantial decrease in unemployment might explain some lower social protection spending in Ireland relative to other OECD countries; however, growth in Irish social welfare spending has not kept pace with growth in Irish GDP or GNP, a situation Alber and Standing (2000) describe as 'arrested development'. With little change in the high reliance on means-tested payments, there is evidence of significant inequality (see table 11.1) and a shift in the risk of poverty towards the non-labour-market poor.

The NESC's (2005) *Developmental Welfare State* document acknowledges that more equitable income support systems have more generous welfare rates. The clear correlation between increased social welfare rates and reductions in income inequality means commitments to increase social welfare rates are a litmus test for wider commitments to equality. Despite considerable debate in Ireland (National Pensions Board, 1998; Government of Ireland, 2001) there is no formal commitment to adopt

Table 11.1 Trends in inequality, 1994–2005

	1994	1998	2001	2003	2005	Change, 1994–2005
Relative income poverty[a]						
50 per cent	6.0	9.9	12.9	11.6	10.8	Increase
60 per cent	15.6	19.8	21.9	19.7	18.5	Increase
70 per cent	26.7	26.9	29.3	27.7	28.2	Increase
Income inequality						
S80/20[b]	5.1	5.0	4.5	5.0	5.0	Steady
Gini[c]	33	33	29	31	32	Decline
Income distribution[d]						
20 per cent	8.6	8.1	8.0	7.9	7.9	−0.7
20–40 per cent	12.0	12.2	12.9	12.8	12.3	0.3
40–60 per cent	16.5	16.9	17.9	18.2	17.0	0.5
60–80 per cent	23.2	22.9	23.2	24.1	22.6	−0.6
Top 20 per cent	39.7	40.0	38.2	37.0	40.1	0.4
Richest/poorest[e]						
0–10 per cent decile	3.8	3.5	3.3	3.0	3.2	−0.6
90–100 per cent decile	24.4	24.2	23.3	23.8	25.6	+1.2

[a] Relative income poverty: percentage living under a particular poverty line (expressed as a specific percentage of average disposable household income).
[b] S80/20: ratio of share of the top 20 per cent of the income distribution to the bottom 20 per cent of the income distribution.
[c] Gini coefficient: an alternative summary measurement of income inequality – the lower the Gini coefficient, the lower the inequality.
[d] Distribution of total national income across five equal parts (quintiles) of the population (poorest 20 per cent, 20–40 per cent, 40–60 per cent, 60–80 per cent, richest 20 per cent).
[e] Comparison of income of poorest 10 per cent and richest 10 per cent of the population (measuring and comparing by dividing the total population into deciles).
Sources: Walsh (2007: 28); Conference of Religious of Ireland (2007: 24).

meaningful social security adequacy benchmarks or indexation formulas that might keep social security incomes on a par with the growth in average earnings, thereby tackling rising relative poverty (defined as living below 60 per cent of median earnings). The 2007 *National Action Plan for Social Inclusion* simply commits the government to maintaining social welfare payments at present levels, and even this commitment is contingent on sufficient resources being available (Government of Ireland, 2007). Nor does the plan adopt any target in relation to income inequality. Containing costs and maintaining flexibility in the face of international trends have outweighed any moves towards indexation, which might benefit people living on low and precarious incomes. Likewise, governments have sought to avoid new costs by ignoring emerging social needs, including those associated with migration. There has been no decision to individualise social welfare payments, a key requirement to address gender inequality and the increased risk of poverty experienced by women. Nor has there been any targeting of child income support towards low-income families with children.

It seems the recent past has consolidated the Anglo-Saxon social security regime in Ireland. Sapir's European welfare typology distinguishes the efficient but unequal Anglo-Saxon (UK, Irish and Portuguese) models from the efficient and equal Nordic models (Austria, Denmark, Sweden, Finland, Netherlands) (Sapir, 2006: 380). He also identifies inefficient and unequal Mediterranean models (Spain, Greece, Italy) and the equal but inefficient continental models of Belgium, Germany, France and Luxembourg. Sapir's analysis suggests there is an optimum combination of policy that maximises equality and efficiency. We can conclude that Ireland could do significantly more to address inequality and that this could be done without threatening or jeopardising efficiency.

The future

It has been concluded that Irish social policy has moved towards greater efficiency. However, given Ireland's keenly felt pressures of international competitiveness, one might have expected that an emphasis on welfare to work would have appeared sooner and to have been stronger (National Economic and Social Forum, 2000; Sweeney and O'Donnell, 2003; Loftus, 2005; One Parent Exchange Network, 2006). Specifically, there has been little progress relating to women's access to employment and there is no policy to index or upgrade 'income disregards' (those means-tested allowances which protect people from unemployment traps, when they are financially worse off from employment). Relative to other liberal regimes, there are fewer requirements to find work and there has been less extension of these to women, lone parents and people with disabilities. In fact, it is only with the publication in 2005 of the NESC's *Developmental Welfare State* document that Irish income-maintenance policy came to reflect the intensity of debate about welfare to work that other liberal regimes and small open economies experienced in the mid-1990s.

The NESC proposal represents a key moment in building consensus about a new Irish welfare state regime. The NESC conceptualises a 'developmental welfare state' with three overlapping domains of welfare state activity: core services, activist measures and income supports. It argues that, in contemporary Ireland, access to core services has 'a wholly new resonance; they underpin the social and economic participation of an increasingly diverse population and enhance labour market flexibility and competitiveness' (NESC, 2005: 155) and emphasises the need for a social dividend to avoid the tipping point where the middle classes may be tempted to abandon support for universal public services. At a local level, the developmental welfare state requires innovative, proactive measures, whereby non-governmental organisations respond to unmet social needs (NESC, 2005: 157–8). There is an attempt to develop a standards-based framework and to rethink governance and regulation issues relating to service contracts for non-governmental organisations in the private and not-for-profit sectors. With regard to income support, the NESC proposal reflects an emerging policy consensus to promote greater social and economic participation and the NESC recommends the extension of conditional work requirements to groups traditionally outside the labour market (O'Connor, 2005).

The NESC proposes that income support measures be differentiated, based on life stages, with particular emphasis on children and the elderly. All others are 'working age' (Cousins, 2005). This focus on working age has shifted Irish social policy into a new paradigm, where social policy is expected to support lifetime attachment to the labour force and participation in employment or other social activities. While the NESC argues for a wide interpretation of participation, it also stresses social inclusion grounded in participation in the labour force and education, arguing that:

> meaningful participation of some form is a legitimate expectation of people of working age (both their expectation of society and society's expectation of them) and that, only in rare cases, should it be accepted that an individual does not have some capacity to develop a greater degree of self-reliance. (NESC, 2005: 219)

It is reasonable to accept that, for most people of working age, participation in paid employment is possible. The 2007 *National Action Plan for Social Inclusion* adopts a strategy to reduce the numbers of working-age social welfare claimants by 20 per cent. However, what of those who cannot participate or whose form of participation is insufficient to lift them out of poverty? What of the income needs of those who choose to pursue some other form of unpaid meaningful activity, such as full-time parenting? Four issues arise here: the level of generosity of the welfare system for those who cannot exercise an employment route out of poverty; the degree to which policy can protect against in-work poverty; the degree of autonomy or choice afforded to welfare recipients; and the degree of state support for those with parenting obligations. With regard to the first, the *Developmental Welfare State* recommends that people of working age should receive a 'basic payment' to enable a 'minimum threshold of income adequacy' to 'guarantee them access to the basic necessities of life' (NESC, 2005: 219) and argues that the target in the *National Action Plan for Social Inclusion* (€150 per week in 2002 terms by 2007) is 'the minimum justified by the present circumstances'. This policy has been affirmed in the 2007 *National Action Plan on Social Inclusion* and in the *Towards 2016* national agreement. However, this level compares poorly to relatively high Dutch and Danish replacement ratios (NESC, 2005: 19). Such a payment would not offer a decent level of social protection and would lock Ireland into a more liberal model, with inequitable outcomes.

Irish social policy assumes a job to be an effective route out of poverty. In 2005, only 1.7 per cent of those in employment were experiencing consistent poverty. However, the number of people in employment at risk of poverty (i.e. those whose household disposable income is less than 60 per cent of national median income) increased from 3.2 per cent in 1994 to 7.4 per cent in 2000 and 9.8 per cent in 2005 (Whelan *et al.*, 2003; Central Statistics Office, 2005a). In-work poverty is likely when low-waged workers are also heads of households, with no other adult working and/or with child dependants. Lone parents are particularly vulnerable, as childcare reduces the possibility of full-time work; low-paid married men with children and non-working spouses are also a high-risk group. Those working in non-standard employment (i.e. in either a temporary or a part-time job) are most at risk of being 'working poor' (Nash, 2004; McCabe, 2006) and lack access to training, pension, health, insurance or sick pay coverage. Policy requires measures targeted at 'working poor' households, for example childcare provision that gives spouses access to employment and lone parents increased hours of employment, maximising take-home pay by improving the family income supplement or by targeted in-work tax breaks, refundable tax credits or enhanced child income support. Education and training policy can play a longer-term role by enhancing the skills levels of low-paid workers and their children and enabling them to break free of occupational segregation. Finally, there is no tracking of the types of employment that unemployed people are accessing through the National Employment Action Plan process, although the economic consultancy Indecon (2005) concludes that most unemployed are exiting the Live Register to low-paid jobs.[3] There was no target in the 2007 social inclusion strategy to limit the increase in the numbers of low-paid workers in poverty, nor was there a policy to monitor trends.

Framing the anti-poverty debate around work requirements can reinforce a type of 'neoliberal individualism' which fails to acknowledge the constraints implied by human interdependency. To date, women are being asked to change their expectations and place themselves on a work continuum. However, little has been done to change the world of care or work to accommodate women's care and employment needs. Without this, women are likely to end up in non-standard and part-time employment; such employment, as we have already seen, is not a route out of poverty (Nash, 2004). Including a care ethic in labour market and employment policy is thus a key requirement for women. There is less equality in the sharing of household tasks between men and women in Ireland than elsewhere (McGinnity *et al.*, 2005). Initiatives to increase the number of working aged in paid employment need to increase the number of hours men spend in unpaid activity and encourage, or indeed compel, men to change their behaviour or broaden the scope of their household activities (Williams, 2004: 13).[4]

One of the major obstacles to achieving a better work–life balance or family-friendly policy is the attitudes of employers who fear greater flexibility for employees will threaten competitiveness. Yet the evidence from Nordic countries shows high levels of compatibility between competitiveness and work–life balance. However, such is the national reverence for competitiveness in the Irish national psyche that even the principle of 'an opportunity to balance work and family commitments' in the 2007 social inclusion strategy has been deliberately qualified and made contingent on being 'consistent with employers' needs' (Government of Ireland, 2007: 40). Employers, rather than providing flexible employment, are increasingly requiring employees to be more and more flexible to suit employers' needs (Duggan and Loftus, 2006; Murphy, 2007). Consideration should now be given to a stronger legislative approach and a regulatory framework for work–life balance (Irvine, 2007).

Full-time family commitments are not on offer in this social inclusion strategy. A labour market strategy that obliges work participation is not necessarily gender or child sensitive and there are potentially negative consequences for child and family well-being from over-concentrating on work solutions to poverty (Sweeney, 2002; O'Brien, 2004; Nicaise, 2004). Various social rights (to care for or to be cared for, to child and family well-being, to a minimum income) could be threatened by an over-zealous or unbalanced approach to employment-based social inclusion. Indeed, this would be the case if government proposals to extend a work obligation to recipients of one-parent family payments and to qualified adults is implemented without due regard for existing care rights of children and parents (Murphy, 2007). A social policy that obliges part-time work without enabling progression to better working conditions will simply lock in poverty (Nash, 2004). It is questionable, from the perspective of the poor, whether the present policy consensus (based on a more conditional but ungenerous means-tested social security system) is a useful direction for Irish income-maintenance policy.

The NESC discourse often refers to the tensions between efficiency and equity or between competitiveness and social inclusion. While arguing that economic and social policy can be made to support each other, the NESC (2005: 1) also argues that 'the social dividend of strong economic performance must take forms that are supportive of the country's ongoing ability to trade advantageously in the world economy'. This suggests social policy is in some way subordinate to economic policy or that efficiency is required before equity.[5] This is consistent with a neoliberal state that prioritises international competitiveness and neoliberal policies of low tax and low social expenditure. An attempt to challenge serious social deficits and inequalities or to conceptualise a social investment state is restricted in the NESC document by an over-emphasis on welfare reform that primarily promotes productivist work-focused values at the expense of care roles. This is consistent with the values of a patriarchal state which under-values care and which passively allows a significant under-representation of women in the political and policy processes. The NESC board which approved the *Developmental Welfare State* document had an 80 per cent gender balance in favour of men. Subsequent political mediation of policy choices offered by the NESC will determine the future direction of welfare reform. But how can change be mediated in a way that rebalances the tendency of a patriarchal competition state away from an overly productivist and inequitable social policy?

The politics

This section considers the political mediation of policy change. Having reflected on recent Irish income support policy and reviewed the content of the NESC's *Developmental Welfare State* and associated policy proposals, the discussion now turns to the dynamic of Irish social policy and what can be done to change it. The discussion focuses on two aspects of social security policy change: why does Irish income policy appear to develop at a slower and less ambitious pace than that of other OECD countries, and what can be done in governance or institutional terms to develop a more equitable policy?

In relation to the first question, path dependence has some explanatory power. The high number of means-tested payments inherited from the past makes restructuring quite complex, and limits the scope and pace of social security reform. This enables those resisting reform to hide behind the complexity of the reform. Change is also rendered less urgent because the Irish social security system is 'lean and mean' and its employment orientation is already broadly consistent with a liberal market economy. High economic growth and the significant growth in employment has meant less pressure to reform and the availability of inward migration to resolve labour market and skills shortages has lessened the pressure to move social security claimants and women into employment.

The nature of the policy system in which policy is developed and decided also determines the type of change that is possible. The NESC's *Developmental Welfare State* reflects the difficulty of promoting debate in a pragmatic political culture with a relatively small, under-resourced social security policy community. Three observations can be made about the political culture in which policy is developed. Ireland is characterised by a number of strong *vetoes*; this leads to a strong consensus style of governance, which can restrict change to small-scale incremental policy change and limit the capacity to implement more significant structural policy reform. Ireland has a narrow form of *coordinative policy discourse*, which engages only a small policy community. A more communicative style of governance is needed to create the type of societal debate that might shift core values and attitudes towards more egalitarian, progressive policy choices. The capacity to 'reinvent' Irish social policy is limited by a '*cognitive lock*', which limits policy makers to examining only that which can be achieved in a low-tax, neoliberal development model (Blyth, 2002). These three features, *vetoes, coordinative discourse* and *cognitive locks*, are now discussed in turn. They combine to reinforce a strong consensus style of governance.

Swank (2002) argues that the type of domestic political institutions and the number of veto points are crucial variables that determine domestic capacity to negotiate restructuring of social security systems. Institutional features of the electoral and political system (e.g. proportional representation, coalition government, a written constitution) and the behaviour of interest groups (e.g. civil servants, social partners and civil society) means Irish political culture is characterised by a significant number of vetoes, so that political actors have a more difficult time negotiating and implementing change (whether regressive or progressive). Ireland's more conservative or consensus-based political culture leans towards consolidation and away from innovation. Tsebelis (2002) and Lijphart (1999) highlight the difference between these Irish consensus institutional features and those found in majoritarian liberal welfare regimes (e.g. Britain, the United States, New Zealand, Canada and Australia). None of the other liberal regimes has this combination of an electoral system based on proportional representation, coalition government and corporatist governance, all of which constitute veto points on more radical change.

This institutional combination is a strong casual factor accounting for Irish path departure from the stronger activation models found in Anglo-Saxon or liberal welfare regimes. In Ditch and Oldfield's (1999) differentiation between 'consolidating' continental European countries and the 'radical innovators' represented by the English-speaking Anglo-Saxon countries, Ireland appears as the exception – an English-speaking liberal regime more inclined to consolidation than radical innovation. An example of this type of consolidation-oriented policy making can be seen in the establishment of the Commission on Social Welfare (CSW) in 1983, the first structural attempt to comment on future options for the social welfare system. Compared with the more negative and threatening UK Fowler report (Lister, 1988), which reviewed UK social security policy options, the CSW produced a positive report that sought to protect basic concepts of the system and that argued for greater generosity, at a time when neoliberal monetarist thinking dominated the international debate. It was a relatively conservative but safe consensus report that has been a positive force in Irish social policy governance. With over 100 recommendations, the report was sufficiently detailed to serve as a 'bible' for senior departmental officials, who regularly turned to it as a source for how to change social security policy incrementally. The CSW's strong focus on consensus protected Irish policy from the more extreme types of change (both progressive and regressive).

This culture of consensus politics pushes the policy-making community away from ideational communicative discourse and towards less controversial problem solving and pragmatic coordinative policy discourse. A dominant governance process which underscores the political culture of consensus is the Irish model of social partnership, where social partners representing the business, trade union, farming and, since 1994, community and voluntary pillars work in common institutions[6] with government to deliberate about economic and social policy. While Cousins (2005: 205) concludes that 'with or without social partnership the Irish social security system would look more or less the same', it is important not to dismiss how social partnership is used by government to garner consensus about reform options. Where such consensus is not found, disagreement on direction can be used to veto change (NESC, 2006: 14). For example, the national agreement Partnership 2000 committed the state to over forty problem-solving processes focused on social inclusion (working groups, taskforces, committees, etc.) some of which serve to take 'off the boil' key policy issues which might otherwise create distributional conflict. The NESC (2006: 13) recognises that social partnership's tendency towards vetoes and towards ruling out radical change can produce the 'lowest common denominator'. However, such vetoes on change may, of course, have a positive function. McCashin *et al.* (2002) attribute the absence of neoliberal rhetoric in Irish social security discourse to social partnership. More broadly, it may be attributed to the 'soft and gentle' (Lijphart, 1999) consensus culture at the heart of Irish policy making.

A core characteristic of the Irish policy style is a conservative approach to policy. Social partnership determines little direct social security change but, since 1987, has played a significant ideational role, building consensus or legitimating the economic development model that sets the context for Irish social policy. Social partnership plays this ideational role by cognitively locking the Irish policy community into a shared understanding based on an economic framework designed to maintain international competitiveness (Kirby, 2002a; Murphy, 2006). This shared understanding is comfortable accommodating high levels of inequality. The early years of the state were dominated by a form of Catholic social teaching which focused on more absolutist forms of poverty reduction and charity (Mahon, 1987; McLaughlin, 2002; Acheson *et al.*, 2004). Addressing equality has never been a core objective of Irish social security policy; rather, there is political acceptance of a 'solidarity without equality' (Ó Riain and O'Connell, 2000: 339). The impact of a shift to more individual values associated with neoliberalism is likely to have further eroded societal support for equality. The patriarchal nature of the state remains markedly ambivalent about women's employment and this is reinforced by unequal gender participation in decision-making matters (O'Connor, 2008). The absence of women and vulnerable groups in such governance processes leads to a focus on protecting the status quo and a limited and conservative menu of policy options. The type of low tax constraints associated with neoliberal economic models and the lack of commitment to the core value of equality differentiates Ireland from other consensus-oriented regimes, which place a higher premium on equality outcomes and achieve a greater equilibrium between social and economic objectives (e.g. the Netherlands and Nordic countries).

The Irish social policy governance process has been transformed in a number of ways, including shifts in participation and the role of social partnership. The international policy community has also had an influence, through, for example, the focus on evidence-based policy making. However, central to governance are the three features identified earlier – the presence of strong institutional and interest-based vetoes, and a coordinative policy discourse embedded in a cognitive lock which restricts policy options to those compatible with a strong variant of a low-tax, flexible political economy. The remaining question is how the governance of income-maintenance policy can be changed to enable the likelihood of more egalitarian outcomes. How can Irish institutions and governance be transformed in a way that makes social policy more ambitious and progressive?

It is not proposed to take the reader into the political debate about reform of proportional representation or social partnership, although both debates are central to answering the question. One less ventilated theme that merits discussion, however, is the participation of civil society and its role in the political construction of policy discourse (Cerny *et al.*, 2005). This space is vital, as it is from here that Polanyi's (1944) 'double movement' or societal reaction to a more productivist or commodified economy and society is likely to emerge.

Frazer (1992) argues 'that public support for the social welfare system is cultivated by open debate and political leadership'. There has been significant debate about the tension over the role of civil society and the community and voluntary sector and how participation in social partnership has affected civil society. Policy debate presently is conducted among a narrow sub-group of policy actors in a tightly controlled coordinative technical discourse in social partnership and other expert fora. Hardiman (1998: 141) concludes that the impact of the community and voluntary pillar is of the 'residual category' and that the growing consultative voice of the sector within and outside formal social partnership 'has not proved enough to change policy priorities'. This sector's capacity to be an effective driver of change has been curtailed by state strategies to control or limit the development of the sector (McCashin, 2004). The Irish state has pro-actively, through funding, regulation and institutional reform, attempted to orientate the community and voluntary sector (and hence civil society) towards a particular development model where it manages its relationship with the state within the narrow confines of social partnership. Since the *Towards 2016* national agreement, the sector has been even more corralled into the confines of a consensus coordinative governance process. This brings considerable opportunity cost for the sector, because such participation is restricted to policy debate that can be progressed within the cognitive lock or shared understanding of the Irish development model. There is less opportunity for more substantive change, which requires ideas to be processed in the type of wide communicative political discourse that is capable of generating social learning and attitudinal change.

One case study illustrates how the community and voluntary sector is perhaps more politically powerful outside the formal confines of social partnership. All the partnership agreements have contained at least a symbolic reference to maintaining and, more recently, to real increases in, the level of social welfare payments. While some genuine progress was evident from 1987 to 2003, arguably real progress was made in the years 2004–6, when the lowest payment increased by over €45. This progress has been attributed to social partnership agreements. However, it is not without coincidence that considerable losses incurred by the governing Fianna Fáil party in the 2004 local elections prompted greater political focus on social inclusion. Various changes followed, including the removal of the then Minister for Finance and the invitation of key community and voluntary activists to major political meetings; for example, the director of the justice commission of the Conference of Religious of Ireland (CORI), Fr Sean Healy, was invited to address the Fianna Fáil party think-in in July 2004, just after the elections. Arguably, the dynamic behind subsequent increases in the social welfare rates was driven by this political rather than social partnership dynamic. While CORI is active and vocal as a social partner, it was its wider social role in arguing the case for change and mobilising support for it (an example of a strong communicative discourse) that contributed to the momentum for increased rates.

Conclusion

The chapter has argued that a shift to a positive social policy and more equitable outcomes requires a shift in power and structures of governance. Irish social policy is mediated between bureaucrats and policy elites in state-controlled patriarchal, exclusive institutional spaces, which prioritise consensus, incremental problem solving over larger-scale structural change. A values-led debate in a more communicative discourse is needed to change priorities at a political level and to identify alternative policy agendas. A key Irish challenge is increasing the capacity of civil society to organise into a more proactive, strong, vested interest group capable of generating public debate about alternative development models. Social policy requires a more public, political discourse that is capable of generating conflict and energy about social change. Progressive political parties and social groups need to build local and national communicative fora to encourage progressive policy actors, including those affected by inequality, to work more in politically open advocacy coalitions – it is only in communicative discourse that sufficient social energy can be created to effect the scale of double movement required to achieve a more equitable development model.

In the evolving negative political and economic environment of late 2008 and 2009, there are opportunities amidst crisis to redefine the role and nature of civil society in relation to the state. Polanyi predicted that it is at times of crisis, when society is most vulnerable, that creative forces and the social energy of civil society can best come together. Perhaps, in Ireland's case, this will be to effect a new public discourse about a more equitable model of Irish development.

Notes

1 Replacement ratios measure the ratio of income when unemployed to income when in work (Callan *et al.*, 1996).
2 Figures sourced from Department of Social and Family Affairs annual statistical reports (various years).
3 The monthly Irish Live Register is published by the Central Statistics Office and records all recipients of Jobseekers Benefit (JB) or Jobseekers Allowance (JA) and those receiving 'PRSI credits' but no payment. It includes relevant part-time, seasonal and casual workers but not systematic short-time workers, smallholders/farm assistants and self-employed people.
4 In 2005, Spain introduced a statutory obligation on men who marry in civil ceremonies to pledge to share domestic responsibilities and the care and attention of children and elderly family members.
5 The *Development Welfare State* document does acknowledge that a society is more than its economy and that there are legitimate objectives for social policy independent of fostering productivity (NESC, 2005: xiv) but stresses how social policy should contribute to the economy.
6 The National Economic and Social Council, the National Economic and Social Forum and the National Centre for Partnership and Performance, all of which are constituted under the umbrella of the National Economic and Social Development Office, and in the various institutions through which national agreements are negotiated and monitored.

12

Contesting the politics of inequality

PEADAR KIRBY

The growth in the power of the market over Irish society, as documented in the chapters of this book, has not happened by accident but is the outcome of a determined politics. Market discourse has a remarkable ability to hide issues of power, and to present itself as if it were some disinterested and benign force standing against the vested interests of trade unions, professional organisations, lobby groups and any other attempts by citizens to influence policy. Yet, behind the seemingly technical and neutral language of the market stand the strongest vested interests of all – the power of global elites, who seek to fashion political rules and social norms that serve the interests of their capital accumulation. Revealingly, in writing his *Brief History of Neoliberalism*, the celebrated academic David Harvey treats it as being 'from the very beginning a project to achieve the restoration of class power', namely the power of 'economic elites and ruling classes everywhere', both in advanced capitalist countries and in many developing countries (he mentions Chile, Mexico and Argentina), who were increasingly worried at their loss of economic and political power during the golden era of welfare capitalism after the Second World War (Harvey, 2005: 15, 16).

At heart, therefore, the project of neoliberalisation, of market liberalisation, of globalisation, has been a political project, though one which has had a remarkable success in concealing that not only from most citizens but even from most analysts of and commentators on the project. In tracing the impact of this project, Harvey documents the turnaround in the share of national income going to the top income earners: in the United States, the top 0.1 per cent of income earners increased their share of the national income from 2 per cent in 1978 to over 6 per cent by 1999; in Britain, the top 1 per cent doubled their share, from 6.5 per cent in 1982 to 13 per cent in 1998. Looking further afield, he shows how 'we see extraordinary concentrations of wealth and power emerging all over the place' – in Russia and eastern Europe, in Mexico and throughout Latin America, and in China (Harvey, 2005: 16–19). Work by Nolan and Maitre shows that a similar process has been happening in Ireland. Using tax returns to examine trends in the share of national income going to the top decile of income earners over the period 1989–2000, they found a substantial increase, from 33 per cent to 38 per cent. The top 1 per cent saw their share rise sharply in the second half of the decade, with all the growth in the share of the top decile being concentrated among this 1 per cent, whose share ended up being twice what it was in the 1970s and 1980s (Nolan and Maitre, 2007: 33–4). In essence, then, the politics of market liberalisation are a politics of the reconstitution of the power of ruling elites and their most visible manifestation is a remarkable growth in economic inequality. It is for this reason that the project is labelled the 'politics of inequality' in this chapter.

The chapter treats the politics of inequality in the Irish case in three sections. The first charts some of the most visible manifestations of inequality in the Ireland of the Celtic Tiger. This is followed by an analysis of how this was achieved politically; the roles of key actors are distinguished and this provides the basis for the analysis in the third section of how an alternative politics may be developed, a politics that could transform Irish society in a more egalitarian and just way. Contesting the politics of inequality constitutes the first step in such a transformation.

Inequality

Most of the focus on the distributional impact of market liberalisation over the period of the Celtic Tiger and beyond has been on poverty. Central to these debates have been the different measures of poverty and the different stories each tells about what is happening. Those who claim the Irish case as one of successful development, particularly those with a vested interest in the maintenance of low taxes and a strongly business-friendly political culture, have pointed to the decline of 'consistent poverty', a measure that combines the numbers falling below percentages of average income with indicators of deprivation of basic necessities, such as new, not second-hand clothes, a warm waterproof overcoat, a meal with meat, fish or chicken every second day, and a week's annual holiday away from home (see Whelan *et al.*, 2003: 35). This is a measure more akin to absolute poverty, as it concentrates on material survival and it is the one that is used by policy makers (e.g. in assessing the success of anti-poverty policy).

An alternative measure, which used to be given greater prominence by state officials, is relative poverty; this calculates the numbers who live with an income that is below 50 per cent, 60 per cent or 70 per cent of mean (or median) income. This is rather more embarrassing to proponents of the Irish success, as it shows a consistent increase in poverty over the years of the economic boom. Perhaps for this reason, it tends to be dismissed as a useful measure of poverty, since, as journalist Brendan Keenan asked, 'should we be concerned that some – the majority indeed – are more better off than others, so long as everybody gets something?' (*Irish Independent*, 7 October 1999). This reveals that what is of importance to policy makers and elite groups is that those on the lowest incomes in Irish society have enough to survive; whether the gap in the distribution of income is growing is considered of no importance. Indeed, as was publicly articulated by the then Minister for Justice, Equality and Law Reform and then leader of the Progressive Democrats, Michael McDowell, inequality is a necessary requirement for 'a dynamic liberal economy like ours … to function' (quoted in Cullen, 2006). Neglecting inequality in analysing the social impact of market liberalisation in Ireland is equivalent to neglecting the shifts in power associated with it. For, following Harvey, what is illustrated through tracing trends in inequality is the reconstitution of the power of a ruling elite, though the actual membership of that elite may, at least partly, be new. This, then, is the focus of discussion in this section.

Table 12.1 gives the headline statistics about the growth in inequality in Ireland between 2000 and 2007. The relative at-risk-of-poverty gap is an agreed EU poverty measure based on the percentage of people whose 'equivalised income' (an income for each individual member of a household estimated on the basis of the total household income) falls below 60 per cent of the national median income. This shows an increase to 2003 but a decline since. The other two measures, however, show a rise over the period, especially the Gini coefficient. The Gini coefficient is a widely used international measure of the cumulative shares of the population arranged according to their level of income and the cumulative share

Table 12.1 Trends in inequality, 2000–7

	2000	2003	2005	2006	2007
Relative at-risk-of-poverty gap	19.3	21.5	20.8	17.5	17.4
Gini coefficient	30.2	31.1	32.4	32.4	31.7
Income distribution	4.7	5.0	4.9	5.0	4.9

Source: Central Statistics Office (2008).

of total income received by them; if everyone received the same income, the Gini coefficient would be 0 per cent, whereas if only one person received all the national income, the Gini coefficient would be 100 per cent. The last measure in table 12.1, income distribution, is the ratio of the total income received by the 20 per cent of persons with the highest income to that of the 20 per cent with the lowest income.

This overall picture, however, needs to be disaggregated to see in more detail what happened to the distribution of income in Ireland. O'Donoghue and McDonough (2006) offer the most comprehensive survey of income inequality and cover trends from 1987 to 2001. Overall, they found 'a remarkable increase in the dispersion of incomes in just a six-year period', namely the height of the economic boom from 1994 to 2000. Yet, there are surprises in who has gained and who has lost out. Those in the bottom 30 per cent of the income distribution did not do well, with income increasing only by an average amount or, in the case of the lowest decile, below the average. However, the gains went not to the top decile, who in fact had the lowest increase over the whole period, but to deciles four to eight. Decile nine also showed only an average increase, less than the five deciles below it.

Overall, then, these data paint a picture of an increasingly middle-class society. However, within this they also reveal a host of other forms of inequality, which alerts us to the fact that inequality is a cumulative reality not easily captured by a single indicator. Among these is a growth in gender inequality, as, between 1994 and 2001, male-headed households increased their income by 67 per cent as against 58 per cent for female-headed households. Age constituted another basis for inequality, with the young and the old, particularly those over sixty-five, doing less well than the middle aged. Regional inequality also persisted: even though the Border, Midland and Western region had increased its income more than the Southern and Eastern region from 1987 to 1994, this was reversed in the later period, as the latter increased more than the former. In occupational terms, professionals and those in crafts and related trades did well, while clerks (in office work and customer service) saw by far the lowest increase in incomes. Within industry, the mining and quarrying sectors saw the highest increase in incomes, followed by construction and the public sector. These latter increases are likely to have had distinct causes – increased demand in a tightening labour market in the first case and the power of public sector unions within social partnership in the second. Finally, home-owners saw a much higher increase in their incomes than did those in the private rented sector (indeed, the latter saw a fall in income between 1987 and 1994).

In surveys of income distribution, however, those in the highest income bracket tend to distort the size of their income, since part of their income derives from trading in assets such as shares or property. Therefore, a true estimate of inequality has to take into account the distribution of wealth or assets such as housing, land, shares and luxury items. Unfortunately, mirroring the neglect of the subject of inequality in Irish public life, our only knowledge of how the distribution of wealth has increased over the course of the economic boom is rather anecdotal. In a survey in 1991, Nolan concluded that the bottom 50 per cent of households had only 12 per cent of total reported wealth, whereas the top 30 per cent had 71.5 per cent. He added, however, that household surveys usually 'seriously understate total wealth and give a misleading picture of its distribution significantly underestimating its concentration at the top' (Nolan, 1991: 14). What evidence we have would indicate that the boom years greatly increased the wealth of an elite in Irish society. A survey of the world's richest people by the information technology services firm Cap Gemini and investment bank Merrill Lynch reported that Ireland's 15,000 wealthiest individuals were worth US$52 billion in 2003, a $1 billion increase on the previous year (*Irish Times*, 16 April 2004). A 2006 report by the Revenue Commissioners on Ireland's top earners indicated that the top 400 of them earned €1 million or more each in 2002 and that they paid an effective tax rate of 24.4 per cent, less than the 28.9 per cent they paid in 2001; one principal way they avoided paying tax was through property-based tax incentives (*Irish Times*, 27 June 2006). This draws attention to one means through which Ireland's housing boom served to fuel inequality: by providing a ready market for lucrative investments by wealthy individuals and reducing their tax liability at the same time. The housing boom had a complex impact on inequality, but while greatly increasing the wealth of home-owners as against non-home-owners, or those who accessed the housing market before the boom as against those who accessed it during the boom, its overall impact is likely to have been to deepen already high levels of inequality in the distribution of wealth.

The growth in inequality finds expression in the growing segmentation of the health and education systems. Wren has documented the two-tier health system, in which public funds subsidise private for-profit hospitals and care by consultants, while an acute crisis has built up particularly in the accident and emergency departments of public hospitals. Meanwhile, the percentage of the population with access to free primary care due to low income declined from nearly 28 per cent in 2003 to 25 per cent at the end of 2005 (Wren, 2003, 2006). Indeed, in a 2006 Euro Health Consumer Index, Ireland ranked second last out of twenty-six European countries on consumer healthcare, on the basis of long waiting times for treatment, bleak medical outcomes and widespread infections with MRSA (*Irish Times*, 27 June 2006). Those on lower incomes bear the brunt of such poor services. Reflecting the social consequences of growing inequality, evidence is emerging that secondary education is being ever more deeply divided by social class, as wealthy parents opt to send their children to fee-paying schools, which again are subsidised out of public funds, while non-fee-paying schools in some areas are finding it harder and harder to recruit students, which undermines their viability over the long run. In these ways, the very structures of the health and education systems are serving to deepen inequality and pass it on to the next generation.

This evidence therefore confirms from the Irish case the validity of Harvey's contention that what is happening is the reconstitution of class rule. While this is happening in different ways in different countries, and some of its worst excesses may be modified in the Irish case by the institutions of social partnership, there is evidence of a trend towards the concentration of wealth. Where this finds its most marked expression is in evidence on the shares of national income going on wages and profits. Table 12.2 gives the share of national income going on employees' wages, profits and taxes in the EU in 2001. Ireland comes after Greece as by far the most unequal of the then fifteen member states. EU data also show that, after 1990, when the wage share of Ireland's gross domestic product was slightly above the EU average (71.3 per cent, to 69.6 per

Table 12.2 Shares of national income (as a percentage of gross domestic product) in the EU, 2001

Country	To employees	To profits	To taxes
Belgium	52.3	35.9	11.8
Denmark	53.4	32.0	14.6
Germany	53.8	35.6	10.5
Greece	32.5	54.6	12.9
Spain	50.0	40.1	9.9
France	52.9	33.3	13.8
Ireland	39.9	48.7	11.5
Italy	40.9	45.6	13.5
Luxembourg	53.0	34.1	12.9
Netherlands	52.0	36.6	11.4
Austria	52.4	35.0	12.6
Portugal	45.0	42.1	12.9
Finland	48.4	40.0	11.6
Sweden	59.5	27.4	13.1
UK	56.3	30.6	13.4
Euro-zone 12	49.8	38.2	12.0
EU 15	51.3	36.3	12.3

Source: Eurostat (2004).

cent), Ireland's wage share fell steadily in comparison with the EU average, so that by 2006 it was 55.1 per cent, to the EU average of 64.4 per cent (Commission of the European Communities, 2007). These data reveal rather more about the structure of power in Irish society and clearly point towards the strength of elite power at the end of the economic boom.

While any conclusions about the extent and nature of inequality in Ireland can only be tentative due to the lack of data on key dimensions (such as the distribution of wealth and how it is changing), the partial evidence at hand indicates that the concentration of wealth and income is now a marked feature of Irish society. International research has pointed to the fact that a correlation exists between income distribution, national mortality rates and general health in terms of psycho-social well-being. Indeed, in their extensive research, Wilkinson and Pickett find 'almost all problems which are more common at the bottom of the social ladder are more common in more unequal societies', not just ill-health and violence but a host of other social problems (Wilkinson and Pickett, 2009: 18). The first report for eighty years on health inequalities in Ireland documented 'the pervasiveness and magnitude of occupational class inequalities on the island' and their effect on health outcomes, with the mortality rate in the lowest occupational class being 100 per cent to 200 per cent higher than the rate in the highest occupational class. Furthermore, this is evident for nearly all the main causes of death: for circulatory diseases it was over 120 per cent higher, for cancers over 100 per cent higher, for respiratory diseases over 200 per cent higher, and for injuries and poisonings over 150 per cent higher (Balanda and Wilde, 2001: 11). Such evidence points to the corrosive effects on society of the failure to address growing inequality.

The politics of inequality

Considering market liberalisation as a project of class restoration draws attention to the fact that it has not happened of its own accord but has been the outcome of political action. This invites examination of how this political project has achieved its aims, with the objective of learning lessons to inform the project of contesting the politics of inequality. Yet both mainstream (Barry, 1999; Nolan *et al.*, 2000) and critical (O'Hearn, 1998; Allen, 2000; Kirby, 2002a) analysts of the Irish boom have devoted little attention to the politics of its emergence; indeed, in all of these analyses it is the state that plays the starring role. Ó Riain (2000, 2004, 2008) is the only analyst to delve more deeply and to identify what he calls 'the ebb and flow of different projects within the Celtic Tiger political economy' (Ó Riain, 2008: 170). What is important for the purposes of this chapter is to identify the different actors promoting these competing projects and the reasons why some gained ascendancy while others were sidelined.

Ó Riain (2008) divides the period since 1987 into three sub-periods. The first, from 1987 to 1994, he labels neo-corporatist stabilisation. This did not mark a major departure from the balance of political forces that had been in the ascendant for decades, although it was characterised by a more serious attempt by the leading political parties and the trade union movement to put differences aside and to cooperate in the effort to stabilise the national finances. Ó Riain emphasises that this period of austerity did not follow neoliberal prescriptions, since tax was not cut in earnest until the subsequent period and foreign investors were attracted not by corporate perks but by the major public investments in education, telecommunications and facilities over the previous two decades. Further-more, state agencies continued to provide the supports for economic development, most notably the Industrial Development Authority (IDA). The state continued in this period to play the decisive role, through an alliance of developmental bureaucrats, particularly those in the IDA, and politicians willing to give them financial support and a large measure of policy autonomy. What Ó Riain's account fails to mention is the role of social partnership in beginning a crucial shift in power among the social partners. As Begg writes, the over-riding objective was to end large-scale unemployment: 'Everything was subordinated to that objective, and busi-ness was given virtually anything it asked for – low corporation taxes, low capital taxes, low social insurance contributions and a virtually unregulated labour market' (Begg, 2005).

The second period, from 1994 to 2000, is the most interesting period, as it marked the emergence of new developmental projects within the state. In Ó Riain's account, these were facilitated by the flow of EU funding, which allowed previously marginalised sectors within the bureaucracy to find the space and resources for new institutional projects and state–society alliances. Among the examples he gives is the alliance between science and technology-oriented state agencies, technical professionals and university centres to deepen technical capabilities and technical learning across the economy, alliances that were crucial to the emergence of the very successful indigenous software sector. Within social partnership also, area-based partnerships for local development were institutionalised, the community and voluntary sector was brought in as a social partner and the National Economic and Social Forum was established. All of these marked a similar developmentalism in the social field. However, Ó Riain makes clear that these developed alongside the old state–society linkages and never chal-lenged them for dominance. Yet, for all its developmentalism, this was also the period in which 'wage inequality increased drastically', as the gap grew between the middle and the top of the income distribution: 'The level and increase in wage inequality was greater than even in the United States' (Ó Riain, 2004: 138). Central to this was the emergence of a new globalised technical/professional class weakly integrated into the institutions of social partnership. In response, public service workers waged intense battles to ensure they did not fall behind in what Ó Riain (2004: 140) calls 'the clash of two middle classes'. Those increasingly left behind were the lowest rung of Irish society, 'caught between a burgeoning service sector of casual employment and a weakening welfare effort' on the part of the state. Paradoxically, therefore, the period of greatest developmentalism by sectors of the Irish state and society also 'only further exposed the raw wounds of the politics of inequality' (Ó Riain, 2004: 140).

The present period, beginning in 2000, Ó Riain calls 'disciplining development and democracy', as it is marked by a neglect of the developmental potentials of the previous period and a reassertion of dominance by the central state and the market across a range of areas. Economic growth is driven by construction and consumption fuelled by tax cuts and tax breaks for the wealthy rather than by innovation and export competitiveness. Meanwhile, social spending has fallen so low that Ireland now spends some of the lowest percentages of its national product on social protection among the members of the EU, and the welfare and taxation systems have operated to penalise the poor and redistribute towards the middle classes and the rich (NESC, 2005). This period, then, marks the flowering of neoliberalism in Ireland, as the state makes itself more and more subservient to the market, complicit in the growth of inequality and less willing to protect the most vulnerable. As Ó Riain describes it:

> In believing their own rhetoric and failing to recognise the social and economic policies that have contributed to economic success, Irish policy makers have contributed to a rising level of inequality. Tax cuts, spending gaps and deregulated markets have created a deeply unequal society in Ireland. While the professional classes and self-employed trades have been able to take advantage of a two-tier system of public subsidies, those living in the poorer urban and rural communities have been left behind – with far fewer services to assist them to compete in the market.... The cold chill of competition is experienced most strongly by those with the least resources to bring to it. (Ó Riain, 2008: 179)

Ó Riain identifies the structural causes for the emergence of higher levels of inequality, and sees these as being the result of the actions of the Irish state. Yet, this does not identify *why* the state acted to prioritise the needs of elites over those of the most vulnerable, nor why its welfare effort has been so weakened. Indeed, through identifying the emergence of new state–society alliances in the sphere of both economic and social development in the mid-1990s, his account raises the added puzzle of why these did not have more success in fashioning a more social democratic model, in which social investment would be seen as a crucial component of sustainable economic success, instead of being seen as a danger to budgetary stability.

The answer lies in the balance of social and political forces. The developmental actors within the Irish state remained small, fragmented and without any clear alternative project to espouse, apart from a capacity for pragmatic experimentalism. Thus, those fostering the emergence of a new professional/technical class in the information technology sector were separate from those working to extend social partnership in developmental ways through the National Economic and Social Forum or the local partnerships. The nearest they came to having a political 'home' that could have provided a forum for incubating an alternative political project, linking the conditions for economic success with the robust social underpinnings needed to sustain it, were parties such as Labour and Democratic Left. It is no coincidence that these developmental efforts emerged during the period of the strongest left-leaning government the state has known. Yet, neither of these parties (either separately or after they merged following electoral defeat in 1997) had a strong enough social base from which an alternative project could be developed. This refers not only to their weak base of support but also to the weaknesses of wider social forces that could help develop such an alternative, key among them a cadre of committed intellectuals. Furthermore, far from providing a forum in which such issues could be debated and an alternative advanced, social partnership institutions served to co-opt the two sectors most likely to provide the social bases for an alternative – the trade union movement and the community and voluntary sector.

This weakness of the basis for developing an alternative project for the Irish state and society derives centrally from the populist nature of Irish party politics. What is most striking about these fundamental changes in Irish society is that they happened by stealth. As Murphy has clearly shown in her detailed survey of the commodification of social security over this period, populism ensured that it never happened as part of a coherent reformist project but rather through a myriad of small incremental moves that ensured opposition was rarely mobilised against it (Murphy, 2006). Thus, the relatively ideological Progressive Democrats could have had a hugely disproportionate influence to their size, though they themselves had to cloak their core neoliberal principles in populist garb if they were to be able to advance them. What populist politics serves to do, therefore, is to obscure the ways in which they serve the interests of key elites (construction, financial services, foreign manufacturing). Furthermore, such a fudging of the issues makes it very hard to mount a frontal assault on them. Bertie Ahern's declaration of himself as one of Ireland's last social-ists is an example – it is difficult to believe he expected anyone to take him seriously but it served to ensure that attempts critically to challenge his stance were similarly deflated. The politics of inequality is therefore dependent on the fragmentation, co-option and marginalisation of the social and political forces that might wish to contest it.

Contesting the politics of inequality

This analysis serves to highlight the difficulties of contesting the politics of inequality in Ireland. What is remarkable about the project of recon-stituting class forces in Irish society is that it has proceeded with so little opposition. This contrasts with the constant challenges it faces in a country like France or the spontaneous mobilisation of a wide range of social forces in Costa Rica in 2000 when the government sought to privatise the state electricity and communications company. In the latter case, what is interesting is that a new political party, the Citizens' Action Party (Partido Accion Ciudadana, PAC), emerged out of that mobilisation and its leader, Ottón Solís, came within a whisker of winning the presidency in the February 2006 election, defying the solid lead that former President and Nobel Peace Prize winner Óscar Arias held in the opinion polls. In other words, the mobilisation of social forces in opposition to an attempt by the state to strengthen the power of private market forces resulted in a very significant new political force emerging. This bottom-up dynamic holds important lessons for contesting the politics of inequality in Ireland.

The first of these is the central importance of civil society. An alternative political project must emerge from the autonomous self-organisation of social forces, just as the radical project of nation building out of which the independent Irish state emerged in the early twentieth century found its incubation in a rich array of civil society organisations over the previous decades – a workers' movement, a rural cooperative movement, an alterna-tive media, various movements of cultural redefinition (foremost among them the Gaelic League), a women's movement, a movement of native sports, and a movement of international solidarity against the Boer War. These were mass popular movements that mobilised significant sectors of Irish society in different forms of opposition to the prevailing state and the socio-economic order over which it presided (see Kirby, 2002b). Many of these movements have echoes in today's civil society but the principal difference lies in the capacity to propose alternatives. Paradoxic-ally, having led a project of nation building, Irish civil society lost many of its imaginative resources following independence and settled for a role that was very dependent on the state. While, at various periods, movements such as Muintir na Tíre or Macra na Feirme emerged that seemed to recapture some of the developmental energy of the earlier period, none of these contested the prevailing political and social order in any serious way. Indeed, as Powell and Geoghegan write of today's co-optation of community development into social partnership: 'The anxiety must be that this is a Faustian bargain in which a state that has embraced neo-liberalism and is replacing welfare policy by an enterprise culture is seeking to incorporate civil society into a project of governance that will fatally compromise its ethical legitimacy' (Powell and Geoghegan, 2004: 260).

So, what are the prospects for a more vigorous civil society to emerge that could provide the foundation for an alternative project, contesting the politics of inequality? One way of addressing this question is to identify the significant shift that is taking place in the relationship of the state to society as it seeks to impose with ever greater determination the disciplines of the market. Aspects of this have been examined in the chapters by Cronin and O'Sullivan in part III of this book. This ever more disciplinary stance by the state towards sectors of civil society who quite legitimately seek to promote their members' interests marks a new moment in state–society relations since the foundation of an independent Irish state and is likely to result in an ever more determined opposition by sectors of civil society. That this coincides with a moment when public anger is growing at the severe inadequacies of public services, especially the health service, is fast eroding the legitimacy of the state and resulting in an upsurge of localised protests. These may remain fragmented and ephemeral or may coalesce into a more significant mobilisation of civil society. For this, leadership is needed, and the articulation by the General Secretary of the Irish Congress of Trade Unions (ICTU), David Begg, of a determined agenda based on a Nordic social democratic agenda at least offers an alternative to today's neoliberal social order (Siggins, 2007). More than any agenda proposed by opposition political leaders, Begg offered a platform around which large sections of civil society could mobilise. Significantly, in responding to Begg, Danny McCoy of the Irish Business and Employers Confederation (IBEC) acknowledged that what remains to be decided in Irish society is not some technically correct or efficient way to grow the economy but a decision about what balance society wishes between efficiency and equity (McCoy, 2006). The emphasis on equity also characterised the ICTU's response to government cutbacks in early 2009, particularly as formulated in its proposal for a Social Solidarity Pact. This is a far cry from the agenda of 'Boston versus Berlin' as articulated by Progressive Democrat leader Mary Harney, which related purely to issues of economic efficiency. Begg and McCoy have now brought social equity into the debate and have focused public attention on the central features of the sort of society Irish people wish to promote; it is an acknowledgement that the public has a choice as to the balance to be achieved between equity and efficiency. The outcome of this choice will depend on the mobilisation of civil society.

Yet, this is only the first step. The second requires political forces to carry and help implement a project that grows out of civil society. This is the clear example being given by the shift to the left throughout Latin America since 2002, as political parties and leaders gain power (or narrowly miss it in the case of Costa Rica and Mexico) in country after country, based on their ability to offer an alternative to neoliberalism that responds to the demands of a mobilised and contestatory civil society. This has happened in Venezuela, Brazil, Argentina, Uruguay, Bolivia, Ecuador and, in a somewhat different way, Chile. So what are the prospects for such an alternative political leadership to emerge in Ireland? The collapse of Fianna Fáil support in late 2008, following its remarkable election victory in 2007, reveals a fundamental volatility has entered Irish politics that creates the conditions for a new alignment, a volatility that was hidden during the years of economic boom. The reverse since 1997 of what had seemed a steady erosion in its support base was largely based on its ability to claim credit for the boom (a claim uncontested by opposition parties in the 2007 general election, which contributed greatly to their loss). As the Irish economy faces more turbulent times, revealing that the years of the Celtic Tiger have camouflaged rather than resolved Ireland's long-term development problems (see Kirby, 2006), Fianna Fáil is being put under severe strain, for two reasons. One is that the party has lost its ability to nip dissent in the bud as it grows ever more out of touch with a vastly changed society less amenable to clientelistic practices. But, paradoxically, the very neoliberalisation of the state which it implemented in office after 1997 robbed the party of many of the traditional levers of patronage. As the many social crises treated in this book intensify and as more and more people are caught with high levels of personal debt amid eroding employment, the conditions are given for a further shift of political allegiances and for the end of Fianna Fáil's dominance of the Irish political system.

The big question that arises in such a situation is whether Fianna Fáil's decline will open the way for the rise of a new political force or whether it will lead to a further splintering, with independent candidates getting elected through championing local issues. The opportunity for a new political alternative to arise in this situation will depend on the emergence of such a force from within civil society. Efforts by some figures to the left of the Labour Party to develop such an alternative are severely hampered by the divisive tactics of Trotskyists and by the failure to appreciate the need for a broad-front strategy that would draw existing progressive parties and social forces, as well as high-profile individuals, into constituting such an alternative. For this, leadership and long-term vision are sorely lacking in contemporary Irish society. Furthermore, there is the added uncertainty of the nature of Sinn Féin's politics as it enters the mainstream. Will it constitute a serious progressive alternative or will it revert to historical form, tolerating 'only a certain type of nebulous, ambiguous rhetoric concerning equality and redistribution' (Ferriter, 2005: 196), as happened in 1919 with the Democratic Programme of the first Dáil? However, Gerry Adams's call at the party's 2009 Ard-Fheis (annual conference) for an alliance of progressive parties – Labour, the Greens and Sinn Féin – shows such a grouping is now in a position to offer a credible alternative, and by early 2009 these three parties together had a consistent lead in the opinion polls over either Fianna Fáil or Fine Gael.

Conclusion

This chapter has argued that growing inequality is not an accidental side-effect of the neoliberalisation of Irish society over the past two decades but is the central social expression of the determined political project that has reconstituted elite power with a success that has few equals in the contemporary world. Few dissenting voices have been raised against this takeover of Irish society by the market and the co-optation of the state to serve global market forces rather than the needs of its citizens. Society has been seduced, sidelined, hoodwinked, fragmented, controlled and, where necessary, disciplined to accommodate itself to this new Ireland, as is well described and documented in the pages of this book. As the inevitable results of this elite project become ever more evident to more and more people in their stressed and pressurised lives, in the inadequate and often crisis-ridden public services they rely upon, in the divided and ever more violent society they inhabit, in the daily pressures of incessant commercial propaganda of a most distasteful kind on their values and sensibilities, the need for a determined counterforce to emerge is ever more obvious and urgent. Whether this can ever happen in the coherent and forceful way that is needed will test the resources of Ireland's progressive social forces to the limit.

13

Transforming Ireland: resources

PEADAR KIRBY, DEBBIE GING
and MICHAEL CRONIN

If there is one common theme running through the chapters of this book, it is the power of the market. Indeed, what the contributors do is to describe and analyse many of the ways in which the market has become an ever more powerful actor in configuring the nature of Irish society and Irish culture. In doing this, they are focusing attention on what is often hidden in mainstream media, political and, indeed, academic treatment of contemporary Ireland and of the changes wrought over the era of the Celtic Tiger. Despite the obsessive attention devoted to economic growth and the lively debates about its social impacts, the nature and role of the market have been subjected to virtually no critical scrutiny, being accepted as an inevitable fact of life and evaluated in the most benign terms.

The foregoing chapters have cast a critical eye over the role of the market in Irish life, putting a real face on what is usually conceived of in highly abstract terms (for we must not forget that the so-called market of neo-classical economics is nothing other than an abstract construct based on a theoretical claim about the role of prices in achieving an equilibrium between supply and demand). In the culture of consumerism, in gender constructions, in the emergence of a disciplinary state, in the role of the media, in the paradigms governing education, in the structuring of migration, in the decline of the Irish language, in understandings of health and its provisioning, contributors have unmasked the role and consequences of the market in contemporary Irish society.

Chapter 12 concluded that growing inequality is not some side-effect of the neoliberalisation of Irish society but the central social expression of a determined political project on the part of an elite. As is well described and documented in the pages of this book, what we are witnessing is a vivid example of the market society so powerfully analysed by Karl Polanyi in his classic book *The Great Transformation* more than half a century ago (Polanyi, 1944). The power of his analysis lies in uncovering the 'conscious and often violent intervention on the part of government which imposed the market organisation on society' (p. 258). This self-regulating market treats labour, land and money as commodities and therefore leads to 'the running of society as an adjunct to the market' (p. 60), which 'required that the individual respect economic law even if it happened to destroy him' (p. 89). According to Polanyi, the creation of a 'market society' results in 'poverty amid plenty', as it inflicts 'lethal injury to the institutions in which [a person's] social existence is embodied' (p. 164). The chapters of this book show just how accurate is Polanyi's work in uncovering the true nature of social transformation in today's Ireland.

But Polanyi's work is also concerned with the spontaneous response of society to the destructive impact of the self-regulating market, the 'double movement' that frames Murphy's analysis in chapter 11. She employs Polanyi's analysis to discuss the possibility of a political response to the changing nature of the Irish welfare state. Indeed, it was one of the explicit instructions of the editors to all authors that they devote some attention in their chapters to the potential for transformation that exists within the areas of society they are discussing. The purpose of this concluding chapter is to draw on their analyses to offer a robust and yet realistic discussion of the potential for social transformation in today's Ireland.

Chapter 1 outlined a theory of social change that draws on the 'historical structures' of Robert Cox. While this gives a central role to the power of civil society to promote an alternative historical structure, it also devotes extensive attention to different forms of power – economic and political power but also the power of ideas and values. It is when the 'fit' between these forms of power becomes unstuck, when tensions arise between these three forms of power, that we begin to see the potential for a transformative politics to emerge. This offers an organising framework for examining the potential for transformation and draws our attention to three aspects of how this happens – values, context and actors. Each is dealt with in turn before final conclusions are drawn.

Values

Values, in the sense used here, are somewhat akin to Cox's ideas, since they constitute the dominant 'common sense' of the age, providing the often hidden structuring principles that guide thought and public discussion. It is significant that they have, to a certain extent, become a battleground in Ireland since the period of the Celtic Tiger. For example, the highly influential Economic and Social Research Institute (ESRI), in its book *Best of Times?*, on the social impact of the Celtic Tiger (Fahey *et al.*, 2007b), takes issue with the account of contemporary Ireland offered by the Ombudsman and Information Commissioner, Emily O'Reilly, at a conference in 2004. In her address, O'Reilly spoke of the 'vulgar fest' of modern Ireland, 'the rampant, unrestrained drunkenness, the brutal, random violence that infects the smallest of our townlands and villages, the incontinent use of foul language with no thought to place or company, the obscene parading of obscene wealth, the debasement of our civic life, the growing distain of the wealthy towards the poor, the fracturing of our community life' (quoted in Fahey *et al.*, 2007b: 1–2). This account had a major impact, with the *Irish Times* reprinting an edited version (6 November 2004), while the conference organisers reported a huge demand for copies of the address and stated that it 'articulated what the majority of people in Ireland feel about the direction Irish society is taking' (quoted in Fahey *et al.*, 2007b: 2). For the ESRI, however, O'Reilly's critique was more a reaction against new-found wealth or a hankering after an idealised past. In his chapter in *Best of Times?*, Erikson asks:

> whether the incidence of violence, drinking, bad language and other utterances of improper behaviour really has increased or whether the image of the past is dimmed by protective mechanisms of memory or perhaps whether the acts have become more visible because those exhibiting them now have the economic resources to do so in contexts where the better-off are present.

As he puts it:

> Suddenly, to the despair of some inhabitants, it seems that the Irish way of life is not the same any longer…. (Erikson, 2007: 275)

Underlying Erikson's rebuttal is the axiomatic belief that change is an absolute rather than a relative value. Change, of course, is not a virtue in itself. The virtue inheres in the consequences. One of the most effective ways of disqualifying criticism in the late modern era is the manner in which the cheerleaders of market-driven politics usurp the language of radical politics to promote vested interests. Hence, the language of 'choice', 'empowerment', 'partnership', 'reform' becomes the preferred rhetoric for the privatisation of public goods and the undermining of workers' rights. If the radicals of yester-year called for radical change, neo-liberalism was more than willing to respond to the call by making a fetish of radical change itself. Anyone opposing these changes was, by definition, reactionary, backward-looking, anti-progressive. Yet, as Denis O'Sullivan demonstrates in chapter 8, on education, and Orla O'Donovan in chapter 9, on the ravages of the medico-pharmaceutical complex in Ireland, the effects of change have been deeply regressive. As Terry Eagleton has noted:

> Capitalism wants men and women to be infinitely pliable and adaptable. As a system it has a Faustian horror of fixed boundaries, of anything which offers an obstacle to the infinite accumulation of capital. (Eagleton 2003: 118)

Much is made of the soft capitalism of high-technology employers in Ireland, such as Google, with their free canteens, gyms, table-tennis tables, casual dress and cooperative teamwork. This is California dreaming on a global scale. Less often mentioned are the complete subservience to the corporate interest, the dramatically anti-social working hours and the culture of permanent surveillance (Dhombres, 2007). In effect, the much-vaunted changes are not so much changes at all but rather business as usual – the expropriation of the labour of many for the benefit of an immensely rich few.

So, if, in calling for a transformative politics, it is necessary to be wary of the instrumentalisation of the language of change, what are the values that might underpin a genuinely radical politics? A belief in the promise of the future has been a feature of progressive thought over the last two centuries and more. Whether the belief took the form of the messianic message of utopian socialism or the incremental pragmatism of social democracy, the notion that the future would be better if struggles were brought to their just conclusion was a central tenet of progressive thinking and praxis. At present, however, the future is viewed increasingly not so much with hope but with a sense of doom. Dramatically widening social inequalities, an excessive and dangerous reliance on highly volatile transnational investment capital, and a deeply worrying deterioration in the natural environment make the future a much less secure place than previously thought. In Ireland, the uncertainty about the future fed the politics of fear, which was used to such powerful effect by the dominant political party, Fianna Fáil, which, through its neoliberal mouthpiece, the Progressive Democrats, had done so much to change Irish society for the benefit of the affluent. Fianna Fáil now decided that change was not so good after all. In an age of uncertainty, as Michael Cronin points out in chapter 7, on modes of coercion, the state often uses the bogeyman of an unpredictable future to make sure that the political present, in terms of the preservation of established interests, is anything but unpredictable. In addition, the long shadows of the murderous pathologies of utopian socialism in the twentieth century can make even progressive movements reluctant to invoke a better or a brighter future for all, for fear of the mocking echo of history. And yet, it is precisely a belief in the value of an alternative future that must be the basis for breaking with the dead hand of conformity and consensualism described so cogently by Mary Murphy in chapter 11.

One way of imagining a different future is to be aware of a different past. As Eagleton observes, 'Over the dreary decades of post-1970s conservatism, the historical sense had grown increasingly blunted, as it suited those in power that we should be able to imagine no alternative to the present' (Eagleton, 2003: 7). A graphic illustration of the politics of historical amnesia in Ireland was Seán de Mórdha's much-lauded *Seven Ages* (2000), a seven-part television documentary about the birth and development of the Irish state. Fixated on a civil war paradigm of what constituted political debate and unerringly statist in its unfolding of a national narrative, the documentary achieved the remarkable feat of almost wholly ignoring the entire post-independence history of the Irish left and the contribution of transformative social movements. The omissions were all the more startling in that modern Ireland would be a radically different place if it were not for the activities of mass language revival and the cooperative movements of the 1890s, the actions of the women's movement in the 1970s and 1980s, or the tireless campaigns of activists to change the legislation on gay rights, environmental protection, disability rights and educational provision. Being reminded of the progressive achievements of the past and the tangible historical results of progressive campaigns shows, among other things, that another future is possible, because our present is the result of others courageously imagining the future to be different.

A value which underlies any movement towards social transformation is solidarity. This is a much more fundamental notion than the rhetorical ploy of 'active citizenship', with its mixture of faith (in the current political system) and good works (charity). Fundamental to the value of solidarity is that the individual consumer, deluded into feelings of omnipotence by credit overdrafts and the personalised narratives of celebrity culture, is neither a viable basis nor a credible argument for the sustainable development of a society. For Aristotle, what defined a slave was that he or she had no ties. As a result, the slave could be moved anywhere, used in whatever way the master saw fit. Pure autonomy, in effect, was a definition of slavery. Free persons, on the other hand, had ties and obligations. Their freedom was defined by their dependence on, not their independence from, others. In the liberal purview, self-realisation is a personal affair. Your development, as long as it does not physically harm others, is a matter of individual striving (Harvey, 2005). The relentless appeal to the appetites of the individual consumer, described in stark terms by Debbie Ging in chapter 4, the fetishisation of school and university league tables, the endless parade of celebrity cooks, gardeners and tap dancers in the media are predicated on a kind of social Darwinism, where the triumph of the individual will is celebrated as the glorious competition of all on all. But people are not monads: they are social animals. That is why we have politics. Our self-realisation comes not through the subjection but through the liberation of others. It is not a question of one person's freedom ending where another person's begins, but rather that the freedom of one is bound up with the freedom of all.

A poor version of freedom in a supposed community of equals is allowing others to die needlessly. Ruth Barrington, head of the Health Research Bureau, noted that, 'It has been estimated that 5,400 fewer people would die prematurely each year if death rates were reduced to match those in Europe by tackling social deprivation and inequalities' (cited in Browne, 2007). Referring to the report by the Institute of Health on inequalities in mortality rates in Ireland, Vincent Browne noted that:

> For all infectious and parasitic diseases in the Republic death rates were over 370 per cent more (that is nearly five times more) among the lowest occupational class as compared with the highest, and the death rate increases as one goes down the social gradient. For tuberculosis, death rates were over 300 per cent more for poor people as compared with the richest, that is four times more. For all neoplasms (cancers), death rates were over 110 per cent more for poor people. (Browne, 2007)

None of these deaths gets the attention of a single high-profile celebrity death, yet it is not the individual success of stars but the collective well-being of a citizenry which defines both the potential for freedom and the quality of life in any given society. And collective well-being *pace* active citizenship means more than coaching for the local soccer club and casting your vote in an election: it means having a say in the shaping of a society which places the interests of the totality of its citizens at its core and not the sociophobic logic of market competition. You cannot have a race to the bottom and expect those at the bottom to applaud their own subjection. There is little point in exhorting families and communities to work together for the common good while extolling the virtues of unbridled competition, which destroys families and communities through long working hours and delocalisation. There is little credibility in telling people that they live in the best of times if thousands of their fellow citizens die every year through avoidable deprivation.

A mantra of neoliberal self-betterment is that anything is possible. Who would have thought two decades ago that liberal democracies would employ private armies to fight their wars? And yet Iraq has been awash with 'security contractors' using lethal force for profit. Possibility is almost invariably pitched at the level of the individual. From mobile phone companies offering the user 'tailored individual packages' to the UK National Lottery's blandishments that 'it could be you', the individual as consumer is ritually infantilised in late modern Ireland. In the fantasy of debt-fuelled consumption, individuals are back to the kingdom of infancy, where they are all-powerful, where needs are instantly met and where there are no Oedipal complications to remind the infant that baby does not always know best. The breathless championing of privatisation, deregulation and competition makes repeated reference to the power of the consumer, to a giddy delirium of possibility, where freedom is not so much the freedom to make choices – too much like democracy – but to choose among the choices presented by private capital. The omnipotence of the consumer almost invariably leads to the impotence of the citizen. As the economic historian Avner Offer points out, prudence generates affluence, but affluence undermines prudence:

> What accounts for this reversal is myopic choice. The strategies of self-control take time to discover, develop, learn, and teach. Affluence is a relentless flow of new and cheaper opportunities. If these rewards arrive faster than the disciplines of prudence can form, then self-control will decline with affluence: even the affluent will become less prudent (a fringe at the top might lose control altogether). Commitment strategies take time and effort to devise and learn. Under the impact of affluence, they become obsolete. (Offer, 2006: 4)

Implicit in the value of solidarity is that strategies of self-control are primarily strategies of commitment to others. In formulating a new politics for Ireland, it is crucial to move from the infantilised world of instant gratification promised by free marketeers to a society that seeks emancipation and self-realisation for its citizens, through a focus on inclusive notions of the collective good and a duty of care to the planet and its inhabitants. Ireland, as indicated in chapter 1, can no longer trade in the coin of exceptionalism. The challenges the society faces are similar to those faced by many countries around the globe. It is for that reason that we must be particularly critical of Ireland being held up as a model for other countries to follow, as somehow as typical in its success as it once was exceptional in its failure. The values underpinning current conventional thinking in Ireland need to be repeatedly challenged, not just because of their baleful influence on the domestic scene but also because of their strategic use elsewhere. Conversely, arguing for alternative sets of values brings Ireland into a meaningful, democratic dialogue with societies everywhere.

Context

The possibilities for radical transformation cannot be discussed without analysing the wider context, which can help or hinder such transformation. In other words, if we live in an era of stability and sustainable development, then we may decide that the prospects for radical transformation are slim. If, however, there is reason to believe that the present era is unstable and unsustainable, then radical transformation is not only more likely but may well be a certainty. If that is the case, then the question changes from one of whether radical transformation is likely, to one of *what sort of* radical transformation is likely. The omission of any discussion of environmental change in this book has meant the neglect of an issue that is more and more likely to dominate all our futures and make radical transformation a vital necessity. Before discussing what kind of transformation this may be, we need first to underline the true nature of the environmental challenges facing us, as our dominant culture has a tendency to minimise their scale and seriousness.

In his book *The Revenge of Gaia*, the eminent scientist James Lovelock (2007) writes that he believes that the understanding scientists have of the Earth 'is not much better than a nineteenth-century physician's understanding of a patient' but that 'we are sufficiently aware of the physiology of the Earth to realise the severity of its illness'. He goes on:

> We suspect the existence of a threshold, set by the temperature or the level of carbon dioxide in the air; once this is passed nothing the nations of the world do will alter the outcome and the Earth will move irreversibly to a new hot state. We are now approaching one of those tipping points, and our future is like that of the passengers on a small pleasure boat sailing quietly above the Niagara Falls, not knowing that the engines are about to fail. (Lovelock, 2007: 7)

While change is a normal part of geological history, what is new about the change now happening is that, for the first time, it is caused by one of the species inhabiting the Earth, namely humans. And, according to Lovelock, nothing like it has happened for 55 million years, when the change was larger than that between the ice age and the nineteenth century, and lasted for 200,000 years. He gives an example of the likely consequences of changes now upon us: if part of the Greenland or Southern glaciers slid into the sea, the level of the sea might rise by a metre all over the world. This event would render homeless millions of those living in coastal cities, making refugees of the populations of London, Calcutta, Miami and Rotterdam. Such conclusions are consistent with the reports of the Intergovernmental Panel on Climate Change (2007).

All the signs are, therefore, that the human race in general is facing a time of major challenges and Ireland is not immune from these challenges. The Environmental Protection Agency (2007) tells us that Ireland warmed up by 0.42 degrees Celsius per decade between 1980 and 2004, about twice as fast as the rest of the world, and it warns that the rate of warming is still accelerating (O'Brien, 2007). When we realise that experts regard it as essential that global temperatures not be allowed to rise by more than 2 degrees Celsius above pre-industrial era levels if we are to avoid catastrophic climate change (see United Nations Development Programme, 2007: 7), then the situation in Ireland is serious. The fast-emerging awareness that the human race is facing a challenge unlike anything it has faced before in its history indicates that the radical transformation of our global and local economies, of our political systems, of our cultural values and of our lifestyles is now imperative if the human race is going to survive. As Kovel puts it in the subtitle of his book *The Enemy of Nature*, it is going to be either 'the end of capitalism or the end of the world' (Kovel, 2007). Kovel's work draws attention to a fact that scientists can often overlook, namely the role that our productive system, based on the principles of the free market and the values of profit maximisation, is playing in the enormous crisis now upon us. Indeed, he sees climate change as a form of imperialism, in this case the domination of the natural environment and its use as a series of commodities from which profit can be extracted, as the source of finite raw materials to aid this extraction as cheaply as possible, and as a sink into which the wastes generated by this extraction can be dumped. The ever greater dominance of these market principles in Irish society over the economic boom, as analysed in this book, is therefore central to the challenges we now face.

The planet is one context for political agency; Europe is another. Ireland has been an enthusiastic member of the EU since its accession. In addition to the economic contribution of structural funds and revenue transfers, the EU was the source of a raft of progressive social and environmental legislation, which had hitherto been stoutly resisted by a motley coalition of economic, religious and political vested interests (Hourihane, 2004). One of the challenges of political transformation is to be critically responsive to general policy directions at EU level without giving hostages to the irredentist fantasies of the European far right. A salient difficulty in terms of democratic accountability is the weakness of the principal instrument of popular sovereignty, the European Parliament. Perry Anderson, in a lengthy review of the achievements of the European project, claimed: 'Constitutionally, the EU is a caricature of democratic federation, since its Parliament lacks powers of initiative, contains no parties with any existence at European level and wants even a modicum of popular credibility' (Anderson,

2007: 17). Power is largely concentrated in the Council of Ministers, the European Commission and the Committees of Permanent Representatives, which means that 'what the core structures of the EU effectively do is to convert the open agenda of parliaments into the closed world of chancelleries' (Anderson, 2007: 17). An average participation rate of less than 50 per cent in the 2004 elections to the European Parliament reflects a legitimate disenchantment with a supranational structure whose operations are increasingly beholden to a self-referential administrative elite.

The difficulty for the citizens of the new Europe is that the ministrations of mandarins are not a remote ritual but an ever-present reality. Jobs, taxes, social services and loan repayments, for example, are all crucially affected by the directives of the European Central Bank, the operation of Stability Pacts and the prescriptions of the Competition Directorate, all striving to make privatisation and deregulation core features of the economic policies of member states. The enlargement of the EU in 2004 and 2007 saw the axiomatic imposition of neoliberal principles on the economies of the new member states, which followed the Irish example in providing business-friendly fiscal regimes, cooperative governments and a pool of cheap labour. Through various competition directives, neoliberalism in effect has acquired the force of law, so not only does it become difficult, it becomes, in fact, illegal to oppose the merciless push towards privatisation. The capture of popular sovereignty by politico-administrative and economic elites is strikingly evident in the extreme reluctance of governments to seek a popular mandate for European treaties; where referenda are used, debates are invariably informed by a predictable politics of fear, where a search for self-understanding is routinely sacrificed to a pandering to self-interest ('all we have to lose'). For this reason, an important context for transformative political thinking in Ireland must be engaging with progressive forces across the EU to build a Union which operates both internally and at a global level as a force for redistributive justice, diplomatic autonomy and ecological integrity. The context is all the more important in that resistance to the vast powers of non-elected elites may result in forms of reactionary populism which are ultimately as hostile to democratic, progressive politics as are the material interests and ideological agendas of bankers and bureaucratic mandarins.

Actors

The previous section argued that the question now facing Ireland (and elsewhere) is not whether radical transformation is likely but, rather, *what kind* of radical transformation is likely. It is paradoxical indeed that the boom years greatly accelerated Ireland's move away from the sort of society that held at least some potential answers to the present crisis. For, what the human race needs to learn again is how to live close to nature in a mutually sustainable relationship, growing and nurturing locally most of the food sources we require, building sustainable communities that can provide for most of the social and cultural needs we have. A sustainable and humane future will therefore be built on a combination of highly imaginative scientific, technological and engineering innovations and very ancient skills of agriculture, holistic medicine, balanced diet and local community supports. This may have overtones of utopianism; however, another future is possible which could be distinctly dystopian and again Lovelock raises it: 'Is our civilisation doomed, and will this century mark its end with a massive decline in population, leaving an impoverished few survivors in a torrid society ruled by warlords on a hostile and disabled planet?' (Lovelock, 2007: 194). In other words, one option will be for the rich and powerful to try to hold on, maintaining their luxuries and way of life at the expense of the rest. There is much in the present ordering of the global system that presages this kind of future. What will make the difference between a more utopian and a more dystopian future will be the actions of human beings in making the challenges necessary for a better future. This brings us to the issue of actors.

Before we examine the potential for social actors to make a difference, it is worth noting that the chapters of this book have already uncovered the dominant actor that is currently shaping Irish society and that is the free market. Of course, as O'Donovan makes clear in chapter 9, speaking of 'the market' simply cloaks the influence of major corporations on our politicians, on our media and, in her example of pharmaceutical companies, on our health and well-being. Flynn's examination in chapter 6 of the power of BSkyB over the Irish government and, ultimately, the viewing choices of Irish soccer fans illustrates the same point in another domain of life. So, any discussion of actors who might change Ireland today has to begin from a recognition of the dominant power of private economic corporations. If political or social actors are to become more influential actors for change, a curtailing will be required of the extensive power market actors have gained for themselves, in particular over the years of the Celtic Tiger boom.

This, however, is no easy task, given post-industrial capitalism's ability to pander to the 'progressive' sensibilities of consumers. Disproportionately optimistic and, in some cases, blatantly misleading discourses about gender equality, cultural integration, active citizenship and quality of life have become commonplace, making it increasingly difficult for anyone to make a case for new, radical forms of political organisation. Now that the environment, social inclusion, gender equality, gay rights and inter-culturalism are all clearly and firmly on the mainstream political and cultural agenda, it appears that our greatest concerns about equality and the repercussions of globalisation are being taken care of. While there is no doubt that the movements which advanced these causes have made phenomenal and tangible gains in Ireland, it is important to remember that these successes are attributable not to the current conjuncture but to a socio-political time and place in which there was a belief in civil society and in the notion that social change could be achieved through political organisation and action. Interestingly, the most optimistic accounts of progress tend to come from those who were neither involved in nor would be involved in such struggles: their optimism is a kind of back-handed compliment, whose real intention is to point to the obsolescence of this type of political action. The rhetorics of 'girl power', cosmopolitan multiculturalism and 'ethical' consumerism are prime examples: rather than raising political consciousness about what needs to be done, these discourses imply that the necessary actions are being or have been taken care of, and are thus effectively geared towards eliminating the guilt of the 'socially conscious' consumer.

An excellent example of this is the relatively recent integration of 'corporate social responsibility' (CSR) within the public profiles of large retail chains, multinational corporations and other large organisations. Naturally, such initiatives are to be welcomed in principle, provided they are about fundamental changes in the structure and philosophy of how these institutions do business. However, this is rarely the case. As Joseph Heath and Andrew Potter (2005) point out in *The Rebel Sell*, it is a good thing if 'products are made by happy workers or eggs are laid by happy chickens' but this in no way undermines, challenges or changes the logic of consumer capitalism. They cite the example of the Blackspot Sneaker, a 'global anti-brand' designed to take on corporate giants such as Nike and Reebok through 'grass-roots capitalism'. Such forms of 'ethical con-sumerism', they argue, are no different to hippies buying VW Beetles in the 1970s to demonstrate their rejection of mass society. Conspicuous consumption, whether it is about consuming organic food, indie music or fair-trade shoes, is not an effective way to change what the counter-culture calls 'the system' because it is 'the system'.

Indeed, the semiotics of 'ethical consumerism' have been hijacked to the point of rendering them completely meaningless. In the British super-market chains which supply most of the food we consume, bread, meat, vegetables, cheese, milk, sugar, chocolates, tea, coffee and even smoothies come packaged with arty black-and-white photos of proud poultry farmers, smiling cheese-makers and celebrity chefs. This personalisation of goods distances the product from the real conditions of its production (i.e. mass production and factory farming), by reappropriating the promotional imagery previously associated with organic and fair-trade foodstuffs. Even in the case of organic foods, which are clearly better for our health and the environment, and fair-trade foods, which go some way to sustaining small agricultural cooperatives in the majority world, little if any significant change is required on the part of the Irish producer, retailer or consumer. That the socially conscious consumer is willing to pay more for a brand of nappies that gives a cut of its profits to charity or for a type of smoothie whose manufacturer plants trees is merely evidence that CSR is good for business. Moreover, one might ask why there are no little black-and-white photos of eight-year-old Xian and twelve-year-old Maya on the packaging that contains the plastic dolls, trucks and host of other imported products that line the shelves of our vastly oversized toy stores.

The highly selective use of CSR in the marketing of products would indicate that globalisation makes us cosmopolitan, informed citizens of the world only insofar as it suits the objectives of the marketplace. For example, the marketing strategies for brands of sportswear which claim to empower (western) women are unlikely to have any resonance with the women who work in the factories in Asia producing that sportswear. But perhaps the more fundamental question concerns how we came to believe that there is a link between material equality or empowerment and wearing a certain brand of sports clothing in the first place. According to Heath and Potter, democratic political action on the left has been supplanted by (counter-)cultural interventions and rhetoric, which they see as not only ineffective but also counterproductive, since the type of individualistic hedonism advocated by the current 'warmed over' versions of the counter-cultural politics of the 1970s 'makes it more difficult to organise social movements, and much more difficult to persuade anyone to make a sacrifice in the name of social justice' (Heath and Potter, 2005: 11). In a society in which (pseudo-)subversion has become a cultural commodity and mediated images have become a substitute for material progress, they argue that the cultural arena is not an effective way of inter-vening politically. The gains of feminism, socialism and anti-racism were not achieved by opting out of 'the mainstream' and consuming particular types of products to make this known but rather 'through the laborious process of democratic political action – through people making argu-ments, conducting studies, assembling coalitions and legislating change' (Heath and Potter, 2005: 11).

Clearly, CSR is an issue that Irish companies are beginning to take seriously, as is demonstrated by the Vodafone Ireland Foundation (VIF), which over the period from 2004 to 2007 gave €2.3 million to 105 projects promoting inclusive citizenship. According to Fintan O'Toole, however, 'The real test of CSR is, perhaps, a company's willingness to lose money in the short term by refusing to engage in practices that harm its workers, the environment or the communities and societies in which it operates' (O'Toole, 2007). Interestingly, the corporate responsibility section on Vodafone's website gives very brief headline summaries of findings from a highly selective number of reports about the dangers of mobile phone use.[1] It is not clear, for example, whether the advice cited from the UK government refers to the Mobile Telecommunications and Health Research (MTHR) programme, which is jointly funded by the British government and the mobile phone industry. Absent are the results of a major study conducted by Professor Kjell Mild of Orbero University, Sweden, which indicate that the risk of cancer among children using mobile phones is higher and that people who have used their mobile phone for a decade are twice as likely to be diagnosed with a tumour on a nerve connecting the ear to the brain (Hardell *et al.*, 2007). When the boundaries between CSR and public relations become unclear, we should be wary of how committed Ireland Inc. will be to real socio-economic change.

Given the attractiveness of a new demographic group of affluent, socially conscious consumers and neoliberalism's inevitable default to short-term profiteering, there is every danger that CSR will fail to entail any kind of radical rethinking about health, the environment, the majority world or ownership of the means of production. While corporate responsibility policies and entrepreneurial philanthropy may be good things in themselves, the crucial question is whether the market is the appropriate place for the advancement of social justice. We argue unequivocally in this book that it is not. O'Toole also asks some pertinent questions which point to the likely limitations of CSR in dealing with issues that are effectively the responsibility of our elected political leaders:

> Can the legal tax avoidance strategies that most companies and business people adopt as a matter of course be squared with CSR? Can investors and stock-markets learn to balance the long-term gains of sustainability against the short-term losses that may be the consequences of the 'economics of enough'? Are there areas of activity – like health and education – that corporations should decline to take over from the state on the ethical grounds that they are not best served by market mechanisms? (O'Toole, 2007: 10)

The logic of CSR, however, is not restricted to the corporate world but is beginning to emerge also in public institutions, most notably in universities. As third-level education becomes both more commercialised and internationalised, it is vital that its pro-diversity and social inclusion strategies are more than just good public relations. At present, the increasingly hierarchical corporate model of academia does not accommodate grass-roots, bottom-up collaborations with community groups because such working models are not considered to be cost-effective in the short term, even though it is clear that they yield the richest social dividends in the long term. It is not uncommon to hear of social-inclusion projects run by universities in which the community stakeholders never actually meet or talk with the project managers. If universities are serious about initiatives such as community-based learning, therefore, they must acknowledge that this requires significant structural and philosophical change. According to Fear and Avila (2005), too often community-based learning is 'valued more for its instrumental value and extrinsic merit – for the funding and publicity it brings – than for its relevance in performing a mission-related responsibility, that is, serving society'.

Conclusion

If Tony Blair's 'legacy' has taught us anything, it is that there is no 'third way', and we are deluded in Ireland if we think that we can square the circles that Britain could not, and have it both ways. As Heath and Potter argue, it is time to cut through the spin-doctoring and media imagery that bombard us with reductive sound-bites and to return to the material realities of people's lives, to the distribution of power and wealth, to what Heath and Potter (2005: 7) refer to as 'the old-fashioned concern for social justice'. It is not in making Ireland a wealthier nation state that the collective challenge now lies, nor in expressing our politically correct credentials through acts of conspicuous consumption, but in finding peaceful, sustainable, inclusive and egalitarian ways to live, work and raise children and in re-empowering those who have been disentitled and disenfranchised by the privatisation and commercialisation of public assets. Three key strategies in the 'war' on neoliberal discourse must be:

1 a genuine commitment to media education at all levels
2 the continued support of public service broadcasting and independent/ investigative journalism
3 resistance to the commercialisation of research in the humanities and social sciences, whose main purpose is to critique our society and culture, uncompromised by vested interests.

Central to these strategies is the notion that an informed and critical population can mobilise for change once it engages with the bigger picture and is not pandered to by simplistic slogans and reductive binarisms.

The media literacy referenced in everyday public discourse, which refers generally to young people's technical sophistication, vast repertoire of cultural references and ability to detect irony or parody, must not be confused with an ability to decode media ideologically or to understand how the media work in terms of ownership or political economy. As Sean Phelan demonstrates in chapter 5, the way in which the discourse of neoliberalism has been internalised by the Irish media calls for the latter sort of media literacy, generally referred to as critical media literacy. Critical skills are crucial to empowering citizens in an increasingly media-saturated world and must be mainstreamed into all levels of the education system. Increased awareness of the limits of ethical consumerism and a more holistic understanding of the impact of consumption are also key to exposing the tokenism of most CSR initiatives. Advocates of liberal capitalism often comment that 'the public gets what the public wants', usually by way of defending the reactionary content of newspapers, the liberalisation of the sex industry or the quantity of unhealthy food available in our supermarkets. However, as Roddy Flynn demonstrates in chapter 6, consumer awareness and empowerment can also force powerful decision makers to change tack. The more we know about the impact of what we consume, the easier it is to demand more fundamental changes. Local initiatives such as the Pearse Street Food Cooperative are viable alternatives to the large supermarket chains. Not only do such initiatives support local producers and minimise negative environmental impact but they also foster other forms of community engagement, such as childcare networks and community action groups.

Another sign of hope pointing the way to the future is the emergence of Ireland's first eco-village, currently being developed in Cloghjordan, County Tipperary, which sees itself as modelling a more sustainable and vibrant way of living amid the crisis now upon us. The eco-village project is far more than simply families and individuals living together in an ecological housing suburb. It involves not just building ecological houses that minimise the use of energy but also providing communal forms of energy production, hot water, waste disposal and food production. The 132 housing units occupy only one-third of the land area of the eco-village; another third is given over to allotments and a farm, where the occupants of each house can produce much of their food ecologically; and a final third is being left as a wilderness for both occupants and other species to enjoy. The Cloghjordan eco-village also sees itself as an educational centre, providing a range of courses, not only on ecological issues but also on the practical skills needed for a good quality of life – health, cookery, therapies and many others. Courses cover political and economic issues, sustainable technologies, dance and music, philosophy, theology and spirituality – indeed, any of the skills and areas of knowledge that people will need for sustainable living and enjoyment in the new era. It is hoped that Cloghjordan will be a model of how vibrant, enjoyable and healthy living is possible without destroying the environment on which we all depend. This, then, is one form of action that holds the potential to make a real difference to the sort of radical transformation that could take place in the new conditions upon us.

Cloghjordan is an example of how civil society can make a real difference in its own right. And this is important to avoid an excessive fixation on the state as both problem and solution in society. But this is by no means sufficient. Transforming *society* will require challenging and changing the power hierarchies that underpin and sustain the present social order, power hierarchies that give a privileged position to the needs of private economic power holders, as this book has illustrated. Challenging power is the arena of politics, an arena discredited in the contemporary world. Yet, as many of the countries of South America are currently showing us, the construction of more popular forms of politics is possible, popular in the sense both that they command widespread support, especially of those marginalised by the power hierarchies of today's neoliberal order, and that they have arisen from the base of society to challenge the status quo. This holds valuable lessons for Ireland and foremost among these lessons is that the construction of such an alternative politics is a task for the long term. Yet, it is worth dwelling on how the 'new left' has emerged in South America, as a way of gaining pointers as to what needs to be done to foster a transformative politics in Ireland.

Three 'moments' of social action can be identified as the steps towards the building of the 'new left'. The first were the many social movements which arose since the late 1970s in the struggles against military dictatorships and for the protection of human rights, in the struggles for economic survival and income generation amid the imposition of neoliberalism, and in the struggles for consciousness raising and new cultural identities as social actors sought to take their future into their own hands. These in turn led to a second 'moment', as new forms of political party arose to give voice to the new social actors empowered through social movements. These took many forms, from the innovative Workers' Party (Partido dos Trabalhadores, PT) in Brazil that arose from the militant trade union struggles in the industrial peripheries of São Paulo but which allowed a remarkable pluralism of political currents of thought to remain organised within, to the broad front, Frente Amplio, of various progressive parties that emerged in Uruguay. The third 'moment' came with the decentralisation of power to municipal governments that happened throughout Latin America after the return to democracy in the 1980s under the pressure of

World Bank advice. Many of these new parties cut their teeth in running these municipalities, using them to introduce such innovative policies as the participative budgetary processes introduced by the Workers' Party in Brazil and now widely used throughout the region. Through their success at municipal level, these parties widened their base of support as a stepping stone to national government. Overall, this process took around thirty years. Having reached national power, they are now preparing for a post-neoliberal era, particularly by making the state again a decisive actor for economic and social development (in countries like Venezuela, Bolivia and Ecuador, where public institutions were most discredited, through a thorough reinstitutionalisation of the state) and through programmes of radical democratisation (see Rodríguez Garavito *et al.*, 2005; Adamovsky, 2007). These 'moments' can be seen to mirror aspects of Cox's alternative historical structure, particularly in the new ideas that emerged through social mobilising and organising and through the new institutions to which these have given rise over time. In this way, the discrediting of the old has opened spaces for the emergence of the new.

The lessons for Ireland are clear. First, as Murphy outlines in chapter 11, social partnership has underpinned a political culture of consensus and has served to maintain a conservative and unambitious welfare regime. Yet, as she tellingly points out, moves towards somewhat more generous benefits resulted not from the pressures of the community and voluntary sector within social partnership but from the major drubbing that Fianna Fáil received from the electorate in the 2004 European and local elections, following which the party quickly rebranded itself as socially caring and sought to distance itself from the Progressive Democrats. This points strongly towards the need to foster the sorts of active social movements that proved to be the seedbed of the new left in Latin America. Arguably, too close an embrace by the state has seriously undermined alternative and contestatory forms of social organisation that are essential for transformation. Second, as Kirby argues in chapter 12, a more activist civil society creates the conditions for the emergence of a new political force (whether an entirely new party or a front of some existing progressive parties) and is a vital necessity for the transformation of society.

The lessons of the Latin American new left remind us that such a political force can emerge only out of a determination to stand aside from the dominant conservative parties and consistently to seek to build the new, even if this allows the conservative parties to maintain a stranglehold on power for some time longer. The failure to develop such alternatives in the Irish party system over any sustained length of time has been one of the great missed opportunities of the past three decades. It is vital now that commitments be made that will ensure Fianna Fáil and Fine

Gael will not continue to dominate the Irish party system for another three decades. Finally, the commitment to elected mayors in Ireland opens another forum that could provide a platform for new parties and leaders to emerge, as has happened in Latin America. While many commentators fear that such positions will reinforce the localist tendencies in Irish politics, with political imagination and skill they could be used as spaces for alternative forms of politics and political leadership to emerge. The hope is that those individuals and groups in the community and voluntary sector, and their many allies in academic life and other parts of Irish society (the media, the civil service and state agencies), who are committed to building an alternative to Ireland's total subservience to global capitalism, might now begin to strategise as to how to move beyond the present impasse and lay the foundations for a transformation. Particularly with the community and voluntary sector, there exists more than enough commitment, seasoned leadership and political imagination to capture this moment of possibility. And the time is certainly ripe.

Note

1 See www.vodafone.com/start/responsibility/mpmh.html (accessed 18 December 2007).

Bibliography

Acheson, Nicholas, Brian Harvey and Arthur Williamson (2004) *Two Paths, One Purpose: Voluntary Action in Ireland North and South*, Dublin: IPA.

Adamovsky, Ezequiel (2007) *Más allá de la vieja izquierda: Seis ensayos para un Nuevo anticapitalismo*, Buenos Aires: Prometeo Libros.

Advisory Committee on Third-Level Student Support (1993) *Report of the Advisory Committee on Third-Level Student Support* (De Buitléir report), Dublin: Stationery Office.

Alber, Jens and Guy Standing (2000) 'Social dumping, catch up or convergence: Europe in a comparative global context', *Journal of European Social Policy*, 10(2): 99–119.

Allen, Kieran (2000) *The Myth of Social Partnership*, Manchester: Manchester University Press.

Allen, Kieran (2003) 'Neither Boston nor Berlin: class polarisation and neo-liberalism in the Irish Republic', in C. Coulter and S. Coleman (eds), *The End of Irish History: Critical Reflections on the Celtic Tiger*, Manchester: Manchester University Press, pp. 56–73.

Allen, Kieran (2007) *The Corporate Takeover of Ireland*, Dublin: Irish Academic Press.

Allen, Theodore W. (1994) *The Invention of the White Race*, New York: Verso.

Anderson, Perry (2007) 'European hypocrisies', *London Review of Books*, 29(18): 13–21.

Angell, Marcia (2004) *The Truth About Drug Companies – How They Deceive Us and What To Do About It*, New York: Random House.

Anson, Brian (1982) *North West Donegal Gaeltacht: A Social and Environmental Study*, report for Údarás na Gaeltachta (unpublished).

Avilés, Luis (2001) 'Epidemiology as discourse: the politics of development institutions in the epidemiological profile of El Salvador', *Journal of Epidemiology and Community Health*, 55: 164–71.

Ayres, Clarence (1944) *The Theory of Economic Progress*. New York: Schocken Books (1962).

Balanda, Kevin B. and Jane Wilde (2001) *Inequalities in Mortality 1989–1998*, Dublin: Institute of Public Health in Ireland.

Balibar, Etienne (1996) 'Existe-t-il un racisme Européen?', *Multitudes*. Available at http://multitudes.samizdat.net/Existe-t-il-un-racisme-europeen.html (accessed 12 May 2007).

Baran, Paul (1958) 'On the political economy of backwardness', in A. N. Agarwala and S. P. Singh (eds), *The Economics of Underdevelopment*, Oxford: Oxford University Press, pp. 75–92.

Barry, Frank (1987) *Between Tradition and Modernity: Cultural Values and the Problems of Irish Society*, Centre for Economic Research, Department of Political Economy, Policy Paper No. 23, Dublin: UCD Press.

Barry, Frank (ed.) (1999) *Understanding Ireland's Economic Growth*, Basingstoke: Macmillan.

Barry, Michael, M. Lesley Tilson and Máirín Ryan (2008) 'Drug expenditure in Ireland – explaining recent trends', in O. O'Donovan and K. Glavanis-Grantham (eds), *Power, Politics and Pharmaceuticals. Drug Regulation in Ireland in a Global Context*, Cork: Cork University Press, pp. 105–16.

Bateman, B., *et al.* (2004) 'The effects of a double blind, placebo controlled, artificial food colourings and benzoate preservative challenge on hyperactivity in a general population sample of preschool children', *Archives of Disease in Childhood*, 89(6): 506–11.

Baughman, Fred A. (2006) *The ADHD Fraud: How Psychiatry Makes 'Patients' Out of Normal Children*, Victoria, BC: Trafford Publishing.

Bauman, Zygmunt (2000) *Liquid Modernity*, Cambridge: Polity Press.

Bauman, Zygmunt (2004) *Wasted Lives: Modernity and Its Outcasts*, Cambridge: Polity Press.

Beaud, Michel and Gilles Dostaler (1997) *Economic Thought Since Keynes: A History and Dictionary of Major Economists*, London: Routledge.

Beck, Ulrich (2006) *Cosmopolitan Vision*, Cambridge: Polity Press.

Begg, David (2005) 'New society requires new labour market standards', *Irish Times*, 17 December.

Benn Michaels, Walter (2006) *The Trouble with Diversity: How We Learned to Love Identity and Ignore Inequality*, London: Metropolitan Books.

Benson, Rodney and Erik Neveu (2005) *Bourdieu and the Journalistic Field*, Cambridge: Polity Press.

Bernstein, Basil (1971) *Class, Codes and Control, Vol. I*, London: Routledge and Kegan Paul.

Billig, Michael (1995) *Banal Nationalism*, London: Sage.

Blommaert, Jan and Jef Verschueren (1998) *Debating Diversity: Analysing the Discourse of Tolerance*, London: Routledge.

Bly, Robert (1992) *Iron John: A Book About Men*, New York: Vintage Books.

Blyth, Mark (2002) *Great Transformations, Economic Ideas and Institutional Change in the Twentieth Century*, Cambridge: Cambridge University Press/Johns Hopkins University Press.

Blythe, Ernest (1958) 'The significance of the Irish language for the future of the nation', *University Review*, 2(2): 3–22.

Bourdieu, Pierre (1998) *Acts of Resistance: Against the New Myths of Our Time*, Cambridge: Polity Press.

Bourdieu, Pierre (1999) 'The state, economics and sport', in H. Dauncey and G. Hare (eds), *France and the 1998 World Cup: The National Impact of a World Sporting Event*, London: Frank Cass.

Bowers, Fergal (2001) 'Drugs body supports relaxed advertising rules'. Available at www.irishhealth.com/?id=2803&level=4) (accessed 20 March 2007).

Boyle, Nicholas (1998) *Who Are We Now? Christian Humanism and the Global Market from Hegel to Heaney*, Edinburgh: T&T Clark.

Boyle, Nigel (2005) *FÁS and Active Labour Market Policy 1985–2004*, Studies in Public Policy No. 17, Dublin: Policy Institute.

Bracken, Ali (2005) 'Taking a dramatic approach to dealing with suicide', *Irish Times*, 8 November.

Bracken, Patrick and Philip Thomas (2005) *Postpsychiatry – Mental Health in a Postmodern World*, Oxford: Oxford University Press.

Bradshaw, Johnathan and Sheila Shaver (1995) 'The recognition of wifely labour by welfare states', *Social Policy and Administration*, 29(1): 10–25.

Breggin, Peter (1991) *Toxic Psychiatry: Why Therapy, Empathy and Love Must Replace the Drugs, Electroshock, and Biochemical Theories of the 'New Psychiatry'*, New York: St Martin's Griffin.

Breggin, Peter and Dick Scruggs (2001) *Talking Back to Ritalin: What Doctors Aren't Telling You About Stimulants and ADHD*, Cambridge, MA: Da Capo Press.

Breheny, Martin (2002) 'No change in our coverage: GAA', *Irish Independent*, 9 July, p. 3.

Brennan, Martin (1969) 'Language, personality and the nation', in Brian Ó Cuív (ed.), *A View of the Irish Language*, Dublin: Stationery Office, pp. 70–80.

Browne, Harry (2006) 'Irish times', *The Dubliner*, May 2006. Available at www.thedubliner. ie/the_dubliner_magazine/2007/04/irish_times.html (accessed June 2006).

Browne, Nick (1987) 'The political economy of the television (super)text', in Horace Newcomb (ed.), *Television: The Critical View* (4th edn), New York: Oxford University Press, pp. 585–99.

Browne, Vincent (2000) 'The public is wrong – teachers must be accountable', *Irish Times Education and Living Supplement*, 25 April.

Browne, Vincent (2002) 'Fairness: it means more than football', *Irish Times*, 17 July, p. 12.

Browne, Vincent (2007) 'Poverty the real killer in Ireland', *Irish Times*, 12 December.

Bruton, Richard (1998) 'Measuring quality', *Irish Times Education and Living Supplement*, 17 March.

Buruma, Ian (2006) *Murder in Amsterdam: The Death of Theo van Gogh and the Limits of Tolerance*, London: Atlantic Books.

Byrne, P. (1996) 'RTE to cover all Ireland's home ties', *Irish Times*, 24 October.

Caherty, Therese (ed.) (1992) *Is Ireland a Third World Country?*, Belfast: Beyond the Pale Publications.

Calhoun, Craig (ed.) (1992) *Habermas and the Public Sphere*, Cambridge, MA: MIT.

Callan, Tim, Brian Nolan and Christopher Whelan (1996) *A Review of the Commission on Social Welfare's Minimum Adequate Income*, Dublin: ESRI.

Campbell, Cefn (2000) 'Menter Cwm Gwendraeth: a case-study in community language planning', in Colin H. Williams (ed.), *Language Revitalization: Policy and Planning in Wales*, Cardiff: University of Wales Press, pp. 247–91.

Canetti, Elias (1986) *The Human Province*, trans. J. Neugroschel, London: Picador.

Casey, Michael (2006) 'The myth of our economic autonomy', *Irish Times*, 19 April.

Castel, Robert (2003) *L'Insécurité sociale: Qu'est-ce qu'être protégé?*, Paris: Seuil.

Castells, Manuel (1996) *The Rise of the Network Society*, Oxford: Blackwell.

Castles, Francis and Deborah Mitchell (eds) (1993) *Worlds of Welfare and Families of Nations: Patterns of Public Policy in Western Democracies*, Aldershot: Dartmouth.

Cave, Martin and Robert W. Crandell (2001) 'Sports rights and the broadcast industry', *Economic Journal*, 111: F4–F26.

Central Statistics Office (2004a) *Census 2002, Vol. 11: The Irish Language*. Available at www.cso.ie/census/Vol11.htm (accessed 1 June 2007).

Central Statistics Office (2004b) Small area population statistics (SAPS) for the Gaeltacht (1981, 1986, 1991, 1996, 2002). Purchased from CSO for purposes of this study.

Central Statistics Office (2005a) *EU Survey on Income and Living Conditions, First Results 2005*, Dublin: Stationery Office.

Central Statistics Office (2005b) *Measuring Ireland's Progress 2005*, Dublin: Stationery Office.

Central Statistics Office (2006) *Women and Men in Ireland 2006*. Available at www.cso.ie/ releasespublications/documents/other_releases/2006/womenandmenireland2006.pdf (accessed 3 May 2007).

Central Statistics Office (2007) *Census 2006: Principal Demographic Results*. Available at www.cso.ie/census/Census2006_Principal_Demographic_Results.htm (accessed 28 May 2007).

Central Statistics Office (2008) *Survey on Income and Living Conditions (SILC) in Ireland 2007*, Dublin: Central Statistics Office.

Cerny, Philip G., Georg Menz and Susanne Soederberg (eds) (2005) *Internalising Globalisation: The Rise of Neoliberalism and the Decline of National Varieties of Capitalism*, Basingstoke: Palgrave.

Chirac, Jacques (1991) Extract from speech by Chirac to party supporters at Orléans, France, 19 June. Available at www.ina.fr/archivespourtous/index.php?vue=notice&from=fulltext&full=chirac+bruit+odeur&num_notice=7&total_notices=8 (accessed 12 May 2007).

Chouliaraki, Lilie and Norman Fairclough (1999) *Discourse in Late Modernity: Rethinking Critical Discourse Analysis*, Edinburgh: Edinburgh University Press.

Chubb, John and Terry Moe (1990) *Politics, Markets and America's Schools*, Washington, DC: Brookings Institution.

Clancy, Patrick (2001) *College Entry in Focus: A Fourth National Survey of Access to Higher Education*, Dublin: HEA.

Clare, Anthony (2000) *On Men: Masculinity in Crisis*, London: Chatto & Windus.

Cleary, Anne (2005) 'Death rather than disclosure: struggling to be a real man', *Irish Journal of Sociology*, 14(2): 155–76.

Coakley, Anne (2005) *Mothers, Welfare and Labour Market Activation*, Research Working Paper No. 05/04, Dublin: Combat Poverty Agency.

Coakley, L. and Piaras Mac Éinrí (2007) *Islands of Difference or Intercultural City? A Study of Refugees and Persons With Leave to Remain in Cork, October 2005–March 2006*, Dublin: Reception and Integration Agency.

Coleman, Marc (2005) 'Swedes warm to Ireland's low-tax regime', *Irish Times*, 19 December.

Coleman, Marc (2007) 'Issue of value for money remains a huge concern', *Irish Times*, 24 January.

Comhairle na Gaeilge (1971) *Institiúidí Rialtais Áitiúil agus Forbraíochta don Ghaeltacht/Local Government and Development Institutions for the Gaeltacht*, Dublin: Stationery Office.

Commission of the European Communities (2003a) *Fourth Report from the Commission to the Council, the European Parliament, the European Economic and Social Committee and the Committee of the Regions on the Application of Directive 89/552/EEC 'Television Without Frontiers'*, COM (2002) 778 Final, Brussels: CEC.

Commission of the European Communities (2003b) 'Publication in accordance with article 3a(2) of Council Directive 89/552/EEC on the coordination of certain provisions laid down by law, regulation or administrative action in Member States concerning the pursuit of television broadcasting activities, as amended by Directive 97/36/EC of the European Parliament and of the Council', *Official Journal*, C100 (26 April): 12–16.

Commission of the European Communities (2007) *Statistical Annex of European Economy*, Brussels: CEC.

Commission on Financial Management and Control Systems in the Health System (2003) *Report* (Brennan report), Dublin: Stationery Office.

Condry, J. C. and S. Condry (1976) 'Sex differences: a study in the eye of the beholder', *Child Development*, 47: 812–19.

Conference of Religious of Ireland (2007) *Socio-Economic Review 2007*, Dublin: CORI.

Connell, R. W. (2002) *Gender*, Cambridge: Polity Press.

Conrad, Peter (2007) *The Medicalization of Society: On the Transformation of Human Conditions into Treatable Disorders*, Baltimore, MD: Johns Hopkins University Press.

Corry, Micheal and Áine Tubridy (2005) *Depression. An Emotion Not a Disease*, Cork: Mercier Press.

Coulmas, Florian (1998) 'Introduction', in Florian Coulmas (ed.), *The Handbook of Sociolinguistics* (2nd edn), Malden: Blackwell, pp. 1–10.

Coulter, Colin (2003) 'The end of Irish history? An introduction to the book', in Colin Coulter and Steve Coleman (eds), *The End of Irish History? Critical Approaches to the Celtic Tiger*, Manchester: Manchester University Press, pp. 1–33.

Coulter, Colin and Steve Coleman (eds) (2003) *The End of Irish History: Critical Reflections on the Celtic Tiger*, Manchester: Manchester University Press.

Council of Education (1954) *Report on the Function and Curriculum of the Primary School*, Dublin: Stationery Office.

Council of Education (1962) *Report on the Curriculum of the Secondary School*, Dublin: Stationery Office.

Cousins, Mel (1995) 'Ireland's place in the world of welfare capitalism', *Journal of European Social Policy*, 7(3): 223–35.

Cousins, Mel (2005) *Explaining the Irish Welfare State*, Lewiston, NY: Edwin Mellen Press.

Cowie, Campbell and Mark Williams (1997) 'The economics of sports rights', *Telecommunications Policy*, 21(7): 619–34.

Cox, Robert W. (1996) 'Social forces, states and world orders: beyond international relations theory' (1981), in Robert W. Cox with Timothy J. Sinclair, *Approaches to World Order*, Cambridge: Cambridge University Press, pp. 85–123.

Cox, Robert W. (2002) *The Political Economy of a Plural World: Critical Reflections on Power, Morals and Civilization*, London: Routledge.

Cromwell Cox, Oliver (1948) *Caste, Class, and Race: A Study of Social Dynamics*, New York: Doubleday.

Cronin, Michael and Barbara O'Connor (eds) (2003) *Irish Tourism: Image, Culture and Identity*, Clevedon: Channel View Publications.

Crossley, Nick (2004) 'On systematically distorted communication: Bourdieu and the socio-analysis of publics', in Nick Crossley and John M. Roberts (eds), *After Habermas: New Perspectives on the Public Sphere*, Oxford: Blackwell/Sociological Review.

Crossley, Nick (2006) 'The field of psychiatric contention in the UK, 1960–2000', *Social Science and Medicine*, 62: 552–63.

Crossley, Nick and John M. Roberts (eds) (2004) *After Habermas: New Perspectives on the Public Sphere*, Oxford: Blackwell/Sociological Review.

Cullen, Elizabeth (2006) 'Growth and the Celtic cancer: unprecedented growth but for whose benefit?', in Tom O'Connor and Mike Murphy (eds), *Social Care in Ireland: Theory, Policy and Practice*, Cork: CIT Press, pp. 112–25.

Davis, Thomas (1843a) 'Self-education', in D. J. O'Donoghue (ed.), *Essays of Thomas Davis: Centenary Edition*, New York: Lemma Publishing Corporation (1974), pp. 90–6.

Davis, Thomas (1843b) 'Our national language', in D. J. O'Donoghue (ed.), *Essays of Thomas Davis: Centenary Edition*, New York: Lemma Publishing Corporation (1974), pp. 97–107.

de Fréine, Seán (1960) *Saoirse gan Só*, Dublin: FNT.

de Fréine, Seán (1965) *The Great Silence*, Dublin: FNT.

Delanty, Gerard (2006) 'The cosmopolitan imagination: critical cosmopolitanism and social theory', *British Journal of Sociology*, 57(1): 25–57.

Department of Communications, Marine and Natural Resources (2003) *Ireland's Submission to the European Commission in Relation to the Review of the Television Without Frontiers Directive*. Available at www.dcenr.gov.ie (accessed 5 April 2004).

Department of Community, Rural and Gaeltacht Affairs (2004) 'Ciste gur fiú €1.56m thar trí bliana fógraithe ag Ó Cuív le haghaidh pleanála teanga sa Ghaeltacht', press release, 27 February. Available at www.pobail.ie/ie/Preaseisiuinti/2004/Feabhra/htmltext,4053,ie.html (accessed 20 May 2004).

Department of Education and Science (2005) *DEIS (Delivering Equality of Opportunity in Schools). An Action Plan for Educational Inclusion*, Dublin: Department of Education and Science.

Department of Education and Science (2007) *Support Services for Post-Primary Education*, Dublin: Department of Education and Science.

Department of Education and Science Inspectorate (2006) *Learning to Teach. Students on Teaching Practice in Irish Primary Schools*, Dublin: Department of Education and Science.

Department of Enterprise, Trade and Employment (2006) *Strategy for Science, Technology and Innovation, 2006–2013*, Dublin: Department of Enterprise, Trade and Employment.

Department of Justice, Equality and Law Reform (2006) *Scheme of the Immigration, Residency and Protection Bill 2006*, Dublin: Department of Justice, Equality and Law Reform.

Department of Social and Family Affairs (various years) *Annual Statistical Reports*, Dublin: Stationery Office.

Devlin, Maurice (2000) *Representations of Irish Youth*, doctoral thesis (unpublished), Maynooth: National University of Ireland.

De Zengotita, T. (2005) *Mediated: How the Media Shape Your World*, London: Bloomsbury.

Dhombres, Dominique (2007) 'Souriez! Vous travaillez chez Google!', *Le Monde*, 11 December, p. 31.

Dicks, Bella (2004) *Cultures on Display: The Production of Contemporary Visitability*, London: Open University Press.

Ditch, John and Nina Oldfield (1999) 'Social assistance: recent trends and themes', *Journal of European Social Policy*, 9(1): 65–76.

Douzinas, Costas (2006) 'Humanitarianism and politics', *Re-Public: Re-imagining Democracy*. Available at www.re-public.gr/en/?p=30 (accessed 1 July 2006).

Downes, Gerard (2008) 'The pharmaceutical industry and the World Trade Organisation's TRIPs agreement: intellectual property, global governance and health', in O. O'Donovan and K. Glavanis-Grantham (eds), *Power, Politics and Pharmaceuticals. Drug Regulation in Ireland in a Global Context*, Cork: Cork University Press, pp. 27–42.

Downing, John and Charles Husband (2005) *Representing Race: Racism, Ethnicity and the Media*, London: Sage.

Doyle, Laura (2001) *The Surrendered Wife: A Practical Guide to Finding Intimacy, Passion, and Peace With a Man*, London: Simon and Schuster.

Dublin Rape Crisis Centre (2005) *25 Years On. Anniversary Report 2005*, Dublin: DRCC. Available at www.drcc.ie/report/anniversary_report.pdf (accessed 12 February 2007).

Duggan, Carmel and Camille Loftus (2006) *A Study of Labor Market Vulnerability and Responses to it in Donegal, Sligo and North Dublin*, Dublin: National Economic and Social Forum. Available at www.nesf.ie/publications.asp (accessed January 2009).

Dukelow, Fiona (2004) 'The path towards a more "employment friendly" liberal regime? Globalisation and the Irish social security system', paper presented at the Foundation for International Studies of Social Security Seminar (FISS), Stockholm, June.

Dunn, Seamus, Valerie Morgan and Helen Dawson (2001) *Establishing the Demand for Services and Activities in the Irish Language in Northern Ireland*, Belfast: Policy Evaluation Research Unit (DCAL/NISRA).

Dutton, Clive (2004) *Ceathrú Gaeltachta: Bunú Bord Forbartha agus Ceisteanna Bainteacha/ Gaeltacht Quarter: The Establishment of a Development Board and Related Issues*, Belfast: DCAL, DSD, DETI.

Eagleton, Terry (2003) *After Theory*, London: Penguin.

Edwards, Elaine (2005) 'Learning to keep a lid on your temper', *Irish Times*, 8 November.

Edwards, Elaine (2006) 'Dark chocolate may relieve symptoms of ME', *Irish Times*, 19 December.

Environmental Protection Agency (2007) *EPA Annual Highlights 2006*, Dublin: Environmental Protection Agency.

Epstein, Debbie (1998) *Failing Boys? Issues in Gender and Achievement*, Buckingham: Open University Press.

Epstein, Debbie and Richard Johnson (1994) 'On the straight and narrow: the heterosexual presumption, homophobias and schools', in Debbie Epstein (ed.), *Challenging Lesbian and Gay Inequalities in Education*, Buckingham: Open University Press, pp. 197–230.

Equality Authority (2008) *Gender Inequalities in Time Use – The Distribution of Caring, Housework and Employment Among Women and Men in Ireland*, Dublin: Equality Authority. Available at www.equality.ie/index.asp?docID=725 (accessed January 2009).

Erikson, Robert (2007) 'Soaring in the best of times?', in Tony Fahey, Helen Russell and Christopher T. Whelan (eds), *Best of Times? The Social Impact of the Celtic Tiger*, Dublin: IPA, pp. 265–76.

Esping-Andersen, Gøsta (1990) *The Three Worlds of Welfare Capitalism*, Cambridge: Polity Press.

Eurobarometer (2007) *Special Eurobarometer: Discrimination in the European Union*, EBS 263, Brussels: European Commission.

European Council (1997) 'Council Directive 97/36/EC of the European Parliament and of the Council of 30 June 1997 amending Council Directive 89/552/EEC on the coordination of certain provisions laid down by law, regulation or administrative action in Member States concerning the pursuit of television broadcasting activities', *Official Journal*, L202 (30 July): 60–70.

Eurostat (2004) *Economy of the Union*, Luxembourg: Eurostat.

Expert Working Group on the Integration of the Tax and Social Welfare Systems (1996) *Report*, Dublin: Stationery Office.

Fagan, G. Honor (2003) 'Globalised Ireland, or contemporary transformations of national identity', in Colin Coulter and Steve Coleman (eds), *The End of Irish History? Critical Approaches to the Celtic Tiger*, Manchester: Manchester University Press, pp. 110–21.

Fahey, Tony, Helen Russell and Christopher T. Whelan (2007a) 'Boom has yielded real social progress', *Irish Times*, 29 June, p. 16.

Fahey, Tony, Helen Russell and Christopher T. Whelan (eds) (2007b) *Best of Times? The Social Impact of the Celtic Tiger*, Dublin: IPA.

Fairclough, Norman (2000) *New Labour, New Language*, London: Routledge.

Fairclough, Norman (2003) *Analysing Discourse: Textual Analysis for Social Research*, London: Routledge.

Fanning, Bryan (2002) *Racism and Social Change in the Republic of Ireland*, Manchester: Manchester University Press.

Fanning, Bryan (2007) *Immigration and Social Change in the Republic of Ireland*, Manchester: Manchester University Press.

Farrell, Warren (1993) *The Myth of Male Power: Why Men Are the Disposable Sex*, New York: Simon & Schuster.

Farrell, Warren (1999) *Women Can't Hear What Men Don't Say: Destroying Myths, Creating Love*, New York: Tarcher/Putnam.

Fear, F. A. and Avila, M. (2005) 'Frames and discourses: exploring the meaning of engagement', *Perspectives on Community Development*, 2.

Ferguson, Harry, with the assistance of Claire Mackinnon (2001) 'Thematic network: the social problem and societal problematisation of men and masculinities', Ireland national report on newspaper representations on men and men's practices, Workpackage 26, available at www.cromenet.org/crome/crome.nsf/resources/2FCB42C251EEF4EEC22 56B6C003C45DA/$file/Ireland.doc.

Ferguson, Harry (2002) 'Critical studies on men in ten European countries', *Men and Masculinities*, 5(1): 5–31.

Ferriter, Diarmaid (2005) *The Transformation of Ireland 1900–2000*, London: Profile Books.

Finegold, David, Laurel MacFarland and William Richardson (eds) (1992) *Something Borrowed, Something Blue? A Study of the Thatcher Government's Appropriation of American Education and Training Policy*, Oxford: Triangle Books.

Fishman, Joshua A. (ed.) (1989) *Language and Ethnicity in Minority Sociolinguistic Perspective*, Clevedon: Multilingual Matters.

Fishman, Joshua A. (1991) *Reversing Language Shift: Theoretical and Empirical Foundations of Assistance to Threatened Languages*, Clevedon: Multilingual Matters.

Fishman, Joshua A. (1996) 'What do you lose when you lose your language?', in G. Cantoni (ed.), *Stabilizing Indigenous Languages*, Flagstaff: Northern Arizona University, pp. 80–91.

Fishman, Joshua A. (ed.) (2000) *Can Threatened Languages Be Saved? Reversing Language Shift Revisited*, Clevedon: Multilingual Matters.

Fiske, John (1990) *Introduction to Communication Studies*, London: Routledge.

Fitzpatrick, James (2006) 'Something beautiful is dying', *Catholic Exchange*, 13 December, p. 14.

Fitzpatrick, Seán (2005) 'Media should spare us the polemics and give us balanced business news', *Irish Times*, 22 September.

Flanagan, Mary and Austin Booth (2002) *Reload: Rethinking Women and Cyberculture*, Cambridge, MA: MIT Press.

Flynn, Roddy (2002) 'Kicking to touch?', *Magill*, August, p. 25.

Flynn, Roddy (2003) 'From promise to practice: broadcasting and the Celtic Tiger', in Peadar Kirby, Luke Gibbons and Michael Cronin (eds), *Reinventing Ireland*, London: Pluto, pp. 160–76.

Football Association of Ireland (2003) 'Review of the Television Without Frontiers Directive'. Available at http://europa.eu.int/comm/avpolicy/regul/review-twf2003/wc_fai. pdf (accessed 5 April 2004).

Foucault, Michel (1977) *Discipline and Punish*, trans. Alan Sheridan, London: Allen Lane.

Foucault, Michel (1980) 'Truth and power', in Colin Gordon (ed.), *Power/Knowledge: Selected Interviews and Other Writings (1972–1977)*, New York: Pantheon Books.

Fox, Patrick (1989) 'From senility to Alzheimer's disease: the rise of the Alzheimer's disease movement', *Milbank Quarterly*, 67(1): 58–102.

Frazer, Hugh (1992) 'The state of welfare', *Poverty Today*, no. 19 (October/December): 3.

Free, Marcus (2005) 'Keeping them under pressure: masculinity, narratives of national regeneration and the Republic of Ireland soccer team', *Sport in History*, 25(2): 265–88.

Free, Marcus and John Hughson (2006) 'Common culture, commodity fetishism and the cultural contradictions of sport', *International Journal of Cultural Studies*, 9(1): 83–104.

Friedman, Milton (1962) *Capitalism and Freedom*, Chicago, IL: University of Chicago Press (1982).

Frome, P. M. and J. S. Eccles (1998) 'Parents' influence on children's achievement-related perceptions', *Journal of Personality and Social Psychology*, 74(2): 435–52.

Frosh, S., A. Pheonix and R. Patman (2002) *Young Masculinities*, Basingstoke: Palgrave.

Gaelic League (1903) *Connradh na Gaedhilge. Árd-Fheis, 1903*, Dublin: Gaelic League.

Gaelic League (1904) *Annual Report of the Gaelic League 1902–3, and Proceedings of Árd-Fheis 1903*, Dublin: Gaelic League.

Gaelic League (1905) *Tuarasgabháil Bliadhna Chonnradh na Gaedhilge, 1903–4, agus Cunntas ar Árd-Fheis 1904*, Dublin: Gaelic League.

Gaelic League (1906) *Connradh na Gaedhilge, Árd-Fheis, 1906. Cunntaisí Bliadhna an Árd-Rúnaidhe, na dTimthirí, 7rl*, Dublin: An Cló-Chumann.

Gaelic League (1907) *Connradh na Gaedhilge, Árd-Fheis, 1907*, Dublin: Gaelic League.

Gaelic League (1908) *Connradh na Gaedhilge. Ard-Fheis 1908*, Dublin: Gaelic League.

Gaelic League (1909) *Ard-Fheis 1909*, Dublin: Gaelic League.

Gaelic League (1910) *Ard-Fheis, 1910*, Dublin: Gaelic League.

Gaelic League (c. 1936) *You May Revive the Gaelic Language*, Dublin: Craobh an Chéitinnigh, Conradh na Gaeilge.

Gaeltacht Commission (2002) *Tuarascáil/Report*. Available at www.pobail.ie/en/AnGhaeltacht/ReportoftheGaeltachtCommission.

Gaeltarra Éireann/SFADCO (1971) *Gníomh don Ghaeltacht: An Action Plan for the Gaeltacht*, report for the Minister for Finance and the Gaeltacht, Dublin.

Gaffney, Maureen (2004) 'Inside the heads of a generation living without constraints', *Irish Times*, 28 February.

Gaffney, Maureen (2007a) 'Retail therapy', *Irish Times Magazine*, 10 March.

Gaffney, Maureen (2007b) 'What's the craic', *Irish Times Magazine*, 25 August.

Gallie, Walter B. (1955) 'Essentially contested concepts', *Proceedings of the Aristotelian Society*, 167–98.

Garland, David (2001) *The Culture of Control: Crime and Social Order in Contemporary Society*, Oxford: Oxford University Press.

Garner, Steve (2004) *Racism in the Irish Experience*, London: Pluto.

Gauchet, M. (1991) 'La société d'insécurité', in J. Donzelot (ed.), *Face à l'exclusion: le modèle français*, Paris: Le Seuil.

Gauntlett, David (2002) *Media, Gender and Identity: An Introduction*, London: Routledge.

Geddes, Andrew (2003) 'Migration and the welfare state in Europe', in Sarah Spencer (ed.), *The Politics of Migration: Managing Opportunity Conflict and Change*, Oxford: Blackwell, pp. 150–62.

Geertz, Clifford (1975) *The Interpretation of Cultures*, London: Hutchinson.

Giddens, Anthony (1982) *Sociology: A Brief But Critical Introduction*, London: Macmillan.

Giddens, Anthony (1994) *Beyond Left and Right. The Future of Radical Politics*, Cambridge: Polity Press.

Giddens, Anthony (2001) *Sociology*, Cambridge: Polity Press.

Giddens, Anthony (2002) *Sociology* (4th edn), Cambridge: Polity Press.

Gill, Rosalind (2003) 'Power and the production of subjects: a genealogy of the new man and the new lad', in B. Benwell (ed.), *Masculinity and Men's Lifestyle Magazines*, Oxford: Blackwell, pp. 34–56.

Gill, Stephen (2003) *Power and Resistance in the New World Order*, Basingstoke: Palgrave Macmillan.

Gilroy, Paul (2004) *After Empire: Melancholia or Convivial Culture?*, London: Routledge.

Ging, Debbie (2005) 'A "manual on masculinity"? The consumption and use of mediated images of masculinity among teenage boys in Ireland', in A. Cleary (ed.), *Irish Journal of Sociology* (*Masculinities*), 14(2): 29–52.

Ging, Debbie (2006) *The Lads from New Ireland: A Textual and Audience Analysis of Marginalised Masculinities in Contemporary Irish Film*, doctoral thesis (unpublished), Dublin: Dublin City University.

Ging, Debbie (2007a) 'All the rage: digital games, female violence and the postfeminiza-tion of cinema's new action heroines', *Film and Film Culture*, 4.

Ging, Debbie (2007b) 'New lads or protest masculinities? Exploring the meanings of male marginalisation in contemporary Irish film', in John Horgan, Barbara O'Connor and Helena Sheehan (eds), *Mapping Irish Media: Critical Explorations*, Dublin: UCD Press.

Giroux, Henry A. (2002) 'Global capitalism and the return of the garrison state', *Arena Journal*, 19: 141–60.

Gleeson, Jim (2000) 'A social partnership: the European Union and Irish vocational educa-tion and training', in Dennis R. Herschbach and Clifton P. Campbell (eds), *Workforce Preparation: An International Perspective*, Ann Arbour, MI: Prakken, pp. 145–60.

Goldberg, David Theo (2002) *The Racial State*, London: Blackwell.

Goldberg, David Theo and John Solomos (2002) *A Companion to Racial and Ethnic Studies*, London: Blackwell.

Goodhart, D. (2004) 'Too diverse?', *Prospect Magazine*, February.

Gorby, Shirley, Selina McCoy and James Williams (2003) *2002 Annual School Leavers' Survey*, Dublin: Department of Education and Science and ESRI.

Gottlieb, Scott (2002) 'Drug companies maintain "astounding profits"', *BMJ*, 324: 1054.

Government of Ireland (1926) *Gaeltacht Commission: Report*, Dublin: Stationery Office.

Government of Ireland (1965) *Athbheochan na Gaeilge: The Restoration of the Irish Lan-guage. White Paper Presented to Houses of Oireachtas*, Dublin: Stationery Office.

Government of Ireland (1997) *Sharing in Progress: National Anti-Poverty Strategy*, Dublin: Stationery Office.

Government of Ireland (1999) *Ireland: National Development Plan 2000–2006*, Dublin: Stationery Office.

Government of Ireland (2001) *Final Report of the Benchmarking and Indexation Working Group*, Programme for Prosperity and Fairness, Dublin: Stationery Office.

Government of Ireland (2002) *National Spatial Strategy for Ireland 2002–2020: People, Places and Potential*, Dublin: Stationery Office.

Government of Ireland (2006) *Ráiteas i leith na Gaeilge 2006/Statement on the Irish Lan-guage 2006*, Dublin: Stationery Office.

Government of Ireland (2007) *National Action Plan for Social Inclusion 2007–2016*, Dublin: Stationery Office.

Graham, Phil and Allan Luke (2005) 'The language of neofeudal corporation and the war on Iraq', *Journal of Language and Politics*, 4(1): 11–39.

Granville, Gary (2004) 'Politics and partnership in curriculum planning in Ireland', in Ciaran Sugrue (ed.), *Ideology and Curriculum: Irish Experiences, International Perspec-tives*, Dublin: Liffey Press, pp. 67–100.

Gray, Breda (2006) 'Migrant integration policy: a nationalist fantasy of management and control?', *Translocations: The Irish Migration, Race and Social Transformation Review*, 1(1): 121–41.

Gray, John (1993) *Men Are From Mars, Women Are From Venus: A Practical Guide for Improving Communication and Getting What You Want in Your Relationships*, London: Thorsons.

Grin, François (1996) 'The economics of language: survey, assessment, and prospects', *International Journal of the Sociology of Language*, 121: 17–44.

Grin, François (2003) 'From antagonism to convergence: economics and linguistic diver-sity', in J. M. Kirk and D. P. Ó Baoill (eds), *Towards Our Goals in Broadcasting, the Press, the Performing Arts and the Economy: Minority Languages in Northern Ireland, the Republic of Ireland, and Scotland*, Belfast: Cló Ollscoil na Ríona, pp. 213–23.

Grin, François and Vaillancourt, François (1999) *The Cost-Effectiveness Evaluation of Minority Language Policies: Case Studies on Wales, Ireland and the Basque Country*, Flensburg: European Centre for Minority Issues.

Gurdgiev, Constantin (2005) 'A story of failure behind the image of prosperity', *Irish Times*, 19 December. Available at www.ireland.com (accessed June 2006).

Habermas, Jurgen (1989) *The Structural Transformation of the Public Sphere*, Cambridge, MA: MIT.

Hage, Ghassan (1998) *White Nation*, London: Pluto.

Hage, Ghassan (2003) *Against Paranoid Nationalism: Searching for Hope in a Shrinking Society*, London: Merlin.

Hall, Jacqueline (2001) *Convivència in Catalonia: Languages Living Together*, Barcelona: Fundació Jaume Bofill.

Hall, Stuart (1980) 'Popular democratic vs. authoritarian populism', in Alan Hunt (ed.), *Marxism and Democracy*, London: Lawrence and Wishart, pp. 157–85.

Hall, Stuart (1996) 'Gramsci's relevance for the study of race and ethnicity', in P. Hamilton (1983), *Key Sociologists: Talcott Parsons*, London: Routledge.

Hall, Stuart, Chas Critcher, Tony Jefferson, John Clarke and Brian Roberts (eds) (1978) *Policing the Crisis: Mugging, the State, and Law and Order*, London: Macmillan.

Hamilton, Peter (ed.) (1985) *Readings from Talcott Parsons*, London: Ellis Horwood & Tavistock.

Hardell, Lennart, Michael Carlberg, Fredrik Söderqvist, Kjell Hansson Mild and L. Lloyd Morgan (2007) 'Long-term use of cellular phones and brain tumours: increased risk associated with use for ≥ 10 years', *Occupational and Environmental Medicine*, 64: 626–32. Available at http://oem.bmj.com/cgi/content/full/64/9/626 (accessed 18 December 2007).

Hardiman, Niamh (1998) 'Inequality and representation of interests', in William Crotty and David Schmitt (eds), *Ireland and the Politics of Change*, London: Longman, pp. 122–55.

Harvey, David (2005) *A Brief History of Neoliberalism*, Oxford: Oxford University Press.

Hay, Colin (2001) 'What place for ideas in the structure–agency debate?' Available at www.theglobalsite.ac.uk/press/109hay.htm (accessed January 2009).

Hayek, Friedrich (1960) *The Constitution of Liberty*, London: Routledge.

Hayes, Michael (2006) *Irish Travellers: Representations and Realities*, Dublin: Liffey Press.

Heath, Joseph and Andrew Potter (2005) *The Rebel Sell: How the Counter Culture Became Consumer Culture*, Bloomington, MN: Capstone Press.

Heidegger, Martin (1962) *Being and Time*, Oxford: Blackwell.

Hennessy, Mark (2002) 'Tough stance on FAI deal only comes during extra time', *Irish Times*, 15 July, p. 5.

Hennessy, Mark (2006) 'Sky likely to fight government over Ryder Cup rights', *Irish Times*, 2 January, p. 3.

Herman, Edward S. and Noam Chomsky (1994) *Manufacturing Consent: The Political Economy of the Mass Media*, London: Vintage.

Herman, Edward S. and Robert McChesney (1997) *The Global Media: The New Missionaries of Corporate Capitalism*, London: Cassell.

Hettne, Björn (1995) *Development Theory and the Three Worlds: Towards an International Political Economy of Development* (2nd edn), Harlow: Longman Scientific & Technical.

Holborow, Marnie (2007) 'Language, ideology and neo-liberalism', *Journal of Language and Politics*, 6(1): 51–73.

Holmer Nadesan, Maija (2002) 'Engineering the entrepreneurial infant: brain science, infant development toys, and governmentality', *Cultural Studies*, 16(3): 401–32.

Holmquist, Kate (2007) 'I want a Barbie the Builder, please, Santa', *Irish Times*, 3 November.

Holt, Eddie (2005) 'Hippocratic hypocrisy', *Irish Times*, 22 October.

Horrocks, Roger (1994) *Masculinity in Crisis: Myths, Fantasies, and Realities*, New York: St Martin's Press.

Horrocks, Roger (1995) *Male Myths and Icons: Masculinity in Popular Culture*, New York: St Martin's Press.

Hourihane, Jim (ed.) (2004) *Ireland and the European Union: The First Thirty Years, 1973–2002*, Dublin: Lilliput Press.

Houston, Muiris (2005) 'Psychiatrist warns of overdiagnosing depression', *Irish Times*, 20 September.

Hudson, John (2001) 'Critically examining the commercialisation of English football: a case for government intervention?', *Sociology of Sport Online*, 4: 1. Available at http://physed.otago.ac.nz/v4i1/v4i1hud.htm (accessed 15 May 2007).

Humphreys, Joe (2004) 'Major security operation starts today', *Irish Times*, 30 April.

Hyde, Douglas (1894) 'The necessity for de-Anglicising Ireland', in *The Revival of Irish Literature: Addresses by Sir Charles Gavan Duffy, Dr. George Sigerson and Dr. Douglas Hyde*, London: T. Fisher Unwin, pp. 115–61.

Hyde, Janet S. (1981) 'How large are cognitive gender differences? A meta-analysis using ω^2 and *d*', *American Psychologist*, 36: 892–901.

Hyde, Janet S. (1984) 'How large are gender differences in aggression? A developmental meta-analysis', *Developmental Psychology*, 20: 722–36.

Hyde, Janet S. (1985) *Half the Human Experience: The Psychology of Women* (3rd edn), Lexington, MA: Heath.

Hyde, Janet S. (2005) 'The gender similarities hypothesis', *American Psychologist*, 60(6): 581–92.

Hyde, Janet S. and E. A. Plant (1995) 'Magnitude of psychological gender differences: another side to the story', *American Psychologist*, 50: 159–61.

Illich, Ivan (1976) *Limits to Medicine. Medical Nemesis: The Expropriation of Health*, London: Marion Boyars (1995).

Indecon (2005) *Review of the National Employment Action Plan Preventative Strategy*, Dublin: Indecon International Economic Consultants, DETE.

Intergovernmental Panel on Climate Change (2007) *IPCC Fourth Assessment Report: Climate Change 2007*. Available at www.ipcc.ch (accessed 30 October 2007).

IPHA (Irish Pharmaceutical Healthcare Association) (2002a) *A Time to Prioritise in Irish Healthcare. Irish Pharmaceutical Healthcare Association Pre-Budget Submission*, Dublin: Irish Pharmaceutical Healthcare Association.

IPHA (2002b) *Submission to the Commission on Financial Management and Control in the Health Services*, Dublin: Irish Pharmaceutical Healthcare Association.

IPHA (2003a) 'The role of medicines in the delivery of a world-class health service', *Medicines Matter*, issue 8. Newsletter of the Irish Pharmaceutical Healthcare Association, available at http://www.ipha.ie/htm/info (accessed February 2009).

IPHA (2003b) *It Is Possible to Build a World-Class Health Service: Irish Pharmaceutical Healthcare Association Pre-Budget Submission*, Dublin: Irish Pharmaceutical Healthcare Association.

IPHA (2004a) *Pre-Budget Submission 2004*, Dublin: Irish Pharmaceutical Healthcare Association.

IPHA (2004b) *Healthcare Facts and Figures 2002/2003*, Dublin: Irish Pharmaceutical Healthcare Association.

IPHA (2005) *Industry Report – Pharma Ireland*, Dublin: Irish Pharmaceutical Healthcare Association.

IPHA (2006a) *Healthcare Facts and Figures 2006*, Dublin: Irish Pharmaceutical Healthcare Association.

IPHA (2006b) *Adverse Side Effects of Pharmaceuticals. Submission to the Sub-Committee on the Adverse Side Effects of Pharmaceuticals*, Dublin: Irish Pharmaceutical Healthcare Association.

Irish Human Rights Commission (2006) *Observations on the Scheme of the Immigration and Residence Protection Bill*. Available at www.ihrc.ie/documents/article.asp?NID=196& NCID=6&T=N (accessed January 2009).

Irish Rugby Football Union (2003) 'Review of the Television Without Frontiers Directive'. Available at http://europa.eu.int/comm/avpolicy/regul/review-twf2003/wc_irfu. pdf (accessed 5 April 2004).

Irvine, Tese (2007) 'Time we considered work life balance as a legal right', *Irish Times*, 2 March.

Jessop, Bob (2004) 'Critical semiotic analysis and cultural political economy', *Critical Discourse Studies*, 1(2): 159–74.

Kearney, Richard (1988) *Across the Frontiers: Ireland in the 1990s*, Dublin: Wolfhound.

Keohane, Kieran and Carmen Kuhling (2004) *Collision Culture: Transformations in Everyday Life in Ireland*, Dublin: Liffey Press.

Keohane, Kieran and Carmen Kuhling (2007) *Cosmopolitan Ireland: Globalisation and Quality of Life*, London: Pluto Press.

Kimmel, Michael (2000) *The Gendered Society*, New York: Oxford University Press.

Kimmel, Michael (2008) *Guyland: The Perilous World Where Boys Become Men*, New York: Harper.

Kimmel, Michael and Michael Kaufman (1995) 'Weekend warriors: the new men's movement', in Michael Kimmel (ed.), *The Politics of Manhood: Profeminist Men Respond to the Mythopoetic Men's Movement (and the Mythopoetic Leaders Answer)*, Philadelphia, PA: Temple University Press, pp. 15–43.

King O'Riain, Rebecca Chiyoko (2006) 'Re-racialising the Irish state through the census, citizenship and language', in Alana Lentin and Ronit Lentin (eds), *Race and State*, Newcastle: Cambridge Scholars Press, pp. 274–91.

Kirby, Peadar (2002a) *The Celtic Tiger in Distress: Growth With Inequality in Ireland*, Basingstoke: Palgrave.

Kirby, Peadar (2002b) 'Contested pedigrees of the Celtic Tiger', in Peadar Kirby, Luke Gibbons and Michael Cronin (eds), *Reinventing Ireland: Culture, Society and the Global Economy*, London: Pluto Press, pp. 21–37.

Kirby, Peadar (2004) *Todhchaí d'Éirinn: Pobal, Féinmheas, Teanga*, Dublin: Coiscéim.

Kirby, Peadar (2005) 'Globalisation, vulnerability and the role of the state: lessons for Ireland', *Administration*, 52(4): 49–68.

Kirby, Peadar (2006) 'Ireland's economic "miracle": challenges from development theory', in Majda Bne Saad and Maura Leen (eds), *Trade, Aid and Development into the Twenty-First Century: A Festschrift in Honour of Helen O'Neill*, Dublin: UCD Press, pp. 301–17.

Kirby, Peadar and Mary Murphy (2008) 'Ireland as a competition state', in Maura Adshead, Peadar Kirby and Michelle Millar (eds), *Contesting the Irish State*, Manchester: Manchester University Press, pp. 120–42.

Kirby, Peadar, Michael Cronin and Luke Gibbons (eds) (2002) *Reinventing Ireland: Culture, Society and the Global Economy*, London: Pluto Press.

Klawiter, Maren (2002) 'Risk, prevention, and the breast cancer continuum: the NCI, the FDA, health activism and the pharmaceutical industry', *History and Technology*, 18(4): 309–53.

Kon, Igor and James Riordan (1993) *Sex and Russian Society*, London: Pluto.

Kovel, Joel (2007) *The Enemy of Nature: The End of Capitalism or the End of the World?* (2nd edn), London: Zed Books.

Kristeva, Julia (1981) *Desire in Language. A Semiotic Approach to Literature and Art*, Oxford: Blackwell.

Kundnani, Arun (2002) *The Death of Multiculturalism*, London: Institute of Race Relations. Available at www.irr.org.uk/2002/april/ak000001.html (accessed 2 July 2006).

Labanyi, David (2005) 'Irish men ignoring weight risks, cancer society study finds', *Irish Times*, 8 November.

Labanyi, David (2006) 'Advertising by another name?', *Irish Times*, 22 August.

Laclau, Ernesto and Chantal Mouffe (1985) *Hegemony and Socialist Strategy*, London: Verso (2001).

Lago, Umberto, Rob Simmons and Stefan Szymanski (2006) 'The financial crisis in European football', *Journal of Sports Economics*, 7(1): 3–12.

Lally, Conor (2004a) 'May Day use of unarmed Gardai criticised', *Irish Times*, 20 April.

Lally, Conor (2004b) 'Wing of prison cleared ahead of possible May Day trouble', *Irish Times*, 29 April.

Lee, J. J. (1989) *Ireland, 1912–1985: Politics and Society*, Cambridge: Cambridge University Press.

Lee, Penny (1996) *The Whorf Theory Complex: A Critical Reconstruction*, Amsterdam: John Benjamins.

Leibfried, Stephan (1993) 'Towards a European welfare state', in Chris Jones (ed.), *New Perspectives on the Welfare State in Europe*, London: Routledge, pp. 133–50.

Lentin, Alana (2004) *Racism and Anti-Racism in Europe*, London: Pluto Press.

Lentin, Ronit (2002) 'Anti-racist responses to the racialisation of Irishness: disavowed multiculturalism and its discontents', in Ronit Lentin and Robbie McVeigh (eds), *Racism and Anti-racism in Ireland*, Belfast: Beyond the Pale Publications, pp. 78–92.

Lentin, Ronit and Robbie McVeigh (2006) *After Optimism: Ireland, Racism and Globalization*, Dublin: Metro Éireann.

Levy, Ariel (2005) *Female Chauvinist Pigs: Women and the Rise of Raunch Culture*, New York: Free Press.

Lewis, Arthur (1955) *The Theory of Economic Growth*, London: Allen & Unwin.

Lewis, Jane (1992) 'Gender and the development of welfare regimes', *Journal of European Social Policy*, 2(3): 159–73.

Lexchin, Joel (2001) 'Lifestyle drugs: issues for debate', *CMAJ*, 164(10): 1449–51.

Lightdale, J. R. and D. A. Prentice (1994) 'Rethinking sex differences in aggression: aggressive behavior in the absence of social roles', *Personality and Social Psychology Bulletin*, 20: 34–44.

Lijphart, Arend (1999) *Patterns of Democracy Government, Forms and Performances, in 36 Countries*, Yale, CT: Yale University Press.

Lillington, Karlin (2006) 'New data retention law raises fears of abuse', *Irish Times*, 14 April.

Lister, Ruth (1988) 'The politics of social security: an assessment of the Fowler review', presented at 'Economy of Social Security', Institute of Fiscal Studies, 15 April.

Loftus, Camille (2005) *Out of the Traps: Ending Poverty Traps and Making Work Pay for People in Poverty*, Dublin: Open and EAPN.

Louw, Eric (2005) *The Media and Political Process*, London: Sage.

Lovelock, James (2007) *The Revenge of Gaia*, London: Penguin.

Loyal, Steve and Kieran Allen (2006) 'Rethinking immigration and the state in Ireland', in Alana Lentin and Ronit Lentin (eds), *Race and State*, Newcastle: Cambridge Scholars Press, pp. 209–28.

Lupton, Deborah (2000) 'Food, risk and subjectivity', in S. Williams, J. Gabe and M. Calnan (eds), *Health, Medicine and Society. Key Theories, Future Agendas*, London: Routledge, pp. 205–18.

Lynch, Kathleen (1999) *Equality in Education*, Dublin: Gill and Macmillan.

Mac An Ghaill, Máirtín (2002) 'Beyond a black–white dualism: racialisation and racism in the Republic of Ireland and the Irish diaspora experience', *Irish Journal of Sociology*, 11(2): 99–122.

Mac Carthaigh, Seán (1999) 'Minister to tackle threat to cultural identity as digital age takes hold', *Irish Times*, 10 June, p. 53.

Mac Donnacha, Joe (2000) 'An integrated language planning model', *Language Problems and Language Planning*, 24(1): 11–35.

Mac Giolla Chríost, Diarmait (2006) *The Irish Language in Ireland: From Goídel to Globalisation*, London: Routledge.

Maddock, Mary and Jim Maddock (2006) *Soul Survivor. A Personal Encounter with Psychiatry*, Stockport: Asylum.

Maguire, Gabrielle (1991) *Our Own Language: An Irish Initiative*, Clevedon: Multilingual Matters.

Mahon, Evelyn (1987) 'Women's rights and Catholicism in Ireland', *New Left Review*, 166: 53–77.

Mahon, Evelyn (2004) 'Families, children and labour markets', paper presented at the Families, Children and Social Policy ISPA Conference, Croke Park, Dublin, 17 September.

Malone, E. (2003) 'Broadcasting deals do little for the home game', *Irish Times*, 17 June.

Mariani, Philomena (1996) 'Law-and-order science', in M. Berger, B. Wallis and S. Watson (eds), *Constructing Masculinity*, London: Routledge, pp. 135–56.

Marshall, Gordon (1998) *Oxford Dictionary of Sociology* (2nd edn), Oxford: Oxford University Press.

Martinussen, John (1997) *Society, State and Market: A Guide to Competing Theories of Development*, London: Zed Books.

Maushart, Susan (1999) *The Mask of Motherhood: How Becoming a Mother Changes Our Lives and Why We Never Talk About It*, New York: Penguin.

May, Stephen (2001) *Language and Minority Rights: Ethnicity, Nationalism and the Politics of Language*, Harlow: Pearson Education.

McCabe, Breda (2006) 'Economic implications of non-standard employment', presentation to Combat Poverty Agency Research Seminar Series, 26 September.

McCann, Donna, Angelina Barrett, Alison Cooper, *et al.* (2007) 'Food additives and hyperactive behaviour in 3-year-old and 8/9-year-old children in the community: a randomised, double-blinded, placebo-controlled trial', *Lancet*, 370(9598): 1560–7.

McCarthy, John (2005) *Hope on a Rope: A Journey from Despair to Joy*, Cork: Elizabeth Press.

McCashin, Anthony (2004) *Social Security in Ireland*, Dublin: Gill and Macmillan.

McCashin, Anthony, E. O'Sullivan and C. Brennan (2002) 'The NESF, social partnership and policy formation in the Republic of Ireland', *Policy and Politics*, 30(2): 263–79.

McCoy, Danny (2006) 'Fabled Nordic model may not suit our economy', *Irish Times*, 25 March, p. 15.

McDonagh, Marese and Gene McKenna (2002) 'FAI snub coalition but offer free game', *Irish Independent*, 10 July, p. 1.

McDonald, Frank (2007) 'A plan that will choke our roads with traffic', *Irish Times*, 20 January, p. 3.

McGarry, Patsy (2006) 'Primate attacks "dehumanising" excess', *Irish Times*, 18 December.

McGauran, AnneMarie (2005) *Plus ca change...? Gender Mainstreaming of the Irish National Development Plan*, Studies in Public Policy No. 15, Dublin: Policy Institute, Trinity College.

McGinnity, Frances, Helen Russell and James Williams (2005) *Time Use in Ireland 2005: Survey Report*, Dublin: Economic and Social Research Institute.

McGinnity, Frances, Philip O'Connell, Emma Quinn and James Williams (2006) *Migrants' Experience of Racism and Discrimination in Ireland*, Dublin: ESRI.

McKay, John (2004) 'Reassessing development theory: "modernisation" and beyond', in Damien Kingsbury, Joseph Remenyi, John McKay and Janet Hunt (eds), *Key Issues in Development*, London: Palgrave, pp. 45–67.

McKay, S. (2006) 'The body threatens technology', *Irish Times*, 19 April.

McLaughlin, Eithne (2002) 'The challenges of a social and economic rights approach to the development of social partnership in Ireland', paper presented to the ISPA Annual Conference, Dublin City University, 12 September.

McLaughlin, Eugene (2001) 'Ireland: from Catholic corporatism to social partnership', in Alan Cochrane and Jonathan Clarke (eds), *Comparing Welfare States*, London: Sage, pp. 203–24.

McMahon, Anthony (1999) *Taking Care of Men: Sexual Politics in the Public Mind*, Cambridge: Cambridge University Press.

McVeigh, Robbie (1992) 'The specificity of Irish racism', *Race and Class*, 33: 4.

McWilliams, David (2005) *The Pope's Children: Ireland's New Elite*, Dublin: Gill and Macmillan.

McWilliams, David (2007a) *The Generation Game*, Dublin: Gill and Macmillan.

McWilliams, David (2007b) 'The future could be so bright', *Sunday Business Post*, 14 October.

Medawar, Charles and Anita Hardon (2004) *Medicines Out of Control? Antidepressants and the Conspiracy of Goodwill*, Amsterdam: Aksant.

Messner, Michael A. and J. Montez de Oca (2005) 'The male consumer as loser: beer and liquor ads in mega sports media events', *Signs: Journal of Women in Culture and Society*, 30(3): 1879–909.

Metzl, Jonathan and Rebecca Herzig (2007) 'Medicalisation in the 21st century: introduction', *Lancet*, 369: 697–8.

Mignolo, Walter (2000) 'The many faces of cosmo-polis: border thinking and critical cosmopolitanism', *Public Culture*, 12(3): 721–48.

Miller, Toby (1996) 'The crime of Monsieur Lange: GATT, the screen and the new international division of cultural labour', in Albert Moran (ed.), *Film Policy: International, National and Regional Perspectives*, London: Routledge, pp. 72–84.

Ministry of Culture (Denmark) (2003) *Consultation on the Television Without Frontiers Directive*. Available at http://europa.eu.int/comm/avpolicy/regul/review-twf2003/wc_d enmark%20ministry%20of%20culture_en.pdf (accessed 5 April 2004).

Mintzes, Barbara (2005) *Educational Initiatives for Medical and Pharmacy Students About Drug Promotion: An International Cross-Sectional Survey*, Geneva: World Health Organization and Health Action International.

Moran, D. P. (1905) *The Philosophy of Irish Ireland* (2nd edn), Dublin: James Duffy & Co., M. H. Gill & Son and The Leader.

Moran, Leo (2005) 'The Swedish fiscal model' (letter to the editor), *Irish Times*, 13 December. Available at www.ireland.com (accessed September 2006).

Morgenroth, Edgar and John Fitz Gerald (eds) (2006) *Ex-ante Evaluation of the Investment Priorities for the National Development Plan 2007–2013*, Policy Research Series 59, Dublin: ESRI.

Moynihan, Ray and David Henry (2006) 'The fight against disease mongering: generating knowledge for action', *PLoS Medicine*, 3(4): e191.

Murphy, Mary (2006) *Domestic Constraints on Globalisation: A Case Study of Irish Social Security 1986–2006*, PhD thesis (unpublished), Dublin: Dublin City University.

Murphy, Mary (2007) 'An emancipatory model of labour market activation', presentation to the Combat Poverty Agency Research Seminar Series, 13 February.

Murphy, Mary and Orla O'Connor (2008) 'Women and Irish social security policy', in Ursula Barry (ed.), *Where Are We Now? New Feminist Perspectives on Women in Contemporary Ireland*, Dublin: New Island Press, pp. 30–52.

Myers, Kevin (2002) 'An Irishman's diary', *Irish Times*, 18 July, p. 15.

Myers, Kevin (2005) 'An Irishman's diary', *Irish Times*, 16 September.

Myint, Hla (1958) 'An interpretation of economic backwardness', in A. N. Agarwala and S. P. Singh (eds), *The Economics of Underdevelopment*, Oxford: Oxford University Press, pp. 93–132.

Nash, Vanessa (2004) 'Wages and poverty risks of atypical workers', presentation to the Combat Poverty Agency Research Seminar Series, 28 May.

National Economic and Social Forum (1995) *First Periodic Report of the Work of the Forum of Income Maintenance Strategies*, Report No. 8, Dublin: Stationery Office.

National Economic and Social Forum (2000) *Alleviating Labour Shortages*, Report No. 19, Dublin: Stationery Office.

National Economic and Social Forum (2006) *Creating a More Inclusive Labour Market*, Report No. 33, Dublin: Stationery Office.

National Pensions Board (1998) *National Pensions Policy Initiative*, Dublin: Stationery Office.

National Women's Council of Ireland (2006) NWCI presentation to DSFA consultation on DSFA proposals for supporting lone parents, Farmleigh House, 27 April.

Negra, Diane (2006) 'The Irish in us: Irishness, performativity, and popular culture', in Diane Negra (ed.), *The Irish in Us: Irishness, Performativity and Popular Culture*, Durham: Duke University Press, pp. 1–19.

NESC (National Economic and Social Council) (1990) *A Strategy for the Nineties*, Dublin: Stationery Office.

NESC (2005) *The Developmental Welfare State*, Dublin: Stationery Office.

NESC (2006) *NESC Strategy Highlights: Challenges for Policy and Partnership, NESC Strategy 2006: People, Productivity, Purpose Report No. 114*, Dublin: Stationery Office.

Nicaise, Ides (2004) *Social Activation Experiments in the Netherlands: Peer Review in the Field of Social Inclusion Practices*, Brussels: European Commission. Available at www.peer-review-social-inclusion.net/peer-reviews/2004 (accessed 8 October 2007).

Nolan, Brian (1991) *The Wealth of Irish Households*, Dublin: Combat Poverty Agency.

Nolan, Brian and Bertrand Maitre (2007) 'Economic growth and income inequality: setting the context', in Tony Fahey, Helen Russell and Christopher T. Whelan (eds), *Best of Times? The Social Impact of the Celtic Tiger*, Dublin: IPA, pp. 27–41.

Nolan, Brian, Philip J. O'Connell and Christopher T. Whelan (eds) (2000) *Bust to Boom? The Irish Experience of Growth and Inequality*, Dublin: IPA.

Norris, Pauline, Andrew Herxheimer, Joel Lexchin and Peter Mansfield (2005) *Drug Promotion. What We Know, What We Have Yet To Learn*, Geneva: World Health Organization and Health Action International.

Northern Ireland Statistics and Research Agency (2002) *Key Statistics (Census 2001)*. Belfast: NISRA. Available at www.nisra.gov.uk/Census/pdf/Key%20Statistics%20ReportTables.pdf (accessed 1 February 2005).

Northern Ireland Statistics and Research Agency (2003) 'Irish language' and 'Education, employment and economic activity', in *Census 2001 Output. Northern Ireland Census 2001 Standard Tables: Local Government District and Ward Level*. Available at www. nisra.gov.uk/census/Census2001Output/standard_tables_lgd.html#irish%20language (accessed 11 November 2004).

O'Boyle, Neil (2006) 'Addressing multiculturalism? Conservatism and conformity; access and authenticity in Irish advertising', *Translocations*, 1(1): 95–120.

O'Brien, Dan (2006) 'The most content of nations', *Open Democracy*, 17 March. Available at www.opendemocracy.net/globalization-vision_reflections/content_3366.jsp (accessed 10 January 2007).

O'Brien, Jason (2002) 'Now fans unite against Sky deal', *Daily Express* (Irish edition), 19 July, p. 2.

O'Brien, Mike (2004) *Workfare: Not Fair for Kids. A Review of Compulsory Work Policies and Their Effects on Children*, Auckland: Child Poverty Action Group.

O'Brien, Tim (2007) 'Ireland warming twice as fast as rest of world, report finds', *Irish Times*, 30 August, p. 1.

Ó Cadhain, Máirtín (c. 1970) *Gluaiseacht na Gaeilge: Gluaiseacht ar Strae*, Dublin: Misneach.

O'Carroll, Aileen (2006) 'Men are from earth, and so are women'. Workers Solidarity Movement. Available at www.wsm.ie/story/1032 (accessed 1 October 2007).

Ó Cinnéide, Mícheál and M. J. Keane (1988) *Local Socioeconomic Impacts Associated with the Galway Gaeltacht*, Galway: University College Galway.

Ó Cinnéide, Mícheál, Michael Keane and Mary Cawley (1985) 'Industrialization and linguistic change among Gaelic-speaking communities in the west of Ireland', *Language Planning and Language Problems*, 9(1): 3–15.

Ó Cinnéide, Mícheál, Seosamh Mac Donnacha and Sorcha Ní Chonghaile (2001) *Polasaithe agus Cleachtais Eagraíochtaí Éagsúla le Feidhm sa Ghaeltacht*, Galway: National University of Ireland.

Ó Cinnéide, Séamus (1998) 'Democracy and the constitution', *Administration*, 46(4): 41–58.

O'Clery, Conor (2004) 'US invested twice as much in Ireland as in China', *Irish Times*, 18 May.

O'Connell, Philip J., David Clancy and Selina McCoy (2006) *Who Went to College in 2004? A National Survey of New Entrants to Higher Education*, Dublin: HEA.

O'Connor, Anne Marie (2005) *An Investigation Into Whether the Contingency Based Nature of Social Assistance Meets Welfare Objectives in the Light of Changes in Irish Society*, masters dissertation (unpublished), Dublin: IPA.

O'Connor, Julia (2003) 'Welfare state development in the context of European integration and economic convergence: situating Ireland within the European Union', *Policy and Politics*, 31(3): 387–404.

O'Connor, Pat (2008) 'The Irish patriarchial state: continuity and change', in Maura Adshead, Peadar Kirby and Michelle Millar (eds), *Contesting the State: Lessons from the Irish Case*, Manchester: Manchester University Press, pp. 165–85.

Ó Doibhlin, Breandán (c. 1973) 'Súil Siar ar an Athbheochan', in *Aistí Critice agus Cultúir*, Dublin: FNT, pp. 230–48.

Ó Doibhlin, Breandán (2004a) 'An enterprise of the spirit', in C. Mac Murchaidh (ed.), *Who Needs Irish? Reflections on the Importance of the Irish Language Today*, Dublin: Veritas, pp. 140–59.

Ó Doibhlin, Breandán (2004b) *An Cultúr Gaelach: Cosaint na Daonnachta*, Dublin: Coiscéim.

O'Donnell, Anne (1999) 'Comparing welfare states: considering the case of Ireland', in Gabriel Kiely, Anne O'Donnell, Patricia Kennedy and Suzanne Quin (eds), *Irish Social Policy in Context*, Dublin: UCD Press, pp. 70–89.

O'Donoghue, Cathal and Terence McDonough (2006) 'The heart of the Tiger: income growth and inequality', in David Jacobson, Peadar Kirby and Deiric O Broin (eds), *Taming the Tiger*, Dublin: Tasc and New Island Books, pp. 45–58.

O'Donovan, Orla (2007) 'Corporate colonisation of health activism? Irish health advocacy organisations' modes of engagement with pharmaceutical corporations', *International Journal of Health Services*, 37(4): 711–33.

O'Donovan, Orla (2008) 'The emergence of pharmaceutical industry "regulation for competition" in Ireland', in O. O'Donovan and K. Glavanis-Grantham (eds), *Power, Politics and Pharmaceuticals. Drug Regulation in Ireland in a Global Context*, Cork: Cork University Press, pp. 61–81.

OECD (Organisation for Economic Co-operation and Development) (1994) *The Jobs Study*, Paris: OECD.

Offer, Avner (2006) *The Challenge of Affluence: Self-Control and Well-Being in the United States and Britain Since 1950*, Oxford: Oxford University Press.

Ó Flatharta, Peadar (2004) 'Cé a cheannóidh Plean?', presentation to conference Tóstal na Gaeilge, Galway, 28 February.

O'Hearn, Denis (1998) *Inside the Celtic Tiger: The Irish Economy and the Asian Model*, London: Pluto Press.

O'Hearn, Denis and Stephen McCloskey (2008) 'Globalisation and pharmaceuticals. Where is the power? Where to resist?', in O. O'Donovan and K. Glavanis-Grantham (eds), *Power, Politics and Pharmaceuticals. Drug Regulation in Ireland in a Global Context*, Cork: Cork University Press, pp. 9–26.

Oliver, Emmet (2001) 'Programme is "totally unsuitable", say parents', *Irish Times*, 21 September.

Oliver, Emmet (2003) 'So it's goodbye to all that', *Irish Times*, 18 March.

Oliver, Emmet (2006) 'Winning new viewers key to Setanta's game', *Irish Times*, 12 May, p. 5.

Ó Murchú, Helen (2003) *Limistéar na Sibhialtachta: Dúshlán agus Treo d'Eagraíochtaí na Gaeilge*, Dublin: Coiscéim.

O'Neill, Brian (2000) 'Media education in Ireland: an overview', *Irish Communications Review*, 8: 57–64.

One Parent Exchange Network (2006) Submission to DSFA 'Proposal on supporting lone parents' consultative meeting in Farmleigh House, 27 April.

O'Reilly, Brendan (2002) 'Letter to the editor', *Irish Times*, 11 July, p. 13.

Ó Riain, Seán (2000) 'The flexible developmental state: globalisation, information technology and the "Celtic Tiger"', *Politics and Society*, 28(2): 157–93.

Ó Riain, Seán (2004) *The Politics of High-Tech Growth: Developmental Network States in the Global Economy*, Cambridge: Cambridge University Press.

Ó Riain, Seán (2008) 'Competing state projects in the contemporary Irish political economy', in Maura Adshead, Peadar Kirby and Michelle Millar (eds), *Contesting the State: Lessons from the Irish Case*, Manchester: Manchester University Press, pp. 165–85.

Ó Riain, Seán and Philip O'Connell (2000) 'The role of the state in growth and welfare', in Brian Nolan *et al.* (eds), *Bust to Boom: The Irish Experience of Growth and Inequality*, Dublin: IPA, pp. 310–39.

Orwell, George (1949) 'Appendix: the principles of Newspeak', in *Nineteen Eighty-Four*, pp. 309–23. New York: Plume.

O'Sullivan, Denis (2005) *Cultural Politics and Irish Education Since the 1950s. Policy Paradigms and Power*, Dublin: IPA.

O'Sullivan, Michael (2006) *Ireland and the Global Question*, Cork: Cork University Press.

O'Toole, Fintan (2005a) 'Rights and wrongs', *Irish Times*, 29 January.

O'Toole, Fintan (2005b) 'Giving our resources to Norway', *Irish Times*, 30 August.

O'Toole, Fintan (2007) 'CSR isn't about how you spend the money you make, it's about how you make the money you spend', *Irish Times Innovation Business Magazine*, 6 December, p. 10.

Payne, Leanne (1995) *Crisis in Masculinity*, Grand Rapids, MI: Baker Book House.

Pettitt, Lance (1999) *Screening Ireland: Film and Television Representation*, Manchester: Manchester University Press.

Phelan, Sean (2003) *The Influence of Neo-liberal Assumptions on Media Treatment of Political Economy in Ireland*, PhD thesis (unpublished), Dublin: Dublin City University.

Phelan, Sean (2005) 'Irish media, Iraq and the charge of anti-Americanism', in Stig Arne Nohrstedt and Rune Ottosen (eds), *Global War – Local Views: Media Images of the Iraq War*, Gothenburg: Nordicom, pp. 171–86.

Phelan, Sean (2007a) 'The discourses of neoliberal hegemony: the case of the Irish Republic', *Critical Discourse Studies*, 4(1): 29–48.

Phelan, Sean (2007b) 'The discursive dynamics of neo-liberal consensus: Irish broadsheet editorials and the privatisation of Eircom', *Journal of Language and Politics*, 5(3): 7–28.

Phillipson, R., M. Rannut and T. Skutnabb-Kangas (1995) 'Introduction', in T. Skutnabb-Kangas and R. Phillipson (eds), *Linguistic Human Rights: Overcoming Linguistic Discrimination*, Berlin: Mouton de Gruyter, pp. 1–19.

Pickstone, John (2000) 'Production, community and consumption: the political economy of twentieth-century medicine', in R. Cooter and J. Pickstone (eds), *Medicine in the Twentieth Century*, Amsterdam: Harwood Academic, pp. 1–14.

Pierson, Paul (2001) *The New Politics of the Welfare State*, Oxford: Oxford University Press.

Plunkett, Horace (1905) *Ireland in the New Century* (3rd edn), Dublin: Irish Academic Press (1983).

Polanyi, Karl (1944) *The Great Transformation: The Political and Economic Origins of Our Time*, Boston, MA: Beacon Press (2001).

Pollock, Sheldon, Homi K. Bhabha, Carol A. Breckenridge and Dipesh Chakrabarty (2000) 'Cosmopolitanisms', *Public Culture*, 12(3): 577–90.

Poole, Steven (2006) *Unspeak: How Words Become Weapons, How Weapons Become a Message, and How That Message Becomes Reality*, New York: Grove Press.

Powell, Fred and Martin Geoghegan (2004) *The Politics of Community Development*, Dublin: A. & A. Farmar.

Quinn, David (2007) 'Walking over majorities to usher in the minorities', *Irish Independent*, 26 January.

Quinn, Stephen (2005) 'Convergence's fundamental question', *Journalism Studies*, 6(1): 29–38.

Radio Telifís Éireann Authority (2002) *Forty-Second Report and Statement of Accounts for the 12 Months Ended 31 December 2002, Presented to the Minister for Communications, Marine and Natural Resources Pursuant to Sections 25 and 26 of the Broadcasting Authority Act, 1960*, Dublin: RTÉ.

Reid, Liam and Conor Lally (2006) 'Intelligence saw no plan for violence, says report', *Irish Times*, 28 February.

Remenyi, Joseph (2004) 'What is development?', in D. Kingsbury, J. Remenyi, J. McKay and J. Hunt (eds), *Key Issues in Development*, London: Palgrave, pp. 22–45.

Reynolds, Brian (1993) *Casalattico and the Italian Community in Ireland*, Dublin: UCD Foundation for Italian Studies.

Ricento, Thomas (2006) 'Theoretical perspectives in language policy: an overview', in Thomas Ricento (ed.), *An Introduction to Language Policy: Theory and Method*, Malden: Blackwell, pp. 3–10.

Riegel, R. and G. Niland (2002) 'Racial timebomb set to explode as crisis deepens', *Irish Independent*, 27 January.

Robertson, Roland (ed.) (1991) *Talcott Parsons: Theorist of Modernity*, London: Sage.

Robinson, Mary (1995) 'Cherishing the Irish diaspora: address to the Houses of the Oireachtas by President Mary Robinson on a matter of public importance', *Dáil Éireann*, 448, 2 February.

Rodríguez Garavito, César A., Patrick S. Barrett and Daniel Chavez (eds) (2005) *La nueva izquierda en América Latina: Sus orígenes y trayectoria futura*, Bogotá: Grupo Editorial Norma.

Roediger, David R. (1999) *The Wages of Whiteness: Race and the Making of the American Working Class*, New York: Verso.

Rolston, Bill and Mary Shannon (2002) *Encounters: How Racism Came to Ireland*, Belfast: Beyond the Pale.

Rose, Nikolas S. (1993) 'Government, authority and expertise in advanced liberalism', *Economy and Society*, 22: 283–300.

Rose, Nikolas S. (2007) 'Beyond medicalisation', *Lancet*, 369: 700–2.

Rostow, W. W. (1968) *The Stages of Economic Growth: A Non-Communist Manifesto*, Cambridge: Cambridge University Press.

Rostow, W. W. (1990) *Theorists of Economic Growth from David Hume to the Present: With a Perspective on the Next Century*, New York: Oxford University Press.

Roughhead, Elizabeth and Joel Lexchin (2006) 'Adverse drug events: counting is not enough, action is needed', *Medical Journal of Australia*, 184(7): 315–16.

Rowe, David (1996) 'The global love match: sport and television', *Media, Culture and Society*, 18: 565–82.

Rowe, David (2004) *Sport, Culture and the Media: The Unruly Trinity* (2nd edn), Maidenhead: Open University Press.

Ryan, Bob (2002) 'Letter to the editor', *Irish Times*, 10 July, p. 13.

Ryner, Magnus J. (2002) *Capitalist Restructuring, Globalisation and the Third Way: Lessons from the Swedish Model*, London: Routledge.

Sadker, Myra and David Sadker (1994) *Failing at Fairness: How America's Schools Cheat Girls*, New York: Touchstone.

Sandberg, A. and I. Pramling-Samuelsson (2005) 'An interview study of gender difference in preschool teachers' attitudes toward children's play', *Early Childhood Education Journal*, 32(5): 297–305.

Sapir, Andre (2006) 'Globalisation and the reform of the European social models', *Journal of Common Market Studies*, 44(2): 369–90.

Sen, Amartya K. (1999) *Development as Freedom*, Oxford: Oxford University Press.

Sennett, R. (2006) *The Culture of the New Capitalism*, New Haven, CT: Yale University Press.

Shaw, Helen (2004) 'Advertising code for children must apply across EU', *Irish Times*, 10 May.

Siggins, Lorna (2002) 'Minister sails stormy seas to keep varied brief on course', *Irish Times*, 19 July, p. 60.

Siggins, Lorna (2007) 'Begg says model should be Nordic social democracy', *Irish Times*, 16 July.

Silverstone, Roger (2006) *Media and Morality: On the Rise of the Mediapolis*, Cambridge: Polity Press.

Skilbeck, Malcolm (2001) *The University Challenged. A Review of International Trends and Issues with Particular Reference to Ireland*, Dublin: HEA in association with CHIU.

Smyth, Brendan (2002) 'Letter to the editor', *Irish Independent*, 12 July, p. 27.

Sparks, Chris (2006) 'The production of the imaginary terrorist as an object of fear: orientalism in the twenty-first century', in Alana Lentin and Ronit Lentin (eds), *Race and State*, Newcastle: Cambridge Scholars Press, pp. 152–68.

Speed, Ewen (2002) 'Irish mental health social movements: a consideration of movement habitus', *Irish Journal of Sociology*, 11: 62–80.

Stavenhagen, R. (1990) *The Ethnic Question. Conflicts, Development and Human Rights*, Tokyo: United Nations University Press.

Steed, J. (1994) *Our Little Secret: Confronting Child Sexual Abuse in Canada*, Toronto: Random House.

Steele, C. M. (1997) 'A threat in the air: how stereotypes shape intellectual identity and performance', *American Psychologist*, 52: 613–29.

Stolcke, Verena (1995) 'Talking culture: new boundaries, new rhetorics of exclusion in Europe', *Current Anthropology*, 36(1): 1–24.

Sugden, J. and A. Tomlinson (2002) 'International power struggles in the governance of world football: the 2002 and 2006 World Cup bidding wars', in J. Horne and W. Manzenreiter (eds), *Japan, Korea and the 2002 World Cup*, London: Routledge, pp. 56–70.

Sugrue, Ciaran (2004) 'Whose curriculum is it anyway? Power, politics and possibilities in the construction of the revised primary curriculum', in Ciaran Sugrue (ed.), *Ideology and Curriculum: Irish Experiences, International Perspectives*, Dublin: Liffey Press, pp. 167–208.

Survey Team (1965) *Investment in Education*, report of the Survey Team appointed by the Minister for Education in October 1962, Dublin: Stationery Office.

Sutherland, H. (1956) *Irish Journey*, London: Geoffrey Bles.

Swank, Dwane (2002) *Global Capital, Political Institutions and Policy Change in Developed Welfare States*, Cambridge: Cambridge University Press.

Sweeney, John (2002) *Ending Child Poverty in Rich Countries: What Works*, Dublin: Children's Rights Alliance.

Sweeney, John (2005) 'Can the Celtic Tiger change its stripes?', paper presented to Irish Social Policy Association Seminar, Royal Irish Institute, Dublin, 11 September.

Sweeney, John and Rory O'Donnell (2003) 'The challenge of linking society and economy in Ireland's flexible developmental welfare state', paper presented to the conference of the Society for the Advancement of Social Economics, Aix en Provence, France, 26–28 June.

Sweeney, Paul (2005) 'Money not the obstacle to completing success story', *Irish Times*, 19 December. Available at www.ireland.com (accessed June 2006).

Tannen, Deborah (2001) *You Just Don't Understand: Men and Women in Conversation*, New York: Harper Paperbacks.

Tasker, Yvonne and Diane Negra (2007) 'Introduction: feminist politics and postfeminist culture', in Y. Tasker and D. Negra (eds), *Interrogating Postfeminism: Gender and the Politics of Popular Culture*, Durham, NC: Duke University Press, pp. 1–26.

Taylor, Charles (1989) *Sources of the Self: The Making of the Modern Identity*, Cambridge: Cambridge University Press.

Taylor, Charles (1994) *Multiculturalism: Examining the Politics of Recognition*, Princeton, MA: Princeton University Press.

Teaching Council (2007) *Draft Codes of Professional Conduct for Teachers*, Maynooth: Teaching Council.

Teather, David (2000) 'No Match of the Day as BBC lose out', *Irish Times*, 15 June, p. 21.

't Hoen, Ellen (2002) 'TRIPs, pharmaceutical patents, and access to essential medicines: a long way from Seattle to Doha', *Chicago Journal of International Law*, 3(1): 27–46.

Thornley, Gerry (1994) 'RTE and FAI sign four year contract', *Irish Times*, 17 September, p. 19.

Titley, Gavan (2008) 'Backlash! Just in case: "political correctness", immigration and the rise of *preactionary* discourse in Irish public debate', *Irish Review*, 38(1): 94–110.

Titley, Gavan and Alana Lentin (2007) 'More Benetton than barricades? The politics of diversity in Europe', in Gavan Titley and Alana Lentin (eds), *The Politics of Diversity in Europe*, Strasbourg: Council of Europe Publishing, pp. 1–26.

Titmuss, Richard (1956) *Essays on the State*, London: George and Allen Unwin.

Tovey, Hilary, Damian Hannan and Hal Abramson (1989) *Cad chuige an Ghaeilge? Teanga agus Féiniúlacht in Éirinn ár Linne/Why Irish? Irish Identity and the Irish Language*, Dublin: Bord na Gaeilge.

Tsebelis, George (2002) *Veto Players, How Political Institutions Work*, Princeton, MA: Princeton University Press.

Tucker, Vincent (1997) 'Introduction: a cultural perspective on development', in Vincent Tucker (ed.), *Cultural Perspectives on Development*, London: Frank Cass, pp. 1–21.

Tynan, Ronan (2002) 'Letter to the editor', *Irish Times*, 9 July, p. 13.

Údarás na Gaeltachta (2005) *Beartas Forbartha 2005–2010*, Na Forbacha: ÚnaG.

United Nations Development Programme (1992) *Human Development Report 1992*, New York: Oxford University Press.

United Nations Development Programme (1996) *Human Development Report 1996*, New York: Oxford University Press.

United Nations Development Programme (2004) *Human Development Report 2004: Cultural Liberty in Today's Diverse World*, New York: United Nations Development Programme.

United Nations Development Programme (2007) *Human Development Report 2007/2008: Fighting Climate Change*, Basingstoke: Palgrave Macmillan.

Urry, John (1990) *The Tourist Gaze: Leisure and Travel in Contemporary Societies*, London: Sage.

Urry, John (2003) *Global Complexity*, Cambridge: Polity Press.

van der Geest, Sjaak, Susan Reynolds Whyte and Anita Hardon (1996) 'The anthropology of pharmaceuticals: a biographical approach', *Annual Review of Anthropology*, 25: 153–78.

Van Hoorhis, Rebecca (2002) 'Different types of welfare states? A methodological deconstruction of comparative research', *Journal of Sociology and Social Welfare*, 28(1): 1–24.

Vertovec, Steven and Robin Cohen (eds) (2002) *Conceiving Cosmopolitanism: Theory, Context and Practice*, Oxford: Oxford University Press.

Walsh, Aidan (2002) 'Letter to the editor', *Irish Independent*, 11 July, p. 25.

Walsh, Jim (2007) 'Monitoring poverty and welfare policy, 1987–2007', in Mel Cousins (ed.), *Welfare Policy and Poverty*, Dublin: IPA/Combat Poverty Agency, pp. 13–58.

Walsh, John (2002) 'Letter to the editor', *Irish Times*, 9 July, p. 13.

Walsh, John (2004) *An teanga, an cultúr agus an fhorbairt: cás na Gaeilge agus cás na hÉireann*, Dublin: Coiscéim.

Walsh, John (2005) *The Influence of the Promotion of the Irish Language on Ireland's Socio-Economic Development*, PhD thesis (unpublished), Dublin: Dublin City University.

Walsh, John (2006) 'Ensuring the Irish language has its place', *Irish Times*, 10 March.

Walsh, John (forthcoming) 'The Irish language: policy and planning', in M. Millar and M. Adshead (eds), *Governance and Public Policy in Ireland*, Dublin: Irish Academic Press.

Walsh, John, S. G. McCarron and E. Ní Bhrádaigh (2005) 'Mapping the Gaeltacht: towards a geographical definition of the Irish speaking districts', *Administration*, 53(1): 16–37.

Waters, John (2001) 'Horrors of feminised education', *Irish Times*, 27 August.

Watson, C. W. (2000) *Multiculturalism*, London: Open University Press.

Watson, Iarfhlaith (2003) *Broadcasting in Irish: Minority Language, Radio, Television and Identity*, Dublin: Four Courts Press.

Werbner, Pnina (2005) 'The translocation of culture: migration, community, and the force of multiculturalism in history', IIIS Discussion Paper No. 48. Available at http://ssrn.com/abstract=739205 (accessed 5 July 2006).

Wernick, Andrew (1991) *Promotional Culture: Advertising, Ideology, and Symbolic Expression*, London: Sage.

West, Candace and Don H. Zimmerman (1987) 'Doing gender', *Gender and Society*, 1(2): 125–51.

Whelan, Christopher T., Richard Layte, Bertrand Maitre, Brenda Gannon, Brian Nolan, Dorothy Watson and James Williams (2003) *Monitoring Poverty Trends in Ireland: Results from the 2001 Living in Ireland Survey*, Policy Research Series No. 51, Dublin: ESRI.

Whelan, Emmett (2007) 'The great divide', *Law Society Gazette*, January/February: 18–22.

Whelehan, Imelda (2000) *Overloaded: Popular Culture and the Future of Feminism*, London: Women's Press.

Wieviorka, Michel (2002) 'The development of racism in Europe', in D. T. Goldberg and J. Solomos (eds), *A Companion to Racial and Ethnic Studies*, London: Blackwell, pp. 460–73.

Wilkinson, Richard and Kate Pickett (2009) *The Spirit Level: Why More Equal Societies Almost Always Do Better*, London: Allen Lane.

Williams, Colin H. (2000) 'Community empowerment through language planning intervention', in Colin H. Williams (ed.), *Language Revitalization: Policy and Planning in Wales*, Cardiff: University of Wales Press, pp. 221–46.

Williams, Fiona (2004) 'Rethinking families, rethinking care', paper presented at the ISPA annual conference 'Families, Children and Social Policy', Croke Park, Dublin, 17 September. Available at www.ispa.ie (accessed 8 October 2007).

Williams, Joan (2000) *Unbending Gender: Why Family and Work Conflict and What To Do About It*, Oxford: Oxford University Press.

Willis, Paul (2000) *The Ethnographic Imagination*, Cambridge: Polity Press.

Wren, Maev-Ann (2003) *Unhealthy State: Anatomy of a Sick Society*, Dublin: New Island Books.

Wren, Maev-Ann (2006) 'A healthier state', in Tom O'Connor and Mike Murphy (eds), *Social Care in Ireland: Theory, Policy and Practice*, Cork: CIT Press, pp. 101–11.

Wrynn, James (2003) 'Universal entitlement gives everyone a stake in society', *Irish Times*, 5 June.

Index